The Psychology of Esports

Seyhan Bekir
Editor

The Psychology of Esports

Springer

Editor
Seyhan Bekir
Department of Psychology
Faculty of Science and Letters
Demiroglu Bilim University
Istanbul, Türkiye

ISBN 978-3-032-25089-6 ISBN 978-3-032-25090-2 (eBook)
https://doi.org/10.1007/978-3-032-25090-2

This Springer imprint is published by the registered company Springer Nature Switzerland AG
The registered company address is: Gewerbestrasse 11, 6330 Cham, Switzerland

The authors acknowledge the grammar assistance and translation provided by ChatGPT (OpenAI) for language editing. The authors made all content decisions and verifications.

This book is dedicated to my beloved son Karel, who was born on February 10, 2026.

—Seyhan BEKİR

Preface

Regardless of whether esports is sports or not, it will hold an important place for individuals who sometimes have a vocational title and sometimes the goal of becoming a player, under the names of science, sports, and entertainment. At the same time, it is important to evaluate it within the scope of sports psychology with a multidisciplinary perspective, such as sports science and psychology, as it marks the beginning of a process that will emerge under the name of esports psychology.

Although esports has a history of approximately 25 years, it combines passion, the desire for success, and entertainment, which can lead to certain psychological needs in esports players. In this regard, addressing both emotional and physiological and sporting requirements will make 'The Esports of Psychology' a groundbreaking book.

This book, ***The Psychology of Esports***, brings together experts from a variety of fields to provide a comprehensive, evidence-based, and practical resource. Topics covered include addiction, attachment, emotions, coaching, recovery, cognition, reaction times, the importance of activity, health, medicine, ethics, and analytical perspectives, which are frequently found in sports psychology.

This work is based on the foundations of psychology and sports psychology and has been interpreted in terms of the theories and application areas within sports psychology. It is designed for researchers and all professionals in the fields of sports science, psychology, education, health, etc., who are interested in esports.

I would like to thank the respected researchers who have contributed to the interpretation of esports by combining different cultures such as Italy, the Netherlands, Belgium, and Turkey in this book. I hope this book will be a source of inspiration for anyone interested in esports psychology who wishes to read and research.

İstanbul, Türkiye — Seyhan Bekir

Contents

Contributors

Yasin Atay Atatürk City Hospital, Sports Medicine Unit, Balıkesir, Turkey

Elif Balıkçı Department of Pychology, Faculty of Art and Social Sciences, Istanbul Galata University, Istanbul, Turkey

Seyhan Bekir Department of Psychology, Faculty of Science and Letters, Demiroglu Bilim University, Istanbul, Türkiye

Burak Bezirganoğlu Speciality Registrar in General Practice, Oxford, UK

Andrea Caputo Department of Psychology, University of Turin, Turin, Italy

Sven Charleer Media, Design & IT, AP University of Applied Sciences and Arts, Antwerp, Belgium

Claudio Giovanni Cortese Department of Psychology, University of Turin, Turin, Italy

Kübra Dombak Deparment of Guidance and Psychological Counseling, Faculty of Educational Science, Sakarya University, Sakarya, Türkiye

Maximilian A. Friehs Psychology of Conflict Risk and Safety, University of Twente, Enschede, Netherlands;
Secondary: Visiting Research Fellow, School of Psychology, University College Dublin, Dublin, Ireland

Laura Herrewijn Media, Design & IT, AP University of Applied Sciences and Arts, Antwerp, Belgium

Cengiz Karagözoğlu Faculty of Sports Science, Fenerbahçe University, İstanbul, Türkiye

Şeval Kayğusuz Istanbul Gedik University, İstanbul, Türkiye

Alp Kaan Kilci Department of Sport Management, Faculty of Sport Sciences, Balikesir University, Balıkesir, Turkey

Fatih Sülün Department of Sports Science, Trakya University, Edirne, Turkey

Ahmet Vatansever Independent Researcher, İstanbul, Turkey

Giuseppe Vercelli Department of Psychology, University of Turin, Turin, Italy; Sport and Human Performance Psychology Center "Umbro Marcaccioli" (ISEF Foundation), Turin, Italy

Serhat Yalçıner Department of Coaching Education, Balıkesir University, Balıkesir, Türkiye

Abbreviations

ADHD	Attention-Deficit/Hyperactivity Disorder
APA	American Psychiatric Association
ARSS	Acute Recovery and Stress Scale
BEAT	Better Esports Analytics for Teams
CIs	Confidence Intervals
CLT	Cognitive Load Theory
CONI	Italian National Olympic Committee
CR-10	Category Ratio-10
CSAI-2	Competitive State Anxiety Inventory-2
DALDA	Daily Analysis of Life Demands for Athletes
DSM-5	Diagnostic and Statistical Manual of Mental Disorders (5th Edition)
EEG	Electroencephalography
EHC	Eye-Hand Coordination
ER	Emotion Regulation
ESIC	Esports Integrity Commission
ESP	Emotional State Profile
fNIRS	Functional Near-Infrared Spectroscopy
FPS	First-Person Shooter
GSR	Galvanic Skin Response
HIIT	High-Intensity Interval Training
ICC	Identification-Control-Correction
ICD-11	International Classification of Diseases (11th Revision)
IGD	Internet Gaming Disorder
IZDy	Individual Zone of Dysfunction
IZOF	Individual Zone of Optimal Functioning
LAN	Local Area Network
LCS	League of Legends Championship Series
LOL	League of Legends
MMOG	Massively Multiplayer Online Game
MMORPGs	Massively Multiplayer Online Role-Playing Games

MOBA	Multiplayer Online Battle Arena
MOBAs	Multiplayer Online Battle Arenas
MUD	Multi-User Dungeon
NASA-TLX	NASA Task Load Index
NIBS	Non-Invasive Brain Stimulation
P-E	Person-Environment
POMS	Profile of Mood States
REST-Q Sport	Recovery Stress Questionnaire for Athletes
SMART	Specific, Measurable, Achievable, Relevant, Time-bound
SPRS	Sport Psychological Recovery Scale
SRSS	Short Recovery and Stress Scale
TMS	Transcranial Magnetic Stimulation
TQR	Total Quality Recovery
TUE	Therapeutic Use Exemption
VR	Virtual Reality
WADA	World Anti-Doping Agency
WHO	World Health Organization
XR	Extended Reality
ZOF	Zone of Optimal Functioning

Chapter 1
Esports Psychology

Seyhan Bekir

1.1 Introduction

Sport is a global activity that is able to connect people from different cultures and backgrounds, no matter what language they speak. There are many different branches of sports. It is possible to say that some countries have specialized in certain branches of sports (Crawford, 2004; Grupe, 1994; Maheu, 1963). For illustrations, the United States leads in basketball, while England is a leader in soccer due to its historical tradition and successful track-record (Georgievski et al., 2019; Sampaio et al., 2010). Popular sports such as soccer, basketball, and volleyball are frequently played at both professional and non-professional standards. In contrast, sports such as shooting and oil wrestling are of limited interest, and the number of players active in these areas remains quite low (Bakhrevskiy, 2019; Gül et al., 2015; Krawietz, 2017). Today, the sense of sport is not limited to traditional branches. With the effect of technological developments, new types of sports such as kite surfing (Bourgois et al., 2014), jogathon, drone racing (Foehn et al., 2022), and esports (Reitman et al., 2020; Rogstad, 2022) have emerged and are becoming increasingly popular. Several of them have obtained official sports status, and the inclusion of some, such as kitesurfing and esports, in the Olympic Games program has recently been discussed. However, there are also some opinions arguing that sports like esports should not be considered "real sports" due to their low level of physical activity (Hallmann & Giel, 2018; Parry, 2021). Leis et al. (2021), meanwhile, state that the real issue is not whether esports should be accepted as a sport, but rather that psychology should have a place in esports and that more studies are required on this topic.

To summarize these studies, the global acceptance of a sport is a complex and lengthy process. In the past, following sports through technological tools such as

S. Bekir (✉)
Department of Psychology, Faculty of Science and Letters, Demiroglu Bilim University, Istanbul, Türkiye
e-mail: Seyhanbekir@yahoo.com

S. Bekir (ed.), *The Psychology of Esports*, https://doi.org/10.1007/978-3-032-25090-2_1

radio was limited, but thanks to television, the internet, and social media, access to sports content has become easier; sports viewership and following have increased globally (Kilci, 2019). Nevertheless, esports came to the fore during the COVID-19 pandemic (Fakazlı, 2020), when physical competitions were banned; it reached millions of spectators, esports players were named "player of the year" in some countries, and discussions about including esports in the Olympics resurfaced. The main point of criticism directed at esports is the very low level of physical activity involved (Parry, 2021). Similarly, sports such as chess, archery, and darts are often not considered sports because they require low physical activity; however, according to the International Olympic Committee's statement, these sports are classified as "mind sports" (Stefani, 2011; 2016). In this context, comparing sports into traditional sports (sports requiring physical strength), low-strength sports, and esports may clarify whether esports should be considered a sport. Table 1.1 below provides details of this comparison.

When the table is analyzed as a whole, it is quite difficult to bring all sports under a single umbrella. That is why it can be said that the view that esports definitely cannot be considered a sport is not supported. In parallel with this, similarities and differences can be observed from time to time. Another similarity is that, as in other

Table 1.1 Comparison between traditional sports, sports requiring low physical strength, and esports

	Traditional sports (Football, Basketball, etc.)	Sports requiring low physical strength (Shooting, Archery, Darts, Chess, etc.)	Esports (League of legends, CS2, Dota, etc.)
Physical Strength Requirements	High	Low	Low
Reaction Time	Medium–High	Medium–High	High
Teamwork/ Individuality	Team	Generally individual	Team
Risk of Injury	High	Medium–Low	Low
Performance Period	Peak at a young age	Wide age range	Peak at a young age
Psychological Pressure	High	High	High
Support equipment	Basic equipment (shoes, etc.)	High-performance equipment (bow, gun, etc.)	High technological equipment
Olympic Status	Yes	Some are Olympic	Not yet officially Olympic
Continuity/ Sustainability	May be limited due to risk of injury	Sustainable even with advancing age	The age range is between 15 and 25. There are very few esports' players over the age of 25

sports, psychology plays a major role in esports performance (Pedraza-Ramirez et al., 2020). In this context, Erdoğan and Kocaekşi (2015) state that, in addition to physical, technical, and tactical elements that are thought to affect athletic performance, there are also cognitive and emotional elements. The scientific study that investigates and researches the cognitive and emotional factors in sports and their impact on performance is now referred to as "sports psychology" (Gill, 2009; Gill & Williams, 2008; Gill et al., 2017).

1.2 Sports Psychology and Esports Psychology

The combination of sports and psychology came about because of players' needs not being fulfilled before, during, and after sports, or because of their psychological needs (Weinberg & Gould, 2023). In another sense, sports psychology is based on understanding how psychological factors affect individuals' physical performance and understanding the psychological development of the individual in their participation in sports and their contribution to well-being. It is not possible to bring all sports disciplines under one umbrella. Therefore, it can be said that interventions to increase players' performance also vary according to the discipline (Football, Basketball, Archery, and Esports). For example, in sports psychology, elements such as running and endurance are evaluated within the scope of physical performance, while in esports, there is no need for such physical performance. Instead, psychomotor performance and perceptual motor processes, etc., come to the fore (Piatysotska et al., 2023; Pluss et al., 2020; Vardal, 2023). Furthermore, factors such as hand–eye coordination, reaction time, and fine motor skills are critical in esports (Koposov et al., 2020; Lachowicz et al., 2025). In fact, elements such as "click timing" (Dahl et al., 2021) or "flick" (Rogers et al., 2024) within the game can be decisive in terms of performance enhancement. However, it is difficult to say that these skills are completely independent of physical performance; because components such as hand–wrist and finger muscle strength, correct body posture, the distance of the keyboard and computer from the body, seat height, keyboard grip, and physical endurance are prerequisites for performing these actions (McGee, 2021; McGee et al., 2024).

Moreover, as in sports psychology, it may be incorrect to address esports psychology under a single umbrella. A review of the literature shows that although there are studies related to "esports psychology," there is no direct definition (Bányai et al., 2019; Cottrell et al., 2019; Pedraza-Ramirez et al., 2020; Sharpe & Birch, 2025). Related studies emphasize how esports players become professional, what mental and motivational factors they possess, issues such as emotion regulation, team management, and anger management in esports, the importance of goal setting, and the necessity of adapting mental skill training programs, attention, self-talk, imagery, mindfulness, relaxation techniques, and that rapid changes in games are important.

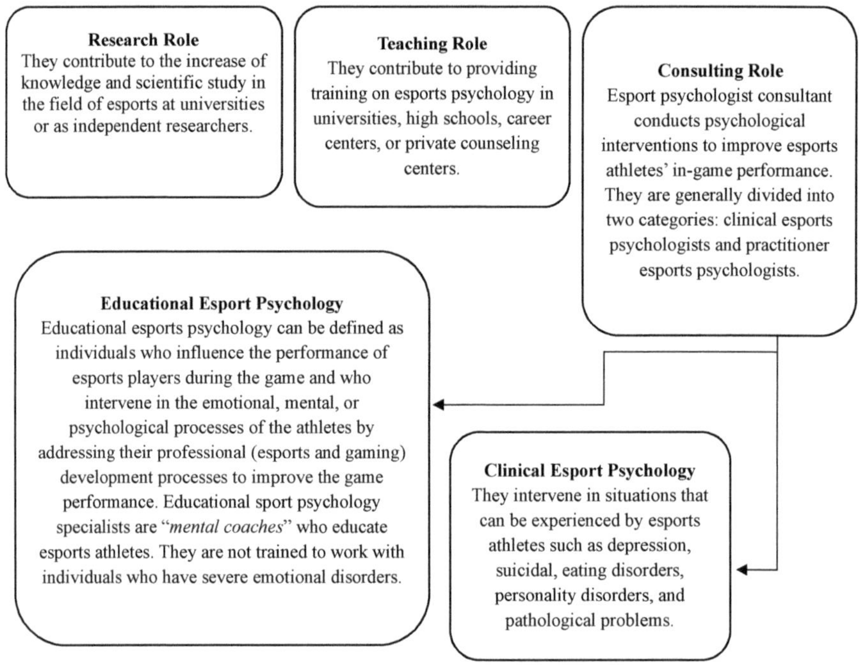

Fig. 1.1 Classification of esports according to sports psychology

In conclusion, esports psychology can be defined as a field that intervenes in the emotional, mental, or psychological processes of players by addressing their professional (esports and gaming) development processes in order to increase their performance in the games they play. At this point, it is important to start from the components of sports psychology to understand esports psychology. Weinberg and Gould (2023) divided the fields of study in sports psychology into three: the researcher role, the teaching role, and the consulting role. The consulting role is further divided into the consulting sports psychologist (which is further divided into the educational sports psychologist and the clinical sports psychologist). Figure 1.1 briefly defines and explains the roles in esports psychology, inspired by this study.

1.2.1 Research Role in Esports Psychology

Academic studies on esports are gradually increasing. At this point, it is also important to highlight that the researchers in esports are growing in number. In the study by Navarro-Lucena et al. (2025), it is stated that the first academic studies on esports were conducted in 2002, but there were only two of them. According to the details of this study, only 19 studies were conducted between 2002 and 2011, and the total number of citations was 626. However, 1,704 scientific studies have been conducted from 2012 to the present, and it is seen that many of these studies have increased with the COVID-19 pandemic. As a result, it is possible to say that esports researchers are growing rapidly. The details of the relevant study are shown in Fig. 1.2.

Based on the scope of academic studies on esports, it can be said that esports has a multidisciplinary structure (Manci et al., 2022). The fields of esports researchers include law (Abanazir & Shinohara, 2024), sports science (Białecki et al., 2024), business and management (Scholz, 2019), psychology (Pedraza-Ramirez et al., 2025), education (Jenny et al., 2024), new media (Hammerschmidt et al., 2024), marketing (Baltezarević et al., 2023), etc.

1.2.2 Teaching Role in Esports Psychology

The academic studies in the field of esports have also contributed to the growth of esports educators. This includes from kindergarten to 12th grade (K12) (Rothwell & Shaffer, 2019), as well as undergraduate programs (Jenny et al., 2024; McGrath, 2019) and graduate programs (Jenny et al., 2024; Shynkaruk et al., 2021). Besides being generally known as a factor that decreases academic achievement (Shukry et al., 2024), online games also have contributions such as increasing academic achievement and creativity in coursework (Cheng, 2025). At such a point, it would be wrong to summarize these benefits and harms under a single heading called "esports training." This is because the topics discussed under the name of esports training are entirely related to games, mechanics, preparation for competitive content, organizing tournaments for relevant online games, and the personal gains that can be obtained from these competitions. Esports is by no means a way to increase knowledge in math class or improve creativity in art class. Integrating esports education into the education system is also not easy because it involves a significant amount of prejudices. For illustrative purposes, one research focused on the satisfaction levels of students, parents, and teachers after adding Minecraft to the curriculum. In the study, 98.5% of participants agreed that the game was fun, and 97.1% stated that it enabled high levels of interaction among its users (Sáez-López et al., 2015). However, other research has also revealed that Minecraft games can lead to situations such as cyberbullying (adults manipulating children in a virtual environment to meet in real life and sexually abuse them) (Bach, 2016; Kopecký & Szotkowski, 2018; Morris, 2017; Szotkowski et al., 2020) and some countries have even banned this practice (NTV, 2015). Therefore, it is important that the education provided in the field of esports does not allow for behavioral addiction and other elements. In addition to this, it can be said that having sufficient knowledge in the field of esports, as well as bachelor's, master's, and doctoral degrees in related fields such as sports/education sciences/psychology, is very important for the proper delivery of esports education.

Jenny et al. (2024) suggest that esports education is offered at the undergraduate, graduate, and certificate programs. These programs include courses in business and management, introduction to esports, media production and communication, and event/event management. Also notable are courses on performance and coaching,

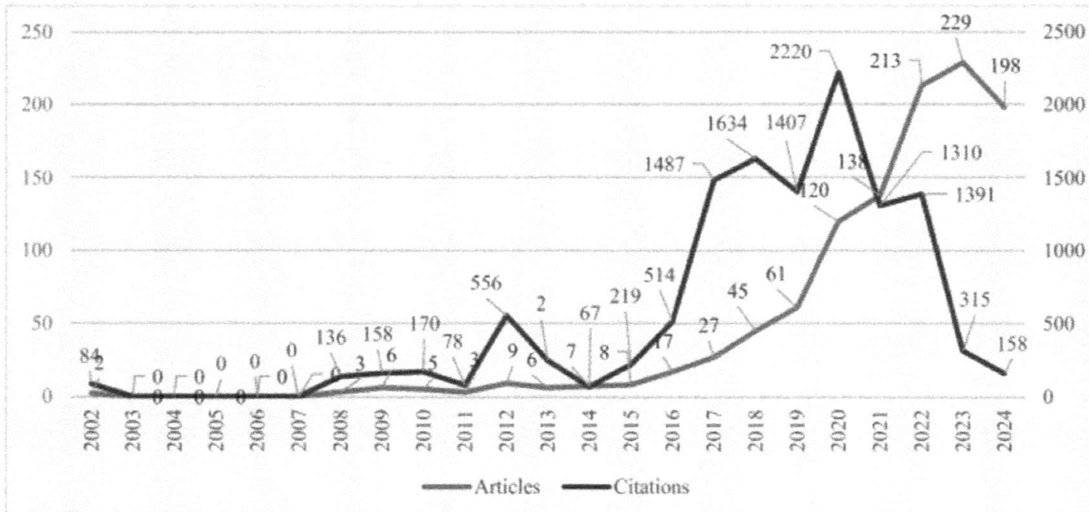

Fig. 1.2 Number of publications by year in esports academic studies (Navarro-Lucena et al., 2025)

game design and studies, and internships/practical application. In parallel, marketing and branding, ethics/law/governance, current trends, and sociology are covered to a lesser extent. The least represented areas are thesis/dissertation, medicine/health, and research methods. In terms of courses, it has been observed that only the University of Copenhagen and the Spanish Sports Psychology and Coaching Association offer education related to psychology. At this point, it can be said that education under the name of esports psychology is currently very limited and is an area that needs to be developed.

1.2.3 Consulting Role in Esports Psychology

To be able to describe the role of the consulting in sports, we will exemplify it via the sports psychology model. In Applied Sports Psychology, clinical sports psychologists and educational sports psychologists are presented as two separate sub-categories (Stapleton et al., 2010; Weinberg & Gould, 2023). Even though their intervention methods are similar, the areas and processes they focus on within the player are different. Clinical sports psychologists mostly focus on pathology-heavy areas such as eating disorders, substance addictions, and personality disorders, but educational sport psychologists deal with performance improvement through imagination, arousal, concentration, and mental processes and sport training processes. In short, clinical sports psychologists deal with issues that affect a player's performance due to their psychological health, while educational sports psychologists deal with mental processes that maximize the use of potential and talent and enhance performance. At this point, it is important to distinguish between the two groups. Although the title of sports psychologist has been debated for years (Anderson et al., 2002; Silva, 1989; Silva et al., 1999), it is accepted that a sports psychologist is a person who applies psychological techniques and strategies aimed at helping players achieve higher performance through a holistic approach to their development (Roper, 2002; Wylleman & Lavallee, 2004).

It is possible to say that there are various challenges in applied esports psychology today. To analyze this issue, the negative perception of applied esports psychology in 2025 can be compared to the negative perception of applied sports psychology in the 1970s. It has been argued that research conducted in the laboratory in the past did not adequately reflect the real context of sport (ecological validity problem), and it has been emphasized that the dynamics of sport on the field must be taken into account (Araújo et al., 2006).

Similarly, in esports, the fact that football players are on the field, basketball players are on the court, boxers are in the ring, skiers are on the slope, and esports players are on the arena can increase the bias in scientific studies. Thus, in applied sports psychology, there are many scales for measuring pre-competition, during competition, and post-competition (Freemantle et al., 2021; Martens et al., 1990; Michel-Kröhler et al., 2023; Willis, 1982). At this point, the scales used are important for identifying the difficulties experienced during the competition and preventing these difficulties from negatively affecting performance. Unfortunately, no such study has yet been conducted in esports. This is because it is unclear where the application of psychology fits into esports. Esports has a mental performance coach and performance coach system, but when looking at professional teams, although sports psychologists are present during certain periods, it is seen that they are not there long-term (García-Lanzo & Chamarro, 2018). It can be said that there are several reasons for this situation. The process in sports psychology actually maximizes in-game performance by facilitating the player's adaptation, etc., but looking at the length of time players stay with teams in esports, it can be said that contract periods are daily, weekly, and at most monthly. In this process, it is thought that there is not enough time for the players to join the team, adapt to the team, and fully establish their position within the team, thus making it difficult to maximize the benefits for the esports players. Performance coaches are responsible for the performance of players in esports (Bekir, 2022). In this context, the role of a sports psychologist can also be defined as a mental performance coach.

Players' demands for improving their game performance due to psychological reasons (Leis et al., 2024, 2025), the stress they experience before/during/after the game (Leis & Lautenbach, 2020), and the need for coaches to communicate with players and other coaches and, indirectly, to manage crises when players fail, among other issues. It can be very difficult for an esports coach to identify a player's pathological condition based on the time they spend training and playing. To facilitate this identification, it is necessary for the coach to convince the player or for an expert in psychology to be part of the team. This is because achieving the necessary successes may be sufficient for the team, and at this point, the player may suppress their discomfort. However, to ensure the player's success remains stable, it is important that the team includes at least a consulting esports psychologist who can evaluate the situation as a potential clinical case and refer the player to a psychiatrist or clinical esports psychologist when necessary. At this point, the short career spans of esports players and the fact that they encounter certain situations at a very young age can be considered a risk.

1.3 Conclusion

Consequently, it is more appropriate to focus on practical applications rather than theory. Increasing practical training and evaluating the effects of physical and mental training from a performance psychology perspective, as well as addressing multidisciplinary aspects such as nutrition and other processes that affect physiology and psychology, are crucial for esports psychology. Therefore, this book also concludes that it is important to first evaluate esports psychology from a sports psychology perspective and to go through these sports psychology processes.

References

Abanazir, C., & Shinohara, T. (2024). Esports governance and esports law. In S. E. Jenny, N. Besombes, T. Brock, A. C. Cote & T. M. Scholz (Eds.), *Routledge handbook of esports* (pp. 482–492). Routledge. https://doi.org/10.4324/9781003410591-53

Anderson, A. G., Mahoney, C., Miles, A., & Robinson, P. (2002). Evaluating the effectiveness of applied sport psychology practice: Making the case for a case study approach. *The Sport Psychologist, 16*(4), 432–453. https://doi.org/10.1123/tsp.16.4.432

Araújo, D., Davids, K., & Hristovski, R. (2006). The ecological dynamics of decision making in sport. *Psychology of Sport and Exercise, 7*(6), 653–676. https://doi.org/10.1016/j.psychsport.2006.07.002

Bach, S. (2016, December). Cyber-Grooming über "Minecraft": Täter im Fall Paul droht lange Haft. N-TV. Retrieved from http://www.n-tv.de/panorama/Taeter-im-FallPaul-droht-lange-Haft-article19228356.html

Bakhrevskiy, E. (2019). History and actual image of oil wrestling. *International Journal of Ethnosport and Traditional Games, 2*(2), 12–36. https://doi.org/10.34685/HI.2020.75.15.002

Baltezarević, R., Baltezarević, V., & Baltezarević, I. (2023). The role of digital marketing in the eSports industry. *Acta Ludologica, 6*(1), 28–45.

Bányai, F., Griffiths, M. D., Király, O., & Demetrovics, Z. (2019). The psychology of esports: A systematic literature review. *Journal of Gambling Studies, 35*(2), 351–365. https://doi.org/10.1007/s10899-018-9763-1

Bekir, S. (2022). Psikolojik danışmanlık bakış açısıyla esporda meslekleşme. In E. Mancı, S. Bekir, & Y. N. Çakır (Eds.), *Espora multidisipliner yaklaşımlar* (pp. 21–27). Nobel Bilimsel Eserler.

Białecki, A., Michalak, B., & Gajewski, J. (2024). Esports training, periodization, and software—A scoping review. *Applied Sciences, 14*(22), 10354. https://doi.org/10.3390/app142210354

Bourgois, J. G., Boone, J., Callewaert, M., Tipton, M. J., & Tallir, I. B. (2014). Biomechanical and physiological demands of kitesurfing and epidemiology of injury among kitesurfers. *Sports Medicine, 44*, 55–66. https://doi.org/10.1007/s40279-013-0103-4

Cheng, Y. H. (2025). The impact of online games on creativity and the role of imagination. *Frontiers in Behavioral Neuroscience, 19*, 1561548. https://doi.org/10.3389/fnbeh.2025.1561548

Cottrell, C., McMillen, N., & Harris, B. S. (2019). Sport psychology in a virtual world: Considerations for practitioners working in eSports. *Journal of Sport Psychology in Action, 10*(2), 73–81. https://doi.org/10.1080/21520704.2018.1518280

Crawford, G. (2004). Consuming sport: Fans, sport and culture. *Routledge*. https://doi.org/10.4324/9780203493922

Dahl, M., Tryding, M., Heckler, A., & Nyström, M. (2021). Quiet eye and computerized precision tasks in first-person shooter perspective esport games. *Frontiers in Psychology, 12*, Article 676591. https://doi.org/10.3389/fpsyg.2021.676591

Erdoğan, N., & Kocaekşi, S. (2015). Elit sporcuların sahip olması gereken psikolojik özellikler. *Türkiye Klinikleri Journal of Sports Sciences, 7*(2), 57–64. https://doi.org/10.5336/sportsci.2014-42993

Fakazlı, A. E. (2020). The effect of COVID-19 pandemic on digital games and eSports. *International Journal of Sport Culture and Science, 8*(4), 335–344. https://doi.org/10.14486/IntJSCS.2020.621

Foehn, P., Brescianini, D., Kaufmann, E., Cieslewski, T., Gehrig, M., Muglikar, M., & Scaramuzza, D. (2022). AlphaPilot: Autonomous drone racing. *Autonomous Robots, 46*(1), 307–320.

Freemantle, A. W., Stafford, L. D., Wagstaff, C. R., Akehurst, L., & Van Laar, D. L. (2021). Development and validation of an in-competition emotion measure: The Brief In-Competition Emotion (BICE) scale. *Psychology of Sport and Exercise, 57*, Article 102050. https://doi.org/10.1016/j.psychsport.2021.102050

García-Lanzo, S., & Chamarro, A. (2018). Basic psychological needs, passion and motivations in amateur and semi-professional eSports players. *Aloma: Revista de Psicologia, Ciències de*

l'Educació i de l'Esport Blanquerna, 36(2), 59–68. https://doi.org/10.51698/aloma.2018.36.2.59-68
Georgievski, B., Labadze, L., & Aboelsoud, M. E. (2019). Comparative advantage as a success factor in football clubs: Evidence from the English Premier League (EPL). *Journal of Human Sport & Exercise, 14*(2), 292–314. https://doi.org/10.14198/jhse.2019.142.04
Gill, D. L. (2009). 2008 CH McCloy lecture: Social psychology and physical activity—Back to the future. *Research Quarterly for Exercise and Sport, 80*(4), 685–695. https://doi.org/10.1080/02701367.2009.10599609
Gill, D. L., & Williams, L. (2008). *Psychological dynamics of sport and exercise* (3rd ed.). Human Kinetics.
Gill, D. L., Williams, L., & Reifsteck, E. J. (2017). *Psychological dynamics of sport and exercise.* Human Kinetics.
Grupe, O. (1994). Sport and culture—The culture of sport. *Journal of Japan Society of Sports Industry, 4*(1), 39–53. https://doi.org/10.5997/sposun.4.39
Gul, M., Turkmen, M., Dogan, A., & Soyguden, A. (2015). Lost tradition in Kirkpinar oil wrestling: Importance of kispet and ceremony of kispet wearing. *International Journal of Wrestling Science, 5*(1), 52–55. https://doi.org/10.1080/21615667.2015.1031622
Hallmann, K., & Giel, T. (2018). ESports—Competitive sports or recreational activity? *Sport Management Review, 21*(1), 14–20. https://doi.org/10.1016/j.smr.2017.07.011
Hammerschmidt, J., Haski, S., Kraus, S., & Heinzen, M. (2024). New media, new possibilities? How esports strategies guide an ambidextrous understanding of tradition and innovation in the German Bundesliga. *Journal of Media Business Studies*, 1–23. https://doi.org/10.1080/16522354.2024.2340310
Jenny, S. E., Gawrysiak, J., O'Hagan, J., & Besombes, N. (2024). Esports education. In *Routledge handbook of esports* (pp. 441–453). Routledge.
Kilci, A. K. (2019). *Spor ve dijital oyunda son nokta: Espor*. Gazi Kitabevi.
Kopecký, K., a Szotkowski, R. (2018). Manifestations of addictive behaviour among the child players of the Minecraft game from the perspective of quantitative research. *Pediatrie pro Praxi [online], 19*(1), 35–40. Dostupné z: https://www.pediatriepropraxi.cz/pdfs/ped/2018/01/07.pdf
Koposov, D., Semenova, M., Somov, A., Lange, A., Stepanov, A., & Burnaev, E. (2020). Analysis of the reaction time of esports players through the gaze tracking and personality trait. In *2020 IEEE 29th International Symposium on Industrial Electronics (ISIE)* (pp. 1560–1565). IEEE. https://doi.org/10.1109/ISIE45063.2020.9152422
Krawietz, B. (2017). The sportification and heritagisation of traditional Turkish oil wrestling. In D. Hassan (Ed.), *Sport in the Middle East* (pp. 47–63). Routledge.
Lachowicz, M., Serweta-Pawlik, A., Konopka-Lachowicz, A., Jamro, D., & Żurek, G. (2025). How does virtual reality training affect reaction time and eye–hand coordination? The impact of short- and long-term interventions on cognitive functions in amateur esports athletes. *Applied Sciences, 15*(8), 4346. https://doi.org/10.3390/app15084346
Leis, O., & Lautenbach, F. (2020). Psychological and physiological stress in non-competitive and competitive esports settings: A systematic review. *Psychology of Sport and Exercise, 51*, Article 101738. https://doi.org/10.1016/j.psychsport.2020.101738
Leis, O., Raue, C., Dreiskämper, D., & Lautenbach, F. (2021). To be or not to be (e) sports? That is not the question! *German Journal of Exercise and Sport Research, 51*(2), 241–247. https://doi.org/10.1007/s12662-021-00715-9
Leis, O., Sharpe, B. T., Pelikan, V., Fritsch, J., Nicholls, A. R., & Poulus, D. (2024). Stressors and coping strategies in esports: A systematic review. *International review of sport and exercise psychology*, 1-31. https://doi.org/10.1080/1750984X.2024.2386528
Leis, O., Trotter, M. G., Birch, P. D., Bubna, K., & Poulus, D. R. (2025). Stressors and coping strategies in amateur esports players: An interview study. *International Journal of Sport Psychology, 56*(1), 47–70. https://doi.org/10.7352/IJSP.2025.56.047
Mancı, E., Bekir, S., & Çakır, Y. N. (Ed.). (2022). *Espora multidisipliner yaklaşımlar*. Nobel Bilimsel Eserler Yayınları.

Maheu, R. (1963). Sport and culture. *Journal of Health, Physical Education, Recreation, 34*(8), 30–49. https://doi.org/10.1080/00221473.1963.10611603
Martens, R., Vealey, R., & Burton, D. (1990). *Competitive anxiety in sports*. Human Kinetics.
McGee, C. (2021). *The ergonomics of esports*. In L. Migliore, C. McGee, & M. N. Moore (Eds.), Handbook of esports medicine (pp. 151–165). Springer. https://doi.org/10.1007/978-3-030-65462-8_13
McGee, C., Ho, K., & Jenny, S. E. (2024). Esports ergonomics and injuries. In *Routledge handbook of esports* (pp. 240–254). Routledge.
McGrath, K. (2019). Leveraging eSports in higher education. In *Understanding esports: An introduction to the global phenomenon* (p. 201).
Michel-Kröhler, A., Krys, S., & Berti, S. (2023). Development and preliminary validation of the Sports Competition Rumination Scale (SCRS). *Journal of Applied Sport Psychology, 35*(2), 265–283. https://doi.org/10.1080/10413200.2021.1961921
Morris, S. (2017, January 20). Welsh gamer jailed for grooming two boys on Minecraft. *The Guardian*. Retrieved from https://www.theguardian.com/uk-news/2017/jan/20/welshgamer-jailed-for-grooming-two-boys-on-minecraft
Navarro-Lucena, F., Molinillo, S., Anaya-Sánchez, R., & Muñoz-Leiva, F. (2025). Levelling up esports research: Mapping the past, present, and future of a thriving digital arena. *Performance Enhancement & Health, 13*(4), Article 100354. https://doi.org/10.1016/j.peh.2025.100354
NTV. (2015). *Minecraft oyuncularına kötü haber*. NTV. https://www.ntv.com.tr/teknoloji/minecraft-oyuncularina-kotu-haber
Parry, J. (2021). Esports will not be at the Olympics. *Journal of Olympic Studies, 2*(2), 1–10.
Pedraza-Ramirez, I., Musculus, L., Raab, M., & Laborde, S. (2020). Setting the scientific stage for esports psychology: A systematic review. *International Review of Sport and Exercise Psychology, 13*(1), 319–352. https://doi.org/10.1080/1750984X.2020.1723122
Pedraza-Ramirez, I., Sharpe, B., Behnke, M., Toth, A. J., & Poulus, D. R. (2025). The psychology of esports: Trends, challenges, and future directions. *Psychology of Sport and Exercise*, 102967. https://doi.org/10.1016/j.psychsport.2025.102967
Piatysotska, S. S., Mulyk, V. V., Huba, A. V., Dolgopolova, N. V., Yefremenko, A. M., & Zhernovnikova, Y. Y. (2023). Study of the psychomotor abilities of athletes in cyclic sports, martial arts and esports. *Slobozhanskyi Herald of Science and Sport, 27*, 19–25.
Pluss, M., Novak, A. R., Bennett, K. J. M., Panchuk, D., Coutts, A. J., Fransen, J., & Pluss, M. (2020). Perceptual-motor Abilities Underlying Expertise in Esports. *Journal of Expertise, 3*(2), 133–143. https://researchoutput.csu.edu.au/en/publications/perceptual-motor-abilities-underlying-expertise-in-esports
Reitman, J. G., Anderson-Coto, M. J., Wu, M., Lee, J. S., & Steinkuehler, C. (2020). Esports research: A literature review. *Games and Culture, 15*(1), 32–50. https://doi.org/10.1177/1555412019840892
Rogers, E. J., Trotter, M. G., Johnson, D., Desbrow, B., & King, N. (2024). KovaaK's aim trainer as a reliable metrics platform for assessing shooting proficiency in esports players: A pilot study. *Frontiers in Sports and Active Living, 6*, 1309991. https://doi.org/10.3389/fspor.2024.1309991
Rogstad, E. T. (2022). Gender in eSports research: A literature review. *European Journal for Sport and Society, 19*(3), 195–213. https://doi.org/10.1080/16138171.2021.1930941
Roper, E. A. (2002). Women working in the applied domain: Examining the gender bias in applied sport psychology. *Journal of Applied Sport Psychology, 14*(1), 53–66. https://doi.org/10.1080/10413200209339011
Rothwell, G., & Shaffer, M. (2019). ESports in K–12 and post-secondary schools. *Education Sciences, 9*(2), 105. https://doi.org/10.3390/educsci9020105
Sáez-López, J. M., Miller, J., Vázquez-Cano, E., & Domínguez-Garrido, M. C. (2015). Exploring application, attitudes and integration of video games: Minecraft Edu in middle school. *Journal of Educational Technology & Society, 18*(3), 114–128.

Sampaio, J., Lago, C., & Drinkwater, E. J. (2010). Explanations for the United States of America's dominance in basketball at the Beijing Olympic Games (2008). *Journal of Sports Sciences, 28*(2), 147–152. https://doi.org/10.1080/02640410903380486

Scholz, T. M. (2019). Stakeholders in the eSports industry. In *eSports is business: Management in the world of competitive gaming* (pp. 43–99). Springer.

Sharpe, B. T., & Birch, P. D. (2025). Psychology of esports special issue: A catalyst for change. *Journal of Electronic Gaming and Esports, 2*(1). https://doi.org/10.1123/jege.2024-0058

Shukry, A. I. M., Zaidi, N. A. S., Nawi, N. A. M. M., Abdullah, N., Rosli, N. N. I. N., & Idris, Z. (2024). Gaming addiction and academic performance: A battle for student success. *Journal of Islamic, 9*(66), 698–706. https://doi.org/10.55573/JISED.096657

Shynkaruk, O., Byshevets, N., Iakovenko, O., Serhiyenko, K., Anokhin, E., Yukhno, Y., & Stroganov, S. (2021). Modern approaches to the preparation system of masters in eSports.

Silva, J. M., Conroy, D. E., & Zizzi, S. J. (1999). Critical issues confronting the advancement of applied sport psychology. *Journal of Applied Sport Psychology, 11*(2), 298–320. https://doi.org/10.1080/10413209908404206

Silva, J. M. (1989). Toward the professionalization of sport psychology. *The Sport Psychologist, 3*, 265–273. https://doi.org/10.1123/tsp.3.3.265

Stapleton, A. B., Hankes, D. M., Hays, K. F., & Parham, W. D. (2010). Ethical dilemmas in sport psychology: A dialogue on the unique aspects impacting practice. *Professional Psychology: Research and Practice, 41*(2), 143–152. https://doi.org/10.1037/a0017976

Stefani, R. (2011). The methodology of officially recognized international sports rating systems. *Journal of Quantitative Analysis in Sports, 7*(4). https://doi.org/10.2202/1559-0410.1347

Stefani, R. (2016). Olympic sports of the future. *The Sport Journal*. https://thesportjournal.org/article/olympic-sports-of-the-future/

Szotkowski, R., Kopecký, K., & Dobešová, P. (2020). *Sexting u českých dětí*. Univerzita Palackého v Olomouci.

Vardal, O. (2023). *Using video games to study the acquisition and performance of psychomotor skills* (Doctoral dissertation, University of York).

Weinberg, R. S., & Gould, D. (2023). *Foundations of sport and exercise psychology*. Human Kinetics.

Willis, J. D. (1982). Three scales to measure competition-related motives in sport. *Journal of Sport and Exercise Psychology, 4*(4), 338–353. https://doi.org/10.1123/jsp.4.4.338

Wylleman, P., & Lavallee, D. (2004). A developmental perspective on transitions faced by athletes. *Developmental sport and exercise psychology: A lifespan perspective*, 507–527.

Chapter 2
Esports, Online Gaming, and Addiction: A Triadic Perspective

Kübra Dombak and Seyhan Bekir

2.1 Introduction

The Internet and computers not only simplify access to information but have also become increasingly important in the world of gaming and leisure. Due to factors such as continuous technological innovations, increasing rate of urbanization, and declining interest in physical games, digital games are increasingly substituting traditional games. In the recent past, gaming was carried out in playgrounds, streets, and homes with large groups of people, involving intense physical activity and interaction, but in recent years it has been carried out behind digital screens. Nowadays, most people prefer to play games on computers and via the internet. This has led to more variety in the gaming industry and the spread of online games. Online games are digital games played via an internet connection, which allow players to interact with other players or the game system in real time (Qu, 2023). The history of online games has been influenced by the types and technologies that have emerged in different periods. In the 1970s and 1980s, before the internet became widespread, text-based MUD (Multi-User Dungeon) games were the first examples of online interaction. Then, in the 1990s, LAN (Local Area Network) and early internet connections made multiplayer games like Quake and StarCraft popular. In the 2000s, with the strengthening of internet infrastructure, MMORPGs (e.g., World of Warcraft) and MOBAs (Dota, League of Legends) emerged, creating large player groups worldwide. After 2010, Battle Royale games (Fortnite, PUBG) becoming a global phenomenon, while

K. Dombak
Deparment of Guidance and Psychological Counseling, Faculty of Educational Science, Sakarya University, Sakarya, Türkiye
e-mail: kbrdmbk10@gmail.com

S. Bekir (✉)
Department of Psychology, Faculty of Science and Letters, Demiroglu Bilim University, Istanbul, Türkiye
e-mail: Seyhanbekir@yahoo.com

S. Bekir (ed.), *The Psychology of Esports*, https://doi.org/10.1007/978-3-032-25090-2_2

online mobile games (Clash Royale, Call of Duty Mobile) reaching users of all ages and furthering the spread of online gaming culture. Consequently, to understand esports psychology, it is helpful to be familiar with the different types of esports games (Ströh, 2017). The most popular games are MOBA and First Person Shooter (FPS) games (Bekir & Çelik, 2019).

MOBA (Multiplayer Online Battle Arena) video games are a type of MMOG (Massively Multiplayer Online Game) (Özenç & Tınmazlar, 2018). They are real-time strategy games that have become one of the most popular types of games in recent years. In a 5 vs. 5 MOBA game, ten players battle on a specific map. Everyone plays as a hero, and the aim is to destroy the opposing team's bases. These heroes have different abilities and skills (Hanke & Chaimowicz, 2017; Silva et al., 2015). These skills allow players to engage in a variety of tactics, such as testing reaction times (Saygı & Odabaş, 2023), setting traps, developing strategies, and executing pressure tactics. Therefore, reasoning, prediction, and tactical research are important in MOBA games (Silva et al., 2017).

FPS video games are action games played from the perspective of the main character, reflecting the perspective of the player (Boudaoud et al., 2022; Demirbaş, 2015; Migliore, 2021). FPS video games are 3D. The virtual worlds created in FPS games imitate the way the human eye perceives the physical world. The player's arms are shown at the bottom of the screen and are equipped with whichever weapons are available. The visible world is then remodeled. To increase the level of realism, many games add sound effects, footsteps, and breathing sounds (Eğüz, 2022). Consequently, it can be said that it is one of the most popular online games (STEAM, 2026).

2.2 Online Gaming and Esports

The spread of online games has led to the growth of tournaments for players, and this process has given rise to the term "*esports*." Esports is defined as a sport in which two people anywhere in the world can meet and play games online (Zhong et al., 2022). Esports has become a leisure activity that is increasingly popular not only among youth but also adults (Bányai et al., 2019). The rapid growth of esports has been significantly influenced by the variety of games and the development of online live streaming technology (Chen, 2022). The diversity of games and live streaming over the internet have increased spectator counts and raised the popularity of esports tournaments (Mao et al., 2022). Although esports gradually developed in the 1990s and 2000s, the real leap occurred after the 2010s. During this period, the number of tournaments increased, and the audience and prize pools expanded significantly. Platforms such as Twitch.tv, YouTube Live, and Facebook Live, in particular, enabled the global spread of esports and created a new market (Korolovych & Liba, 2023). Twitch, launched by Amazon in 2011, was a catalyst for the industry's growth, creating a revenue stream for both professional and amateur players to engage with their audience (Watanabe et al., 2021). Currently, the esports market is forecast to reach $4.8 billion by 2025 and reach over 896 million users by 2029 (Statista, 2025).

The two most important components of esports are esports players and spectators. Esports offer a space where digital games are not only played but also created and co-experienced, combining consumer and producer roles through both in-game interactions and game-based content to create a new media experience (Sjöblom et al., 2020). In this new media experience, esports has disrupted the traditional understanding of media by blurring the boundaries between spectators and players, creating a more participatory culture (Scholz, 2019). Some esports spectators play the games they watch, while others watch esports broadcasts even though they do not play. Even though those who play esports games are more likely to also be spectators (Hedlund, 2021), according to Newzoo's 2017, Global Esports Market Report, 42% of spectators do not play the games they watch (Pannekeet, 2017). This percentage is quite high and actually gives us important clues about the growth potential of esports. With the growth of the esports industry, every stakeholder in the ecosystem actually wants to make money from the audience (Scholz, 2019). In terms of viewers' gains from esports, some studies (Bowman et al., 2022; Yin et al., 2023) have found that watching esports streams creates a state of flow in individuals, relieves them from work and daily stress, provides an enjoyable experience, and this situation affects individuals' sense of well-being.

The widespread use of online games and esports is based on a confluence of technological, sociocultural, and economic factors. Primarily, the global strengthening of internet infrastructure and the proliferation of high-speed connectivity have made it possible for players from different regions to connect in real time. Improvements in computer hardware, game consoles, and mobile devices have increased user interest by offering high-resolution graphics, smooth gaming experiences, and advanced interaction capabilities. The rise of social media and live streaming platforms (e.g., Twitch, YouTube Gaming) has enabled gaming and esports events to reach wider audiences, transforming players into not only participants but also content creators and viewers. Competition, reward systems, and professional tournament organizations have transformed esports into an attractive career field, strengthening its economic dimension through sponsorship and advertising revenues. Furthermore, the social interaction, teamwork, and sense of belonging offered by online games are powerful attractions, especially among younger generations. All these factors have ensured that online games and esports have evolved beyond being merely a form of entertainment to become a widespread digital culture phenomenon on a global scale. Individuals who cannot detach themselves from the gaming world are shifting their gaming behavior to the center of their lives. This situation has many positive and negative repercussions for the individual.

2.3 Opportunities and Risks of Online Gaming for Esports Players

Online games offer esports players cognitive, social, emotional, and motivational benefits beyond mere entertainment. According to Mihaly Csikszentmihalyi's Flow Theory, when players encounter challenges that match their skill level, they experience flow, which both gives them pleasure and improve their performance (Deci & Ryan, 2000). Task-and goal-oriented structures support intrinsic motivation by giving players a sense of progress (Coelho et al., 2025). Furthermore, serious games contribute to the development of esports players by increasing attention span, openness to learning, and behavioral changes (Nanjundan et al., 2024). Gaming encourages problem solving, quick decision making, and creativity increases cognitive capacity; strategy games have a positive effect on memory and cognitive functions (Cahill & Dhamala, 2025). Socially, online games strengthen cultural interaction, encourage prosocial behavior, and reduce loneliness (Tushya et al., 2025). In addition, they provide psychological support with their stressful-reducing functions (Pallavicini et al., 2021). As a result, the right game selection and balanced use make online games a versatile development tool for esports players.

Although the widespread use of online games offers many opportunities for esports players, it also carries serious psychological, social, and physical risks. Overuse of gaming has been linked to decrease academic achievement, communication difficulties, anxiety disorders, and increased aggressive behavior, especially among young esports players (Düll et al., 2024). Furthermore, increased gaming time and problematic gaming behavior elevate the risk of depression, anxiety, and loneliness (Pallavicini et al., 2022). Physically, prolonged screen time can cause sleep disorders, eye dryness, and obesity, as well as back and hand pain (Nakshine et al., 2022). Furthermore, intense gaming tempo increases the risk of musculoskeletal disorders, particularly carpal tunnel syndrome (Lam et al., 2022). Decreased sleep quality and physical fatigue are also common among gamers with gaming addiction (Nakshine et al., 2022).

Game content also carries a risk factor for esports players. Games involving violence have been linked to decreased empathy and increased aggression (Gandolfi et al., 2025). For players under performance pressure, excessive participation can lead to academic failure, health problems, and weakened family relationships (Alzahrani & Griffiths, 2024). Furthermore, players who develop alternative identities in MMORPG-type games identify intensely with virtual worlds; this is associated with depression, low self-esteem, and decreased life satisfaction (Snodgrass et al., 2025). Competitive aspects, instant prizes, and constantly updated content accelerate addiction, leading to functional impairments in professional esports players' family, work, and educational lives (Sharma & Verma, 2025). Therefore, online gaming addiction is one of the most critical threats to not only individual health but also the career sustainability of esports players.

2.4 Online Game Addiction

While digital games are an important source of entertainment for many people, they can lead to serious problems when played for extended periods of time and uncontrollably. Game addiction is one of the most common problems. The concept of game addiction was first mentioned by Soper and Miller (1983), and over time, it began to be considered among behavioral addictions. In literature, game addiction has been referred to by various terms, including problematic online game use, video game addiction, problematic gaming, gaming disorder, pathological gaming, and online game addiction. This diversity demonstrates that game addiction is addressed in different ways. Online games are considered more appealing because they offer rapid feedback, near-realistic visuals, and provide players with the opportunity to interact with others (Griffiths, 2010). Furthermore, the ability of players to create alternative identities in virtual worlds increases the persistence of gaming behavior and increases the risk of addiction. Online game addiction is defined as an individual who develops a habit of playing games and finds it difficult to quit despite negative consequences (Charlton & Danforth, 2007). This addiction stems not only from a need for entertainment but also from psychosocial factors.

While offline games offer solitary pleasure, online games offer the opportunity to communicate with others, develop shared goals, and provide a sense of social belonging (Zervas & Maronitis, 2025). Research shows that addicted players try to fulfill needs that cannot be met in real life through games. Online games create a sense of belonging to a group, providing a sense of accomplishment and connection. This sense of belonging, in turn, increases the risk of addiction. Online gaming addiction manifests itself not only through the frequency of gaming but also through psychological and behavioral symptoms. Common symptoms include social isolation, the development of obsessive–compulsive beliefs about gaming, persistent gaming behavior despite realizing it is harmful to oneself, withdrawal, conflict, relapse, and behavioral salience (Xu et al., 2012). In short, online gaming addiction is a type of behavioral addiction that profoundly affects both the social and psychological lives of individuals. This activity, which seems fun for players, can turn into serious individual and social problems when control is lost.

Considering the increasing prevalence of online gaming and its associated problems, the American Psychiatric Association (APA) has recommended that problematic online gaming be included as "Internet Gaming Disorder" in the Diagnostic and Statistical Manual of Mental Disorders (DSM-5) to recognize it as a condition requiring further research and to clarify the diagnostic process (APA, 2022). Before the APA defined gaming addiction, the World Health Organization (WHO) began examining gaming addiction by recognizing it as a psychological health problem. In the 11th revision of the International Classification of Diseases (ICD11), published in 2019, WHO classifies problematic gaming as "Gaming Disorder" within the scope of behavioral addiction (WHO, 2019). The point that needs to be emphasized before discussing online gaming addiction is to define a general framework regarding the extent to which online gaming occupies an individual's daily life. However, Gentile

(2009) argues that prolonged gaming does not necessarily mean an individual has a gaming disorder. In this context, higher gaming frequency and longer durations are associated with the development of online gaming disorder (Kuss & Griffiths, 2012). Therefore, it can be argued that not every individual who plays games is addicted, and that for addiction to be considered, frequency and duration must exceed normal limits.

2.4.1 The Prevalence of Online Gaming Addiction

The number of online games and players is increasing every year. It is estimated that the number of individuals playing online games worldwide will reach approximately 3.32 billion by 2025. This figure represents almost half of the world's population and demonstrates that online gaming has become a widespread form of digital interaction globally. When examining the regional distribution, Asia leads with 1.48 billion players, followed by Europe and Latin America. Furthermore, approximately 83.6% of internet users play games. This rate is even higher in some countries; for example, in the Philippines, 97.1% of internet users play online games. This demonstrates that games go beyond being merely a means of entertainment and create a broad spectrum of participation at the socio-cultural level. According to Statista data, the number of people playing games worldwide increased from 760 million in 2017 to 1.31 billion in 2024 and is expected to reach 1.47 billion in 2027 (Clement, 2024). As of the third quarter of 2023, the gaming rate among internet users was reported as 83.1%. By country, Indonesia (96.5%), the Philippines (95.9%), and Turkey (94.8%) had the highest rates. These high rates highlight the importance of awareness of the negative effects of gaming behavior and the risk of Online Gaming Disorder.

While online gaming addiction is seen in a small portion of society, it is a growing problem on a global scale. Prevalence rates in literature vary across countries, age groups, and measurement methods. For example, studies have shown that this rate can range from as low as 0.2% to as high as 15%. While prevalence among adolescents in Europe is around 1–3%, it can reach up to 12% in some Asian countries, especially among male adolescents (Festl et al., 2013). Among the most important reasons for these differences are the diversity of measurement tools used, cultural factors, and differences in research samples (Kuss & Griffiths, 2012). Furthermore, cultural norms and societal expectations can also influence gaming behavior and its evaluation as an addiction. Therefore, it is not possible to provide a definitive prevalence rate for online gaming addiction. This demonstrates that addiction is a complex phenomenon shaped not by universal criteria but by the influence of cultural, societal, and individual factors.

2.4.2 Online Game Addiction Risk Factors

Online game addiction is considered a growing public health problem. According to a recent meta-analysis, game addiction may affect approximately 7% of the population, while this rate can exceed 20% among adolescents; the risk of addiction also tends to decrease with age (Stevens et al., 2021). Male gender, early internet use, low family income, and metropolitan living are among the important demographic risk factors for addiction (Kuss & Griffiths, 2012). Furthermore, personality traits such as impulsivity, sensation seeking, low self-management, low self-esteem, and introversion facilitate the development of addiction (Marinaci et al., 2021). Psychopathological problems are also closely related to addiction. Depression, anxiety, social phobia, and attention-deficit/hyperactivity disorder (ADHD) frequently coexist with online gaming addiction, creating a mutually reinforcing cycle (André et al., 2022). Furthermore, inadequate emotion regulation and stress management skills make gaming a short-term escape, increasing the risk of addiction.

Socio-environmental factors also play a determining role in the addiction process. Family dysfunction, poor parental support, and lack of supervision are among the factors that predispose to the development of addiction (Gentile et al., 2011). Lack of social skills, loneliness, and low empathy are also factors that drive individuals to use online games (Pallavicini et al., 2022). The social identity-building and opportunity to participate in virtual communities offered by games are particularly appealing to socially isolated individuals. However, cultural and environmental factors, particularly the prevalence of internet cafes, the promotion of a competitive gaming culture, and the aggressive marketing strategies of gaming companies, also play a critical role in the development of addiction. Design features of massively multiplayer online role-playing games (MMORPGs), such as "unlimited progression" and "being left behind when offline," make it difficult for individuals to quit the game and increase the risk of addiction (Kuss & Griffiths, 2012).

Esports players, as a particular risk group, also attract attention for online gaming addiction. Professional and semi-professional gamers participate in intense training sessions lasting more than 20–25 h per week, exceeding critical thresholds associated with addiction. Indeed, a study conducted in Hungary found the rate of internet addiction among adult recreational esports players to be 19.9% (Kósa et al., 2022). Similarly, a longitudinal study conducted with professional gamers found that 16.8% of gamers experienced functional problems due to gaming, compared to 9.8% in the non-professional group. Furthermore, professional players reportedly played an average of 36.4 h per week, while non-professionals played 26.7 h (Soffner et al., 2023). Prolonged gaming practices lead to a decrease in interest in activities outside of gaming and an increase in gaming-related mental preoccupation. Furthermore, the performance anxiety, tournament pressure, and constant competitive stress experienced by esports players are among the psychological factors that increase the risk of addiction.

Gaining identity and social status through gaming, sponsorship deals, and the pressure of popularity are leading games to become not just a means of entertainment but also a central part of life. Indeed, a large-scale survey of the esports community reported that 73% of participants exhibited mild symptoms of internet addiction, while 27% exhibited moderate symptoms (Poulus et al., 2024). Similar findings are observed in esports samples from different countries. For example, a study conducted in Jordan reported a prevalence of IGD among esports players of approximately 19% (Karasneh et al., 2021). In an Indonesian sample, 20% of esports players were found to meet the criteria for gaming addiction (Pritalia et al., 2024). In this context, online gaming addiction is considered not only an individual health problem for esports players but also a critical threat to their professional performance and sectoral sustainability.

2.4.3 Protective Factors for Online Game Addiction

Protective factors against online gaming addiction vary at the individual, familial, and environmental levels. Psychological resilience and self-control are among the strongest protective variables; research has emphasized that high self-regulation skills reduce the risk of addiction (Hidalgo-Fuentes et al., 2023). Similarly, emotional intelligence and stress coping skills serve as buffers against gaming addiction (Hawi & Samaha, 2023). At the familial level, parental support, open communication, and warm family relationships are among the protective factors against the development of addiction. Strong family ties, particularly in adolescents, have been associated with lower rates of online gaming addiction symptoms. At the social level, peer support and healthy social relationships play a role in mitigating the negative effects of excessive gaming behavior. In terms of education and leisure time management, participation in sports and physical activities stands out as one of the protective factors against addiction. Studies show that young people who engage in regular physical exercise have a lower risk of gaming addiction (Salmensalo et al., 2024). Additionally, time management skills and alternative pursuits reduce the risk of addiction by preventing games from becoming the center of life. Finally, psychoeducation programs and school-based awareness programs also support the development of healthy digital usage habits in individuals and offer an important protective mechanism against addiction. All these findings highlight the importance of multidimensional and holistic approaches to combating online gaming addiction.

2.5 Conclusion

This chapter demonstrates that online gaming addiction and esports are two phenomena that develop on the same digital cultural landscape but produce different outcomes. While online gaming addiction diminishes individuals' psychological, social, and biological functioning, reducing their quality of life, esports open new doors for individuals through disciplined work, strategic thinking, team spirit, and economic opportunities. This suggests that the impact of games on individuals is not unidirectional but varies depending on the context and usage. Therefore, holistic approaches must be developed at the individual, societal, and institutional levels to mitigate the negative effects of online gaming and effectively utilize the potential offered by esports. In this regard, family guidance, educational institutions' awareness-raising programs, and policymakers' regulatory frameworks play a critical role. Only then can online gaming be considered not only a risk factor but also a powerful opportunity space that supports cognitive, social, and economic development.

References

Alzahrani, A. K. D., & Griffiths, M. D. (2024). Problematic gaming and students' academic performance: A systematic review. *International Journal of Mental Health and Addiction*, 1-34. https://doi.org/10.1007/s11469-024-01338-5

American Psychiatric Association. (2022). *Diagnostic and statistical manual of mental disorders DSM 5*. American Psychiatric Publishing.

André, F., Munck, I., Håkansson, A., & Claesdotter-Knutsson, E. (2022). Game addiction scale for adolescents—Psychometric analyses of gaming behavior, gender differences and Adhd. *Frontiers in Psychiatry, 13*, Article 791254. https://doi.org/10.3389/fpsyt.2022.791254

Bányai, F., Griffiths, M. D., Király, O., & Demetrovics, Z. (2019). The psychology of esports: A systematic literature review. *Journal of Gambling Studies, 35*(2), 351–365. https://doi.org/10.1007/s10899-018-9763-1

Bekir, S., & Çelik, E. (2019). Examining the factors contributing to adolescents' online game addiction. *Anales de Psicología, 35*(3), 444–452. https://doi.org/10.6018/analesps.35.3.323681

Boudaoud, B., Spjut, J., & Kim, J. (2022). Firstpersonscience: An open source tool for studying fps esports aiming. In *ACM SIGGRAPH 2022 talks* (pp. 1–2).

Bowman, N. D., Rieger, D., & Tammy Lin, J. H. (2022). Social video gaming and well-being. *Current Opinion in Psychology, 45*, Article 101316. https://doi.org/10.1016/j.copsyc.2022.101316

Cahill, K., & Dhamala, M. (2025). Structurally constrained functional connectivity reveals efficient visuomotor decision-making mechanisms in action video gamers. *bioRxiv*, 2025–06. https://doi.org/10.1101/2025.06.13.659455

Charlton, J. P., & Danforth, I. D. W. (2007). Distinguishing addiction and high engagement in the context of online game playing. *Computers in Human Behavior, 23*(3), 1531–1548. https://doi.org/10.1016/j.chb.2005.07.002

Chen, D. M. (2022). Issues and strategies of localising sensitive audiovisual elements in game streaming: A case study on Overwatch League (OWL) Chinese streaming. *British Journal of Chinese Studies, 12*(2), 154–179. https://doi.org/10.51661/bjocs.v12i2.191

Clement, J. (2024). Share of internet users worldwide who play video games on any device as of 3rd quarter 2023, by region [Infographic]. Statista. https://www.statista.com/statistics/195768/global-gaming-reach-by-country/

Coelho, F., Rando, B., Aparício, D., Pontífice-Sousa, P., Gonçalves, D., & Abreu, A. M. (2025). The impact of educational gamification on cognition, emotions, and motivation: A randomized controlled trial. *Journal of Computers in Education*, 1–48. https://doi.org/10.1007/s40692-025-00366-x

Deci, E. L., & ve Ryan, R. M. (2000). The "What" and "Why" of goal pursuits: Human needs and the self-determination of behavior. *Psychological Inquiry, 11*(4), 227–268. https://doi.org/10.1207/S15327965PLI1104_01

Demirbaş, K. Y. (2015). Dijital oyunlara, "oyun türü" yaklaşımlarının sorunları: Platform oyunları türüörneği. *Selçuk İletişim, 9*(1), 363–387. https://doi.org/10.18094/si.05694

Düll, L., Müller, A., & Steins-Loeber, S. (2024). Negative consequences experienced by individuals with gaming disorder symptoms: A systematic review of available longitudinal studies. *Current Addiction Reports, 11*(3), 528–550. https://doi.org/10.1007/s40429-024-00554-2

Eğüz, E. B. (2022). Video oyunları içerisindeki ürün yerleştirmeler (gamevertising) üzerine bir içerik analizi. *Maltepe Üniversitesi İletişim Fakültesi Dergisi, 8*(2), 287–323.

Festl, R., Scharkow, M., & Quandt, T. (2013). Problematic computer game use among adolescents, younger and older adults. *Addiction, 108*, 592–599. https://doi.org/10.1111/add.12016

Gandolfi, E., Ferdig, R. E., Krause, K., Copus, A., Ostrowski-Delahanty, S., & Alemagno, S. (2025). Problematic gaming at a crossroad: Exploring the interplay between internet gaming disorder, toxic attitudes, and empathy in digital entertainment. *Games and Culture, 20*(5), 633–656. https://doi.org/10.1177/15554120231211991

Gentile, D. (2009). Pathological video-game use among youth ages 8 to 18: A national study. *Psychological Science., 20*(5), 594–602. https://doi.org/10.1111/j.1467-9280.2009.02340.x

Gentile, D. A., Choo, H., Liau, A., Sim, T., Li, D., Fung, D., & Khoo, A. (2011). Pathological video game use among youths: A two-year longitudinal study. *Pediatrics, 127*(2), https://doi.org/10.1542/peds.2010-1353

Griffiths, M. (2010). The role of context in online gaming excess and addiction: Some case study evidence. *International Journal of Mental Health Addiction, 8*(1), 119–125. https://doi.org/10.1007/s11469-009-9229-x

Hanke, L., & Chaimowicz, L. (2017). A recommender system for hero line-ups in MOBA games. In *Proceedings of the AAAI conference on artificial Intelligence and interactive digital entertainment* (Vol. 13, No. 1, pp. 43–49).

Hawi, N., & Samaha, M. (2023). The relationship between obsessive-compulsive disorder and gaming disorder. *International Journal of Cyber Behavior, Psychology and Learning (IJCBPL), 13*(1), 1–15. https://doi.org/10.4018/ijcbpl.330133

Hedlund, D. P. (2021). A typology of esport players. *Journal of Global Sport Management, 8*(2), 460–477. https://doi.org/10.1080/24704067.2021.1871858

Hidalgo-Fuentes, S., Martí-Vilar, M., & Ruiz-Ordoñez, Y. (2023). Problematic internet use and resilience: A systematic review and meta-analysis. *Nursing Reports, 13*(1), 337–350. https://doi.org/10.3390/nursrep13010032

Karasneh, R., Al-Azzam, S., Alzoubi, K. H., Nusair, M. B., Hawamdeh, S., & Nusir, A. T. (2021). Patterns and predictors of internet gaming disorder: An observational study from jordan. *Clinical Practice and Epidemiology in Mental Health: CP & EMH, 17*, 217. https://doi.org/10.2174/1745017902117010217

Korolovych, O., & Liba, N. (2023). Game streaming platforms and their impact on the development of esports as a new sphere of Ukraine's digital economy. *Економічна наука, 13*, 36–40. http://dspace.msu.edu.ua:8080/jspui/handle/123456789/11552

Kósa, G., Feher, G., Horvath, L., Zadori, I., Nemeskeri, Z., Kovacs, M., Fejes, É., Meszaros, J., Banko, Z., & Tibold, A. (2022). Prevalence and risk factors of problematic internet use among Hungarian adult recreational esports players. *International Journal of Environmental Research and Public Health, 19*(6), 3204. https://doi.org/10.3390/ijerph19063204

Kuss, D. J., & Griffiths, M. D. (2012). Internet gaming addiction: A systematic review of empirical research. *International Journal of Mental Health and Addiction, 10*(2), 278–296. https://doi.org/10.1007/s11469-011-9318-5

Lam, W. K., Liu, R. T., Chen, B., Huang, X. Z., Yi, J., & Wong, D. W. C. (2022). Health risks and musculoskeletal problems of elite mobile esports players: A cross-sectional descriptive study. *Sports Medicine-Open, 8*(1), 65. https://doi.org/10.1186/s40798-022-00458-3

Mao, Z., Du, Z., Yuan, R., & ve Miao, Q. (2022). Short-term or long-term cooperation between retailer and MCN? New launched products sales strategies in live streaming e-commerce. *Journal of Retailing and Consumer Services, 67*, 102996. https://doi.org/10.1016/j.jretconser.2022.102996

Marinaci, T., Venuleo, C., Ferrante, L., & Della Bona, S. (2021). What game we are playing: The psychosocial context of problem gambling, problem gaming and poor well-being among Italian high school students. *Heliyon, 7*(8). https://doi.org/10.1016/j.heliyon.2021.e07872

Migliore, L. (2021). What is esports? The past, present, and future of competitive gaming. In *Handbook of esports medicine: Clinical aspects of competitive video gaming* (pp. 1–16). Springer International Publishing.

Nakshine, V. S., Thute, P., Khatib, M. N., & Sarkar, B. (2022). Increased screen time as a cause of declining physical, psychological health, and sleep patterns: A literary review. *Cureus, 14*(10). https://doi.org/10.7759/cureus.30051

Nanjundan, P., Chinnasami, S., Saravanan, V., & Ramachandran, M. (2024). Contrasting the impact of online games and offline games: A comparative analysis. *Contemporaneity of English Language and Literature in the Robotized Millennium, 2*(4), 28–36.

Özenç, O. E., & Keskin, H. (2018). *Türkiye'de e-spor ve league of legends: Dijital oyunlar serisi-3 profil kitap.*

Pallavicini, F., Pepe, A., & Mantovani, F. (2021). Commercial off-the-shelf video games for reducing stress and anxiety: Systematic review. *JMIR Mental Health, 8*(8), Article e28150. https://doi.org/10.2196/28150

Pallavicini, F., Pepe, A., & Mantovani, F. (2022). The effects of playing video games on stress, anxiety, depression, loneliness, and gaming disorder during the early stages of the COVID-19 pandemic: PRISMA systematic review. *Cyberpsychology, Behavior, and Social Networking, 25*(6), 334–354. https://doi.org/10.1089/cyber.2021.0252

Pannekeet, J. (2017). Esports, a franchise perspective: 70% watch only one game and 42% do not play. Retrieved August 10, 2025, from https://newzoo.com/resources/blog/esports-franchises-70-watch-only-one-gameand-42-dont-play

Poulus, D., Nicholson, M., Obine, E., Drew, M., Fisher, K., Vella, S., & Sharpe, B. (2024). The state of mental health research in esports: A scoping review. *Retrieved from ResearchGate:* https://shorturl.at/1h7Tb. https://doi.org/10.31234/osf.io/g78kd

Pritalia, G. L., Rahayu, F. S., Brahmandika, L., & Nastiti, P. (2024). An empirical study on Internet Gaming Disorder (IGD) among Indonesian esports players. In *2024 International Conference on Information Technology Systems and Innovation (ICITSI)* (pp. 14–20). IEEE. https://doi.org/10.1109/icitsi65188.2024.10929428

Qu, X. (2023). An overview of online games and their effects on adolescents. *Open Journal of Social Sciences, 11*(11), 310–320. https://doi.org/10.4236/jss.2023.1111021

Salmensalo, M., Ruotsalainen, H., Hylkilä, K., Kääriäinen, M., Konttila, J., Männistö, M., & Männikkö, N. (2024). Associations between digital gaming behavior and physical activity among Finnish vocational students. *Journal of Public Health, 32*(1), 53–63. https://doi.org/10.1007/s10389-022-01788-y

Saygı, T., & Odabaş, İ. (2023). Comparing the accuracy and reaction times of esports players and sport sciences students. *Eurasian Research in Sport Science, 8*(2), 80–94.

Scholz, T. (2019). *Esports is business. Management in the world of competitive gaming.* Palgrave-Macmillan. https://doi.org/10.1007/978-3-030-11199-1

Silva, M. P., do Nascimento Silva, V., & Chaimowicz, L. (2015, November). Dynamic difficulty adjustment through an adaptive AI. In *2015 14th Brazilian symposium on computer games and digital entertainment (SBGames)* (pp. 173–182). IEEE.

Silva, M. P., do Nascimento Silva, V., & Chaimowicz, L. (2017). Dynamic difficulty adjustment on MOBA games. *Entertainment Computing, 18*, 103–123.

Sjöblom, M., Macey, J., & Hamari, J. (2020). Digital athletics in analogue stadiums: Comparing gratifications for engagement between live attendance and online esports spectating. *Internet Research, 30*(3), 713–735. https://doi.org/10.1108/INTR-07-2018-0304

Snodgrass, J. G., Sagstetter, S. I., Branstrator, J. R., Giardina, A., Lacy, M. G., Bollinger-Deters, A. T.,Callendar, C. L., Zhao, K. X., Dengah II, H. J., & Billieux, J. (2025). Player-avatar bonds and gaming benefits and risks: Assessing self-discrepancy theory against a broader range of character and play experiences. *Cyberpsychology: Journal of Psychosocial Research on Cyberspace, 19*(3). https://doi.org/10.5817/cp2025-3-10

Soffner, M., Bickmann, P., Tholl, C., & Froböse, I. (2023). Dietary behavior of video game players and esports players in Germany: A cross-sectional study. *Journal of Health, Population and Nutrition, 42*(1), 29. https://doi.org/10.1186/s41043-023-00373-7

Soper, W. B., & Miller, M. J. (1983). Junk-time junkies: An emerging addiction among students. *The School Counselor, 31*(1), 40–43.

Statista. (2025). eSports market revenue worldwide 2025–2029. Retrieved August 10, 2025, from https://www.statista.com/outlook/amo/esports/worldwide

STEAM. (2026). Steam User Status. Retrieved January 12, 2026, from https://store.steampowered.com/stats/stats/?l=turkish

Stevens, M. W., Dorstyn, D., Delfabbro, P. H., & King, D. L. (2021). Global prevalence of gaming disorder: A systematic review and meta-analysis. *Australian & New Zealand Journal of Psychiatry, 55*(6), 553–568. https://doi.org/10.1177/0004867420962851

Ströh, J. H. A. (2017). *The eSports market and eSports sponsoring* (1st ed.). Tectum Verlag Marburg. ISBN: 978-3828838918.

Sharma, I., & Verma, N. (2025). Addiction to online gaming and its effects on youth mental health: A psychological analysis and new approaches to treatment. *Shodhbodhalaya, 3*(1), 206–223.

Tushya, Chhabra, D., & Abraham, B. (2025). Social networking or social isolation? A systematic review on socio-relational outcomes for members of online gaming communities. *Games and Culture, 20*(3), 355–383. https://doi.org/10.1177/15554120231201760

Watanabe, N. M., Xue, H., Newman, J. I., & Yan, G. (2021). The attention economy and esports: An econometric analysis of Twitch viewership. *Journal of Sport Management, 36*(2), 145–158. https://doi.org/10.1123/jsm.2020-0383

World Health Organization. (2019). *International statistical classification of diseases and related health problems* (11th ed.). https://icd.who.int/

Xu, Z., Turel, O., & Yuan, Y. (2012). Online game addiction among adolescents: Motivation and prevention factors. *European Journal of Information Systems, 21*(3), 321–340.

Yin, C., Huang, Y., Kim, D., & Kim, K. (2023). The effect of esports content attributes on viewing flow and well-being: A focus on the moderating effect of esports involvement. *Sustainability, 15*(16), 12207. https://doi.org/10.3390/su151612207

Zervas, K., & Maronitis, K. (2025). Digital bonds: A gamers' perspective on the role of online gaming communities in fostering social interaction and identity. *International Review for the Sociology of Sport*, 10126902251349297.

Zhong, Y., Guo, K., Su, J., & Chu, S. K. W. (2022). The impact of esports participation on the development of 21st century skills in youth: A systematic review. *Computers & Education, 191*, Article 104640. https://doi.org/10.1016/j.compedu.2022.104640

Chapter 3
Attachment and Relational Regulation in Esports Psychology: Understanding Performance in Digital Environments

Elif Balıkçı

3.1 Introduction

Today, digital technologies and virtual environments have become not merely tools of communication, but social contexts in which relationships are established, maintained, and regulated (Boellstorff, 2008; Possamai-Inesedy & Nixon, 2017). In this context, esports presents a distinctive performance domain characterized by digital mediation, high levels of competition, continuous evaluation, and synchronous social interaction (Castronova, 2005). From this perspective, although debates regarding whether esports constitutes a "real" sport have largely been surpassed, it remains necessary to emphasize the importance of focusing on the psychological characteristics of this distinctive performance environment (Leis et al., 2021). While the literature has frequently highlighted the cognitive load, decision-making processes, and emotion regulation demands of esports (Pedraza-Ramirez et al., 2025), the relational and regulatory components as part of its psychosocial dimension have received comparatively less attention. However, esports is not merely a domain in which cognitive and motor skills are displayed; it is also an environment in which relational regulation takes place under conditions of threat, uncertainty, and social evaluation. Intra-team communication, coach feedback, social media evaluations, and digital visibility shape not only players' performance but also their perceptions of security and their ways of coping with stress (Kavanagh et al., 2022). In this respect, esports can be conceptualized as a hybrid relational system characterized by digital mediation (Sitnik-Warchulska et al., 2023).

E. Balıkçı (✉)
Department of Pychology, Faculty of Art and Social Sciences, Istanbul Galata University, Istanbul, Turkey
e-mail: elif.balikci@galata.edu.tr

S. Bekir (ed.), *The Psychology of Esports*, https://doi.org/10.1007/978-3-032-25090-2_3

This section seeks to examine the relationships individuals establish with the digital world and with one another through the digital world, addressing the psychosocial dimension of esports practices, which involve stressful moments of competition and team interactions largely taking place in virtual environments, both from a foundational perspective and without overlooking their structural distinctiveness. Bowlby's (1969) Attachment Theory is one of the foundational theories in psychology that explains the relationships individuals form with themselves, with others, and with the world in stressful contexts, as well as their internal regulatory mechanisms. Explaining the stress-inducing competitive environment of esports and the digitally mediated relationships established by esports players on the basis of the fundamental principles of attachment theory will provide a theoretical grounding for discussing the psychosocial dimension of esports.

3.2 Fundamental Concepts of Attachment Theory and Its Place in Sport Psychology

Attachment theory, which explains the internal regulatory mechanisms individuals develop in stressful situations through reliance on close relationships in their search for security, offers a deeply rooted and comprehensive theoretical framework within the psychology literature (Bowlby, 1969). Its central assumption is that from birth, individuals are biologically oriented toward seeking safety and proximity, that internal regulatory mechanisms are formed through experiences in the early years of life, and that this working system continues to function throughout the lifespan. In early childhood, attachment patterns are shaped according to the sensitivity and consistency of the caregiver figure, forming internal working models that determine individuals' perspectives on themselves and others (Ainsworth et al., 1978).

Exploratory behavior, defined as the tendency to establish effective and competent interaction with the environment (White, 1959), is innate, just like the need for attachment characterized by a tendency toward security and proximity. Attachment theory explains that the attachment system, activated in stressful moments, functions like an alarm that interrupts the exploratory system. The fundamental condition for these two systems to function together in a healthy manner is associated with the caregiver's sensitive and consistent responsiveness to the individual's need for proximity during stressful moments in the early years of life (Ainsworth et al., 1978; Elliot & Reis, 2003). In addition to proximity, the caregiver—who provides the function of a "secure base" as a psychological foundation enabling the individual to explore the environment and of a "safe haven" as a source to which the individual can turn in order to achieve emotional regulation in stressful moments—gradually becomes an attachment figure. According to the theory, close relationships that fulfill these functions in an individual's life may become attachment figures and take their place as relationships that regulate the attachment system (Bowlby, 1988). The adult attachment literature conceptualizes attachment patterns along the dimensions of anxiety and avoidance, describing them as patterns of emotion, cognition, and behavior that move toward more secure attachment as attachment anxiety and avoidance decrease, and toward more insecure attachment as they increase (Brennan et al., 1998). As attachment anxiety rises, individuals become more sensitive to the possibility of rejection and disapproval, engage in greater reassurance-seeking in relationships, experience greater disruption of the exploratory system, and display less functional coping strategies in dealing with stress; when attachment avoidance increases, individuals appear as those who suppress the need for proximity, tend to preserve their autonomy, experience less disruption of the exploratory system yet are unable to conduct exploration within a sufficiently healthy framework, and more often choose suppression as a coping strategy. In the secure pattern, where low anxiety and low avoidance are evident, the individual is seen as possessing the capacity to maintain the exploratory system in a healthy manner, establish closeness, and demonstrate independent and functional coping mechanisms in stressful moments (Mikulincer & Shaver, 2016).

This theoretical framework explaining attachment possesses the capacity to account for the sport context in a fundamentally detailed manner. The sport environment constitutes a field of exploration through performance and competition; at the same time, with its inherent stress and perception of uncertainty, it is a potentially threatening environment capable of activating attachment (Carr, 2009a; Elliot & Reis, 2003; Forrest, 2008). According to the theory, contexts involving evaluation, the possibility of failure, and social comparison are stressful environments that increase threat perception and intensify the search for security (Mikulincer & Shaver, 2016). The sport environment, with its structure in which performance is constantly observed, success is conditionally rewarded, and failure and mistakes are highly visible, precisely meets these characteristics (Mellalieu et al., 2009). Recognizing the theory's capacity to explain the sport context, researchers have examined factors such as athlete–coach relationships, peer relationships within teams, and social support mechanisms on the basis of attachment theory. It has been observed that athletes with higher attachment security develop greater trust, open communication, and mutual commitment with their coaches and peers, thereby positively influencing their performance satisfaction and psychological well-being. In contrast, as attachment anxiety increases, athletes respond more sensitively to coach feedback and report higher feelings of rejection and disapproval within the team; as attachment avoidance rises, help-seeking behavior decreases and athletes are found to remain more distant from their coaches or peers (Carr, 2009b; Davis & Jowett, 2010, 2014; Jowett & Cockerill, 2003). Moreover, the stress-inducing environment of sport is not limited to the performance "field"; rather, it encompasses the ecosystem of the sport environment, including organizations, travel, competition and training routines, training camps, and all individuals associated with the context (Arnold et al., 2017). Such environments are defined in attachment theory as unfamiliar environments that activate the attachment system by triggering the need for security and proximity (Ainsworth et al., 1978). The threat perceived from this unfamiliar environment is not physical but related to disconnection in relationships (Johnson, 2019). Owing to its structural characteristics, the sport environment frequently creates this type of stressful setting, potentially confining athletes within a cycle of uncertainty, loss of control, and diminished social support (Mikulincer & Shaver, 2016).

3.3 A Perspective on the Distinctive Environment of Esports Within the Framework of Attachment Theory

The esports environment offers a performance domain in which intense, synchronous interactions are established predominantly within a virtual rather than a physical space. While players are often situated in relatively isolated physical settings, they perform in coordination through digital communication networks and are subjected to social evaluation (Boellstorff, 2008; Possamai-Inesedy & Nixon, 2017). As in other sport environments, threat and uncertainty are present within a stressful field of competition in esports; however, within the distinctive structure and setting of esports performance, elements related to attachment are not directly transferred to the digital environment but are reorganized within it. Sitnik-Warchulska et al. (2023) note that these interactions across physical and virtual environments create a hybrid world. That is, attachment in the esports environment does not emerge merely as a digital version of the physical context, but rather unfolds within a hybrid relational system. While the player is physically alone, they are digitally and continuously evaluated and observed. This situation may create a distinctive regulatory process within the attachment system that requires simultaneous processing of both proximity and threat signals.

In the digital performance environment of esports, elements such as high spectator pressure, instant performance feedback, post-error visibility, and evaluation through digital platforms render the threat perception of the competitive environment continuous. The simultaneous observation of performance, its openness to evaluation, and the esports player's concurrent exposure to these evaluations constitute, according to the sport psychology literature, one of the primary factors that increase performance anxiety. It is well established that environments characterized by high levels of evaluation and error visibility increase athletes' cognitive anxiety while weakening their self-regulation skills (Mellalieu et al., 2009). In their review of esports psychology, Pedraza-Ramirez et al. (2025) noted that esports performance occurs under high cognitive load and that emotion regulation is critical. When this situation is evaluated from an attachment perspective (Mikulincer & Shaver, 2016), in the esports environment players with high attachment anxiety may attend excessively to performance-related evaluations and, following an error, seek greater reassurance in interactions with their team or coach; whereas in players with high attachment avoidance, evaluations may be experienced as distressing, leading to reduced communication after mistakes, resistance to coach feedback, or withdrawal from team coordination. In addition to this perspective, as Sitnik-Warchulska et al. (2023) indicate, part of attachment-based regulation occurs through "mediated digital contact". In other words, researchers suggest that the search for proximity, necessary for internal regulation in attachment theory, may provide emotional and physiological regulation through digital cues in online interactions. Translated into the esports context, this means that in stressful moments players may utilize voice communication, instant messages, and digital indicators that signal the presence and support of the coach or team in order to fulfill the functions of a secure base and safe haven. However, secure bases in digital environments may be more fragile in terms of sensitivity and consistency; inconsistencies such as the variability of team structure, disruptions in online communication, and instantaneous negative social media evaluations may lead to greater activation of the attachment system (Mikulincer & Shaver, 2016). Indeed, in line with this entire theoretical explanation, Leis et al. (2021) reported that esports players often regulate performance stress through intra-team support, communication, and social bonds.

When explaining esports within the framework of attachment theory, there are findings that warrant discussion regarding the function of attachment avoidance in digital environments. Research indicates that increased attachment avoidance heightens the tendency to avoid face-to-face social evaluation, directing individuals to spend more time in digital environments, and this has been found to be associated with both internet and gaming addiction (Arpaci et al., 2017; Eichenberg et al., 2017; Sung et al., 2020). In this context, considering that digital environments may be more preferable and functional for individuals displaying an avoidant attachment pattern, it may be inferred that the esports environment could appear more efficient for players with avoidant attachment. This is because individuals high in attachment avoidance, unlike anxiously attached individuals, do not exhibit visible stress responses by employing hyperactivating regulatory strategies; instead, they rely on deactivating strategies—such as suppressing emotions, inhibiting emotional experience, and distancing themselves from stress-related cognitive content—that do not overtly display stress responses (Mikulincer & Shaver, 2003). This regulatory pattern in avoidance may appear more controlled from an external perspective compared to anxiety. While online environments provide individuals high in attachment avoidance with the social isolation they seek and may appear adaptive in the esports context in the short term, it can be argued that in the long term they carry the risk of problematic digital engagement and indirectly affecting performance (Sung et al., 2020). This is because individuals high in attachment avoidance, while benefiting from the isolation in which they feel comfortable, may make social errors such as failing to recognize their need for closeness, misperceiving threat, and missing social signals (Coulson et al., 2017). In the esports context, this may translate into a form of perceptual blindness among avoidant attached players, such as failing to notice intra-team tensions, disregarding coach or team feedback, and not recognizing that social disconnection is affecting their performance. Therefore, although "not appearing stressed" during performance may seem advantageous, attachment avoidance constitutes an invisible risk, and its long-term consequences may be detrimental.

3.4 Contribution of Attachment Theory to Applied Esports Performance

This evaluation within the framework of attachment theory demonstrates that focusing solely on cognitive and technical skills is insufficient in applications aimed at esports performance. For sport psychologists and performance specialists, assessing players' attachment patterns and addressing intra-team communication dynamics, feedback processes, and regulatory strategies under stress within this framework present an important area of application. In particular, interventions aimed at regulating evaluation sensitivity among players with anxious attachment patterns, and efforts to strengthen the ability to recognize social signals and utilize support among players with avoidant attachment patterns, may enhance the sustainability of performance. Furthermore, structuring digital communication channels in ways that support the functions of a "secure base" and "safe haven" may contribute to strengthening relational regulation within hybrid performance environments. In this regard, the development of protective and regulatory technologies aimed at preventing the uncontrolled spread of aggressive and hostile expressions in online interactions emerges as a particularly important area of application. In this respect, an attachment-based approach allows for the development of a more holistic and long-term performance model in esports psychology.

3.5 Conclusion

In conclusion, esports is not merely a platform in which players display the psychological skills of performance and sport psychologists focus solely on training these skills. It also emerges as a field of application in which attachment—fundamental to the individual's emotional and social development—can be examined in its manifestation within the digital age. Bowlby's theoretical framework, by explaining how individuals organize their search for security, regulation of proximity, and exploratory behavior in stressful and uncertain environments, provides a strong theoretical foundation for understanding the distinctive performance context of esports. On the one hand, the esports environment contains threat elements capable of activating the attachment system through high cognitive load, simultaneous social evaluation, and error visibility. On the other hand, through digital communication channels, it creates a hybrid relational domain in which the functions of secure base and safe haven can be reorganized. In this respect, esports constitutes a distinctive environment demonstrating that attachment-based regulatory processes may operate not only through physical proximity but also through mediated and digital contact.

The evaluation sensitivity, reassurance-seeking, and risks of emotional fluctuation among players high in attachment anxiety, as well as the seemingly "controlled" but deactivating regulatory strategies of players high in attachment avoidance—who risk missing social signals and failing to benefit from support—demonstrate that esports performance cannot be explained solely by cognitive and motor skills. These different attachment patterns may generate effects across a broad spectrum, ranging from intra-team communication to coach feedback, from performance identity to long-term well-being. Therefore, the sustainability of performance in the esports context depends not only on technical and psychological skill training but also on understanding players' relational patterns and how they regulate themselves under stress.

As a final remark, it is necessary to move beyond a common mistake occasionally made in the literature: viewing esports players as robots who merely display cognitive performance. Esports players should be understood as subjects positioned within a digital relational ecosystem, carrying a search for security and a need for belonging. At this point, attachment theory offers a holistic and in-depth framework for explaining the psychosocial dimension of esports and for making sense of the new regulatory dynamics emerging within the performance environments of the digital age.

References

Ainsworth, M. D. S., Blehar, M. C., Waters, E., & Wall, S. (1978). *Patterns of attachment: A psychological study of the strange situation*. Erlbaum.

Arnold, R., Fletcher, D., & Daniels, K. (2017). Organizational stressors, coping, and outcomes in competitive sport. *Journal of Sports Sciences, 35*(7), 694–703. https://doi.org/10.1080/02640414.2016.1184299

Arpaci, I., Baloğlu, M., Özteke Kozan, H. İ., & Kesici, Ş. (2017). Individual differences in the relationship between attachment and nomophobia among college students: The mediating role of mindfulness. *Journal of Medical Internet Research, 19*(12), e404. https://doi.org/10.2196/jmir.8847

Boellstorff, T. (2008). Coming of age in Second Life: An anthropologist explores the virtually human. *Princeton University Press*. https://doi.org/10.1515/9781400874101

Bowlby, J. (1969). *Attachment and loss: Vol. 1. Attachment*. Basic Books.

Bowlby, J. (1988). *A secure base: Parent-child attachment and healthy human development*. Basic Books.

Brennan, K. A., Clark, C. L., & Shaver, P. R. (1998). Self-report measurement of adult attachment: An integrative overview. In J. A. Simpson & W. S. Rholes (Eds.), *Attachment theory and close relationships* (pp. 46–76). Guilford Press.

Carr, S. (2009a). Implications of attachment theory for sport and physical activity research: Conceptual links with achievement goal and peer-relationship models. *International Review of Sport and Exercise Psychology, 2*(1), 95–115. https://doi.org/10.1080/17509840902759173

Carr, S. (2009b). Adolescent–parent attachment characteristics and quality of youth sport friendship. *Psychology of Sport and Exercise, 10*(6), 653–661. https://doi.org/10.1016/j.psychsport.2009.04.001

Castronova, E. (2005). Synthetic worlds: The business and culture of online games. *University of Chicago Press*. https://doi.org/10.7208/9780226096315

Coulson, M., Oskis, A., & Gould, R. L. (2017). Avoidance of the real and anxiety about the unreal: Attachment style and video-gaming. *Contemporary Issues in Early Childhood, 18*(2), 240–249. https://doi.org/10.1177/1463949117714085

Davis, L., & Jowett, S. (2010). Investigating the interpersonal dynamics between coaches and athletes based on fundamental principles of attachment. *Journal of Clinical Sport Psychology, 4*(2), 112–132. https://doi.org/10.1123/jcsp.4.2.112

Davis, L., & Jowett, S. (2014). Coach–athlete attachment and the quality of the coach–athlete relationship: Implications for athletes' well-being. *Journal of Sports Sciences, 32*(15), 1454–1464. https://doi.org/10.1080/02640414.2014.898183

Eichenberg, C., Schott, M., Decker, O., & Sindelar, B. (2017). Attachment style and internet addiction: An online survey. *Journal of Medical Internet Research, 19*(5), Article e170. https://doi.org/10.2196/jmir.6694

Elliot, A. J., & Reis, H. T. (2003). Attachment and exploration in adulthood. *Journal of Personality and Social Psychology, 85*(2), 317–331. https://doi.org/10.1037/0022-3514.85.2.317

Forrest, K. A. (2008). Attachment and attention in sport. *Journal of Clinical Sport Psychology, 2*(3), 242–257. https://doi.org/10.1123/jcsp.2.3.242

Johnson, S. M. (2019). Attachment theory in practice: Emotionally Focused Therapy (EFT) with individuals, couples, and families. *Guilford Press.* https://doi.org/10.4324/9781351168366

Jowett, S., & Cockerill, I. M. (2003). Olympic medalists' perspective of the athlete–coach relationship. *Psychology of Sport and Exercise, 4*(4), 313–331. https://doi.org/10.1016/S1469-0292(02)00011-0

Kavanagh, E., Litchfield, C., & Osborne, J. (2022). Social media, digital technology and athlete abuse. In *Sport, social media, and digital technology: Sociological approaches* (pp. 185–204). Emerald Publishing. https://doi.org/10.1108/S1476-285420220000015022

Leis, O., Raue, C., Dreiskämper, D., & Lautenbach, F. (2021). To be or not to be (e)sports? That is not the question! Why and how sport and exercise psychology could research esports. *German Journal of Exercise and Sport Research, 51*(2), 241–247. https://doi.org/10.1007/s12662-021-00715-9

Mellalieu, S. D., Hanton, S., & Fletcher, D. (2009). A competitive anxiety review: Recent directions in sport psychology research. In S. D. Mellalieu & S. Hanton (Eds.), *Advances in applied sport psychology* (pp. 1–45). Nova Science Publishers.

Mikulincer, M., & Shaver, P. R. (2003). The attachment behavioral system in adulthood: Activation, psychodynamics, and interpersonal processes. *Advances in Experimental Social Psychology, 35*, 56–152. https://doi.org/10.1016/S0065-2601(03)01002-5

Mikulincer, M., & Shaver, P. R. (2016). *Attachment in adulthood: Structure, dynamics, and change* (2nd ed.). Guilford Press.

Pedraza-Ramirez, I., Sharpe, B., Behnke, M., Toth, A. J., & Poulus, D. R. (2025). The psychology of esports: Trends, challenges, and future directions. *Psychology of Sport and Exercise,* 102967. https://doi.org/10.1016/j.psychsport.2025.102967

Possamai-Inesedy, A., & Nixon, A. (2017). A place to stand: Digital sociology and the Archimedean effect. *Journal of Sociology, 53*(4), 865–884. https://doi.org/10.1177/1440783317744104

Sitnik-Warchulska, K., Izydorczyk, B., & Wajda, Z. (2023). E-attachment and online communication: The changing context of the clinical diagnosis and psychological treatment. *Routledge.* https://doi.org/10.4324/9781003221043

Sung, Y., Nam, T. H., & Hwang, M. H. (2020). Attachment style, stressful events, and internet gaming addiction in Korean university students. *Personality and Individual Differences, 154*, Article 109724. https://doi.org/10.1016/j.paid.2019.109724

White, R. W. (1959). Motivation reconsidered: The concept of competence. *Psychological Review, 66*, 297–333. https://doi.org/10.1037/h0040934

Chapter 4
Esports and Emotion Regulation: The Role of the Individual Zone of Optimal Functioning (IZOF) Model

Cengiz Karagözoğlu

4.1 Introduction and Individual Zone of Optimal Functioning (IZOF)

Esports is characterized by rapid decision-making, high-pressure environments, and intense competitive challenges. Athletes experience "a complex range of emotional responses" (Beres et al., 2023) during gameplay. Emotional experiences are regarded as an inseparable component of human functioning, reflecting the nature of past, ongoing, or anticipated person-environment (P-E) interactions within sport psychology literature, emotion regulation (ER) remains a central domain of area. Hanin (2007) describes ER in practice as often involving the reframing of an athlete's attitude toward specific emotional experiences.

Since the 1960s, research on performance-related emotions (Hanin & Syrija, 1995) has driven athletes, coaches, and psychologists to exert significant effort in uncovering the emotion-performance relationship under varying conditions. To this end, numerous theoretical and applied approaches have been developed. The Individual Zone of Optimal Functioning (IZOF) model is currently recognized as one of the most prominent theory-to-application methodologies (Hanin, 1980). Initially conceptualized as the Zone of Optimal Functioning (ZOF), the model evolved into IZOF due to the idiosyncratic nature of emotions and the use of individualized assessment procedures to identify optimal and non-optimal emotional states. In this regard, Hanin known as the pioneer of individualized emotional profiling (Jones et al., 2005).

The IZOF model posits that athletes are most likely to achieve peak performance when pre-competition emotional intensities align with those observed during optimal performances (Robazza et al., 2000). A key feature of the model is its

C. Karagözoğlu (✉)
Faculty of Sports Science, Fenerbahçe University, İstanbul, Türkiye
e-mail: cengiz.karagozoglu@fbu.edu.tr

S. Bekir (ed.), *The Psychology of Esports*, https://doi.org/10.1007/978-3-032-25090-2_4

emphasis on interindividual variability in the intensity and content of idiosyncratic optimal and dysfunctional emotions as they relate to successful and poor performances (Robazza et al., 2004). Unlike group-based evaluations, IZOF interventions prioritize individual experiences. Emotions are viewed as components of the psychobiosocial state a situational, multimodal, and dynamic representation of complete human functioning (Hanin, 1997). Accordingly, intervention strategies are designed based on athletes' situational, multifaceted, and long-term emotional experiences. Performance related states include five interrelated modalities as dimensions: Form, content, intensity, time, and context. Form, content, and intensity represent the athletes subjective experiences; time and context dimensions characterize the dynamics of these experiences (Ruiz & Hanin, 2010).

Emotion content is conceptualized into two interacting independent factors of the hedonic tone (pleasant or unpleasant) and functional impact on performance (optimal or dysfunctional). Negative, Unpleasant and Dysfunctional (N–), Negative, Unpleasant-Functional (N +), Positive, Pleasant-Functional (P +), and Positive, Pleasant-Dysfunctional (P–) respectively (Hanin & Syrija, 1995, Robazza, 2006). The emotions stimulus list in the beginning comprised of 40 positive and 37 negative emotions (Hanin & Syrija, 1995). During the application, if an athlete cannot describe their emotion from the list, he/she can generate their own.

Application of the IZOF Model: The IZOF process begins with a comprehensive list of emotions, from which athletes identify functional and non-functional states while differentiating their positivity or negativity during a sports psychologist's interview. Athletes asked to answer about their exact feeling, not how he/she would like to feel in the given situation. The Emotional State Profile (ESP)—a structured emotion list—simplifies this process for both athletes and psychologists. The ESP consists of 10 emotions per category. The instrument is organized into four columns of 10 rows each, the ESP requires athletes to compare the four emotional items in each row and assign the highest weight to the emotion most representative of their state. The emotion with the highest valence should be given 4 points, the next item will be given 3, and so on. In this way, an athlete describes the intensity of each emotion. When indicating each row, he/she also indicates the intensity of each N-, N + , P + , and P- category. Athletes complete the ESP for three scenarios: (a) Before competition or preparation, (b) During competition or task execution, and (c) After competition or evaluation. Below, you can see a sample of the ESP emotions list (Ruiz & Hanin, 2014):

[] Tired	[] Tense	[] Energetic	[] Easy-going
[] Sluggish	[] Dissatisfied	[] Confident	[] Tranquil

This methodology enables comparisons of psychological conditions across different contexts. For optimal or poor performances, athletes provide additional details, explaining their emotional responses. Over long-term follow-ups, recurring emotional patterns emerge for both optimal and poor performances. A core assumption of IZOF is that sport competitions involve repetitive experiences, wherein similar emotional states correlate with situational factors (e.g., winning or losing). For example, a table tennis player may experience anger after failing to return a critical serve, and in similar situations, the athlete may feel similar emotions. Hanin termed these consistent responses "*emotional patterns*" (Hanin, 2007; Ruiz & Hanin, 2004), which refers to relatively stable, repeated experiences.

According to Robazza (2006), there are three main elements apparent in the working conceptualization of emotions: subjective experience, physiological response, and action tendencies. At this point, psychologists need to ask the athlete about their subjective experiences related to their IZOF profile. For example, an athlete may not know the possible contribution of any experienced negative emotion to their athletic performance. Athletes may drop into Individual Zone of Dysfunction (IZDy) when they cannot learn to manage their emotional experiences. Kamata et al. (2002) proposed IZDy to define when an athlete's emotional intensity is outside the optimal functional zone. If the intensity is higher or lower than the optimal emotional zone, the performance is expected to be suboptimal. This state is referred to in the methodology as being "out of zone." Hanin developed the ICC (Identification-Control-Correction) program, which includes developing emotion- and action-focused strategies (Hanin, 2010) and rapid correction of habitual errors (Hanin & Hanina, 2009) to address these types of mental obstacles of athletes.

By analyzing multiple responses, performance-related emotions can be evaluated. Discussions with athletes and interpretations of emotional patterns in relation to performance outcomes clarify how emotions influence athletic success. Emotion regulation interventions often address questions such as: "*Will the athlete regulate negative thoughts and emotions linked to prior performance*?" (Balk & Englert, 2020). At this stage, psychological intervention programs can be tailored based on ESP-derived patterns and interpretations. Through prolonged ESP applications and competition analysis, Yuri Hanin gradually reduced the number of ESP items. Initially comprising 40 items, the list can be refined to 20 through athlete discussion, eventually narrowing to as few as 12 key emotions. Once athletes identify the most salient emotional content for both optimal and poor performances, individualized, evidence-based interventions, and self-regulation programs can be developed.

To predict an optimal emotion-performance relationship, success is most likely when maximized facilitating effects and minimized debilitating effects (i.e., "in-the-zone" conditions) are observed (Robazza et al., 2004). Hypothetically, graphing an athlete's ESP results should yield an "iceberg" profile—similar to the Profile of Mood States (POMS)—where Positive-Functional (P +) and Negative-Functional (N +) states exceed both Positive-Dysfunctional (P–) and Negative-Dysfunctional (N–) states. While IZOF examines each emotional state individually, it also considers aggregate scores. In order to estimate an athletes' emotional intensity, Hanin also used Category Ratio (CR-10) scale for draw an iceberg profile. When athletes filling this scale, they score each IZOF emotions according to a modified version of Borg Scales. This way visualized graphic shape provides an iceberg shape to see optimal interaction effects between the maximum intensity of strong optimal (P + , N +) emotions and the dysfunctional emotions which shown a minimum intensity (N-, P-)

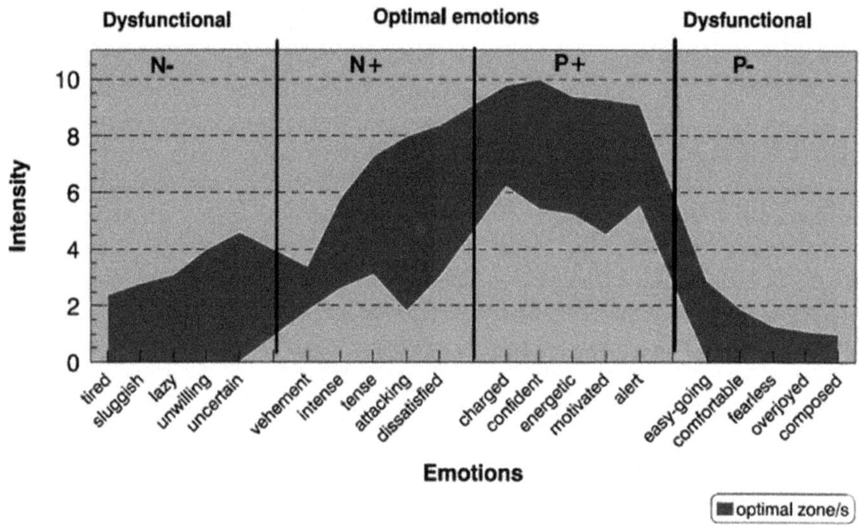

Fig. 4.1 An Iceberg profile of IZOF for football players

as well (Hanin, 2000a). Below it can be seen a sample of iceberg profile when Hanin (2000b) studied with football (soccer) players in Fig. 4.1:

4.1.1 Metaphors and Psychobiosocial States

In his work, Hanin used metaphors to generate emotion profiling as well. In their study with Ruiz (Ruiz & Hanin, 2004), they recruited karate athletes who self-generated metaphors according to the general application methodology of IZOF. Metaphors describing athletes' states prior to, during, and after their best and worst competitions were collected. The study revealed the states underlying the metaphoric expressions. The IZOF model delineates performance states across six dimensions. These states are categorized as "cognitive" (e.g., "focused"), "affective" (e.g., "calm"), "motivational" (e.g., "unwilling"), "bodily" (e.g., "tired"), "kinesthetic" (e.g., "heavy"), and "operational" (e.g., "I missed the timing"). When classified for an individual athlete, these categories provide a comprehensive list of performance factors that interact with emotions. This study revealed that cognitive and affective connotations were more frequent in optimal performances. Ruiz and Hanin employed a long-term follow-up strategy in their research and observed that athletes' metaphors changed over time. This suggests that intervention strategies need to be adjusted accordingly.

4.1.2 Esports: Unique Emotional and Psychological Demands

If we take a look of a definition, "esports" is an area of sport activities in which people develop and train mental or physical abilities (Wagner, 2006). A review of the literature reveals that the emotional characteristics of esports and gaming athletes remain understudied. Research highlights that esports differs fundamentally from "traditional physical sports" (Beres et al., 2023), suggesting distinct physical and psychological profiles—or more accurately, player profiles. Esports settings are inherently different from non-esports disciplines. While all sports exhibit discipline-specific differences, esports uniquely involves: Seated, screen-based competition (Behnke et al., 2022), interaction with virtual environments, and tasks demanding mental effort (e.g., strategizing, decision-making) rather than physical exertion (Mancı & Günay, 2023). Another important factor is that the characteristic of the communication between players is not face-to-face but digital connectivity (Poulus et al., 2026). Under these digital circumstances, cyberpsychological effects need to be taken into account. It is known that, under online interactions have a negative influence on emotions.

4.1.3 Esports-Related Emotions Include

It is possible to say that emotions are important in sport and even frequently occur throughout every stage of the competition *(pre-, during-, and post-competition)*. For instance, in FPS (first-person shooter) games, the disappointment experienced after missing a shot, the joy felt after winning a match, the frustration encountered during training, and the fear of toxic behavior within the game may be present (Beres et al., 2023). But the literature on esports is still scarce, some studies call esports research within the field of psychology is in its infancy (Fuentes & Sanchez, 2025); also, rather than esports, many studies focus on gaming (Machado et al., 2022). Additionally, it is reported that, esports environment is created a toxic gamer culture where players harass, cheat, cyberbully others (Türkay et al., 2020). Toxicity in online gaming can exert additional psychological pressure on players, affecting their mental well-being and overall esports experience. Probably it can play a role that the nature of some games contains fighting, more likely players experience frustration, anger, or disappointment. Despite the research findings above, Hagiwara et al. (2020) found cognitive skill (procession speed) and selective attention improved after esports activity. In another study Hagiwara et al. (2021) also found before and after the activity of using car racing-type esports is related with ability to focus (concentration). As sum, we can assume that esports help to improve players' mental abilities, but the players need to learn how to regulate their emotions. In this context, it is essential to explain IZOF in terms of the importance of emotions and the stages before, during, and after the competition.

4.1.4 Emotion Regulation in Esports with IZOF

When individuals lose control over their gaming habits, prioritize gaming over other activities, and continue despite negative consequences, their personal, social, or professional lives may be significantly impaired (World Health Organization, 2019). From a sports psychology perspective, emotion regulation can be examined through two key lenses. First, it involves analyzing performance-related emotional states using methodologies such as the IZOF model—to enhance esports performance. Second, it serves as a protective mechanism to mitigate gaming disorder (now formally recognized in diagnostic criteria) and other problematic gaming behaviors, thereby fostering greater well-being and a healthier lifestyle. Similarly, just as in pre-esports versions of certain games, the ability to successfully regulate negative emotions and manage related psychological processes has become increasingly critical in their esports adaptations. Details regarding these harms are elaborated in Chapter 2. In parallel to these harms, there is another factor that affects in-game performance. This can be described as tilt.

The tilt experience is associated with frustration, rage, and deterioration of gameplay ability which generates negative emotions (McLinton & Pascale, 2024; Wu et al., 2021). Tilt manifests across poker players regardless of expertise; however, successful and veteran esports players exhibit significantly greater efficacy in mitigating its adverse effects and shortening its persistence compared to inexperienced or less successful players (Fuentes & Sánchez, 2025). This result shows us that such as tilt, athletes with previous experiences have a capability to acquire some sort of emotional control such as coping with pressure. In esport literature there are a limited number of studies in emotion regulation. Leis et al. (2024) written by one such article is it. In this study, internal regulation refers to attempts to manage internal resources in response to stress, framing it as an emotion regulation task. In team-based games and settings, unregulated emotions can lead to the rapid spread of one player's negative emotions to others (Kou & Gui, 2020). Beyond the individual level, emotion regulation thus plays a multifaceted role in esports. Here, the aim or the emotion regulation is clustering around two groups of esports emotional consequences:

1. Emotion regulation for performance optimization,
2. Emotion regulation for coping with negative emotions.

Esports related literature shows that, in the first step an emotion regulation program needs to be focused on controlling negative emotions, in the next step, focusing on performance optimization could be better. In an evidence-based study, Abramov et al. (2021) designed a system to record the esports players' voice and detect the emotional positivity or negativity using computer software. According to the results, more successful teams generated more positive tones than the less successful teams. The angry tone was also slightly lower in winners. At the end, researchers concluded that emotions closely related to team performance in esports. From this perspective, an angry tone can quickly spread to teammates, given that effective communication is critical in team-based games. Thus, Eldadi et al. (2025) examined the verbal communication of expert and non-expert esports teams, revealing that non-expert teams relied more on non-task-related and emotionally charged communication during gameplay. In another study, Eldadi and Tenenbaum (2025) confirmed that expert esports teams, relative to nonexpert teams, demonstrate more frequent-, concise-, and acknowledgment- oriented communication. This means that those individuals actively recognize, validate, and respond to the emotions, perspectives, or contributions of others. Based on these findings, emotion regulation programs in esports should also prioritize the management of communicative emotions.

Emotion regulation means the individual regulates their own emotional experiences, while interpersonal emotion regulation refers to the act of regulating others' emotions (Kou & Gui, 2020). Under the reality of presence of team events in esports, a "team emotion regulation" aim can be added into the model. After collecting emotional profiles of individual esports players, it could be consolidated as team profiles. In this regard, having team emotional profiles gives a chance to compare each individual between team. If there are "negative contributions" of some team members, this can be another emotion regulation work for the team.

Previous IZOF Based Emotion Regulation and intervention studies focused on state-like emotions and trait-like (stable) emotions than meta-experiences. In their study, Woodcock et al. (2012) applied an IZOF framework for consultant practice and athlete reflections on emotional regulation for a cross-country runner. In this study, the emotion regulation program consisted of an introductory session, optimal and non-optimal zone identification with previously explained CR-10 intensity ranking, identify emotion regulation techniques, apply imagery to build feelings of competence, goal setting for performance and process goals for competitive races, review and refine current use of self-talk during races and lastly, review of the emotion regulation program. In this program, subjective emotions, cognitions, and physiological symptoms are examined in relation with optimal zone perspective.

In another study, Robazza et al. (2004) employed an applied IZOF Emotion self-regulation program for eight elite Italian athletes from several disciplines. Steps of the procedure were started identifying optimal and dysfunctional emotional states, prediction of emotion–performance relationships, then following an applied intervention study of emotion self-regulation. This section synthesizes key contributions from leading authors to explore effective applications of IZOF emotion regulation, positioning esports as an emerging field in this domain—particularly in comparison to traditional sports. At this stage, the IZOF model will be provided as an esports intervention program.

4.1.5 Application of the IZOF Methodology into Esports

Phase 1: Compiling esports-specific Emotional Profiles To systematically identify the emotional experiences unique to esports athletes, the initial phase of this study employs an Individualized Zones of Optimal Functioning (IZOF) emotion inventory preferably the most comprehensive available version to capture context-specific affective responses. The inventory is administered to the target athlete cohort under three distinct competitive conditions: Pre-competition, In-competition, and Post-competition respectively. Through this triphasic assessment, frequently recurring emotional descriptors are extracted to generate a tailored, esports-specific emotion lexicon. This methodological approach aligns with prior research by Ruiz and Hanin (2004), who utilized a similar protocol to elicit metaphor-based emotional narratives from karate athletes. Researchers may opt to replicate their metaphor-generation technique if qualitative depth is prioritized.

For studies constrained by time or resources, an abbreviated protocol may be adopted by directly applying a pre-existing IZOF Emotional State Profile inventory (e.g., Hanin's, 2000 or 2007 versions). This streamlined approach remains valid for preliminary data collection, though it may sacrifice granularity in esports-specific emotional nuance.

Phase 2. Control the level of anxiety for optimal performance. IZOF methodology assumes elite athletes' best performances comes when they have an ideal anxiety-state zone. Robazza et al. (2008) emphasized that anticipated effects of pre-performance anxiety intensity upon forthcoming performance can be similarly facilitative or debilitative in different athletes. Nogueira et al. (2019) designed an IZOF based model for controlling anxiety and self-efficacy of volleyball players. In this study, researchers applied Competitive State Anxiety Inventory—2 (CSAI) reduced version and Individual Self-Efficacy Scale for Volleyball instruments to collect anxiety and self-efficacy data. As frequently mentioned, participants' questionnaire scores showed significant variability such as ranging from 3 to 5 points for cognitive anxiety, 2 to 7 points for somatic anxiety, 2 to 14 points for self-confidence, and 12 to 54 points for self-efficacy. As a result, IZOF's found to be quite different both inter-individual and intra-individual levels. Different athletes' optimal zones were presented in different areas. When exact competition scores and questionnaire scores are matched for a while, it is possible to talk which zone is called an optimal zone for each individual. IZOF model shows individual differences in the optimal worry zones of several athletes (Robazza, 2006). It is specified below in the relevant table (Fig. 4.2).

In this phase, athletes emotion profile and performance relations need to be matched. In order to Robazza et al. (2004) predicted of emotion–performance relationships in their study, examined the optimal pleasant and unpleasant emotions for availability of resources and their effective recruitment and utilization by producing energizing (enhanced effort) and organizing (enhanced skill) effects, in the light of maximum enhancing and minimum debilitating effects (to be in the zone condition). There are non-linear findings regarding the emotion profile and performance situations due to the idiosyncratic nature of emotions. For instance, Hagtvet and Hanin (2007) found that the worst performance situations might not be characterized by a single consistent and distinct emotion profile, because "each athlete applies her/his own unique set of construct indicators."

Before starting the next phase, it is essential that players have a thorough understanding and introspection of their profiles. Considering the emotional state they have chosen, how they feel in the current situation, what this means, and how it relates to their current performance, is crucial for further progress. Some individuals tend not

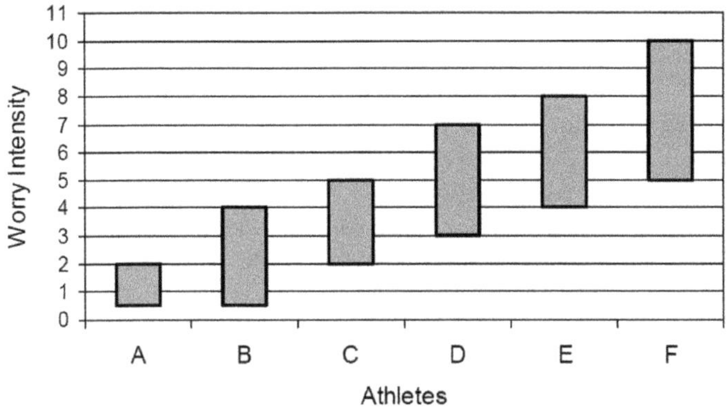

Fig. 4.2 Individual differences of optimal zones

to accept their emotions. Gratz and Roemer (2004) evaluated the factors contributing to emotion regulation and developed an emotion regulation scale. According to this study, six factors were found to be related to incomplete emotion regulation. These factors are nonacceptance of emotional responses, difficulties in engaging in goal-directed behavior, impulse control difficulties, lack of emotional awareness, lack of emotional clarity, and limited access to emotion regulation strategies. Castro and Neto (2025) conducted a study using the mentioned Difficulties in Emotion Regulation Scale (DERS) among gamers and found that, men with lower academic qualifications exhibited higher emotional regulation dysregulation behavior. In light of these findings, after emotional profiling, it is necessary to seek opportunities for better understanding each participant's own emotions and how to apply emotion regulation strategies in real-life situations. Previously it is mentioned above there are gender differences related with perceiving emotions. Here also it is revealed that, a good evaluation of gender, educational level, age, and other personal characteristics including game behaviors can help create a better emotional regulation program.

Phase 3. In this phase, it is necessary to decide on the approach to emotion regulation. The team's or player's situation, level, and goals can help inform the choice of approach. Naragon-Gainey et al. (2017) identified two distinct emotion regulation approaches:

Strategy-based approach: Several strategies have been proposed, including behavioral avoidance, situation selection, expressive suppression, acceptance, and thought suppression.

Ability-based approach: This approach encompasses emotion recognition, responses to emotions, moderation of the negative effects of emotions, and related abilities.

After examining the emotional profiles, the next step is to select a suitable emotion regulation strategy to control or modify the emotions. In their previous study, Kou and Gui (2020) proposed two strategies—situation selection and attentional deployment—out of five distinct strategies (situation modification, cognitive change, and response modulation) to help esports players manage their emotions. Situation selection aims to teach players to approach or avoid certain situations. The authors recommended that if a player feels tilted, they should listen to music, watch videos, or take a break instead of continuing to play. They believed that by avoiding the negative situation, a player can effectively manage their negative emotions. Ultimately, strategy-based or ability-based approaches will focus on identifying the "tilt triggers" that lead players to tilt and the "tilt responses" that they commonly exhibit after experiencing this phenomenon. In a qualitative study, Aras and Algün Doğu (2025) examined esports players' psychological perspectives through their sports psychologists and identified two primary approaches: goal-setting strategies and individual performance analysis.

During IZOF based self regulation program mentioned above, Robazza et al. (2004) scheduled several meetings with athletes to maintain to learn the necessary psychological skills including imagery, self-talk, self-assessment and pre-competition routines, goal setting, and focusing. An esport player needs to learn the basic psychological training skills for adopt a successful personal emotion regulation. While using those skills, players improve the ability to reduce their performance related bodily negative symptoms, replaced them with facilitating ones. Kou and Gui (2020) reported several emotion factors related with League of Legends (LoL) players:

Achievement-related situations: Where players anticipate whether they would reach or fail to reach certain achievements.

Teammate-related situations: Where teammates' in-game performance or behavior trigger emotions.

Game design-related situations: Like new applied game patches usually trigger emotional responses where players respond based on how the patches would affect their gameplay.

Social identity-related situations: Where players experience emotions as they identify or disassociate with a community or a group.

When the emotion regulation program is under preparation, it is better that esports psychologists take into account the above-mentioned esports-related emotional situations. The above situations need to be matched with emotional states to regulate. For instance, if a player feels a negative emotion in team-related situations, an emotion regulation program can be structured to control (or avoid) possible high-pressure situations. Each player's emotion profile and performance relations will probably be better covered with this evidence-based approach and esports-specific situations. Furthermore, adopting a team perspective and implementing team emotion regulation programs is a crucial aspect of these efforts. Trotter et al. (2023) emphasized the importance of understanding how cognitive and behavioral regulation unfolds within esports teams. In order to choose an emotion regulation methodology, the gender of the player is another factor to take into consideration. Guisti (2024) revealed that male and female characters showed different emotional expressions; as expected, male characters showed more anger, while female ones stayed more neutral. In light of these results, and in line with the existing literature, emotion regulation programs for male players should address the issue of controlling anger and reducing the intensity of emotions. This is because the literature shows that anger plays a determining role—alongside personality—in esports performance (Mateo-Orcajada et al., 2022), often accompanied by sadness and fear. In particular, anger has been identified as a key cause of the "tilt" experience (Kou et al., 2018). Additionally, winning and losing affect players' anger differently. When players win, a significant decrease is found in their anger levels. Therefore, emotion regulation for anger may be more critical in losing situations. For female players, however, such programs should encourage the spontaneous expression of emotions rather than blocking them. As sum, positivity is mentioned as one of the most important affective factors in esports. For instance, Gursesli et al. (2023) found that higher-ranked Italian players in League of Legends (LoL) showed more positive affect toward the game. When conducting intervention programs, team communication, positivity, and anger management methods need to be included.

In the near future, as psychologists conduct new applied studies with esports players, the acquired knowledge will help us develop esports-specific methodologies and tools, as well as design better emotion regulation programs. As sport psychologists, we expect that this improved understanding and integration of esports with other sports disciplines will foster broader collaborations.

References

Abramov, S., Korotin, A., Somov, A., Burnaev, E., Stepanov, A., Nikolaev, D., & Titova, M. A. (2021). Analysis of video game players' emotions and team performance: An esports tournament case study. *IEEE Journal of Biomedical and Health Informatics, 26*(8), 3597–3606.

American Psychiatric Association. (2013). *Diagnostic and statistical manual of mental disorders* (5th ed.). https://doi.org/10.1176/appi.books.9780890425596

Aras, H., & Algün Doğu, G. (2025). E-sports from the perspective of sports psychologists. *InnovatioSports Journal, 3*(2), 146–160.

Balk, Y. A., & Englert, C. (2020). Recovery self-regulation in sport: Theory, research, and practice. *International Journal of Sports Science & Coaching, 15*(2), 273–281.

Behnke, M., Gross, J. J., & Kaczmarek, L. D. (2022). The role of emotions in esports performance. *Emotion, 22*(5), 1059.

Beres, N. A., Klarkowski, M., & Mandryk, R. L. (2023). Playing with emotions: A systematic review examining emotions and emotion regulation in esports performance. In *Proceedings of the ACM on Human-Computer Interaction, 7(CHI PLAY)* (pp. 558–587).

Brand, M., Young, K. S., Laier, C., Wölfling, K., & Potenza, M. N. (2016). Integrating psychological and neurobiological considerations regarding the development and maintenance of specific Internet-use disorders: An interaction of person–affect–cognition–execution (I-PACE) model. *Neuroscience & Biobehavioral Reviews, 71*, 252–266. https://doi.org/10.1016/j.neubiorev.2016.08.033

Castro, C. M., & Neto, D. D. (2025). Profiling gamers: The role of mental health, attachment and social factors in gaming behaviors. *Addictive Behaviors, 169*, Article 108390.

Eldadi, O., Fitoussi, S. J., & Tenenbaum, G. (2025). Verbal communication, coordinated effort, and performance in esports teams: An expert–nonexpert paradigm study. *Journal of Sport & Exercise Psychology, 47*(5), 320–332. https://doi.org/10.1123/jsep.2024-0343

Eldadi, O., & Tenenbaum, G. (2025). Between-rounds verbal communication in expert and nonexpert esports team players. *Sport, Exercise, and Performance Psychology*. Advance online publication. https://doi.org/10.1037/spy0000384

Fuentes, R., & Sanchez, X. (2025). A qualitative examination of tilt in league of legends esports players. *International Journal of Sport and Exercise Psychology*, 1–21. https://doi.org/10.1080/1612197X.2025.2594513

Giusti, F. S. (2024). The emotional landscape of league of legends: A gendered analysis. In *Companion Proceedings of the 2024 Annual Symposium on Computer-human Interaction in Play* (pp. 420–423).

Gratz, K. L., & Roemer, L. (2004). Multidimensional assessment of emotion regulation and dysregulation: Development, factor structure, and initial validation of the difficulties in emotion regulation scale. *Journal of Psychopathology and Behavioral Assessment, 26*(1), 41–54.

Gursesli, M. C., Masti, F., Duradoni, M., Bostan, B., Sungu, E., Zilbeyaz, P. C., & Guazzini, A. (2023). Psychological and behavioral effects of League of Legends rank system for Italian competitive players. In *International Conference on Videogame Sciences and Arts* (pp. 59–71). Springer.

Hagiwara, G., Akiyama, D., Furukado, R., & Takeshita, S. (2020). A study on psychological training of esports using digital games: Focusing on rhythm game. *Journal of Human Sport and Exercise, 15*(3), S495–S503.

Hagiwara, G., Kawahara, I., & Kihara, S. (2021). An attempt to verify the positive effects of esports: Focusing on concentration and cognitive skill. *Journal of Digital Life, 1*(1), S1–S7.

Hagtvet, K. A., & Hanin, Y. L. (2007). Consistency of performance-related emotions in elite athletes: Generalizability theory applied to the IZOF model. *Psychology of Sport and Exercise, 8*(1), 47–72.

Hanin, Y. L. (1980). A study of anxiety in sports. In W. F. Straub (Ed.), *Sport psychology: An analysis of athlete behavior* (pp. 236–249). Mouvement.

Hanin, Y. L. (1997). Emotions and athletic performance: Individual zones of optimal functioning model. *European Yearbook of Sport Psychology, 1*, 29–72.

Hanin, Y. L. (2000a). Individual Zones of Optimal Functioning (IZOF) model. In Y. L. Hanin (Ed.), *Emotions in sport* (pp. 65–89). Human Kinetics.

Hanin, Y. L. (2000b). Soccer and emotion: Enhancing or impairing performance. In J. Bangsbo (Ed.), *Soccer and science* (pp. 69–89). University of Copenhagen.

Hanin, Y. L. (2007). Emotions in sport: Current issues and perspectives. In G. Tenenbaum & R. C. Eklund (Eds.), *Handbook of sport psychology* (pp. 22–41).

Hanin, Y., & Syrjä, P. (1995). Performance affect in junior ice hockey players: An application of the individual zones of optimal functioning model. *The sport psychologist, 9*(2), 169–187.

Hanin, Y. L., & Hanina, M. (2009). Optimization of performance in top-level athletes: An action-focused coping approach. *International Journal of Sports Science & Coaching, 4*(1), 47–91.

Hanin, Y. L. (2010). Coping with anxiety in sport. In A. R. Nicholls (Ed.), *Coping in sport: Theory, methods, and related constructs* (pp. 159–175). Nova Science.

Jones, M. V., Lane, A. M., Bray, S. R., Uphill, M., & Catlin, J. (2005). Development and validation of the sport emotion questionnaire. *Journal of Sport & Exercise Psychology, 27*(4), 407–431.

Kamata, A., Tenenbaum, G., & Hanin, Y. L. (2002). Individual Zone of Optimal Functioning (IZOF): A probabilistic estimation. *Journal of Sport and Exercise Psychology, 24*(2), 189–208.

Kou, Y., & Gui, X. (2020). Emotion regulation in esports gaming: A qualitative study of league of legends. *Proceedings of the ACM on Human-Computer Interaction, 4*(CSCW2), 1–25.

Kou, Y., Li, Y., Gui, X., & Suzuki-Gill, E. (2018). Playing with streakiness in online games: How players perceive and react to winning and losing streaks in League of Legends. In *Proceedings of the 2018 CHI Conference on Human Factors in Computing Systems* (pp. 1–14).

Leis, O., Sharpe, B. T., Pelikan, V., Fritsch, J., Nicholls, A. R., & Poulus, D. (2024). Stressors and coping strategies in esports: A systematic review. *International Review of Sport and Exercise Psychology,* 1–31.

Machado, S., de Oliveira Sant'Ana, L., Cid, L., Teixeira, D., Rodrigues, F., Travassos, B., & Monteiro, D. (2022). Impact of victory and defeat on the perceived stress and autonomic regulation of professional esports athletes. *Frontiers in Psychology, 13*, 987149. https://doi.org/10.3389/fpsyg.2022.987149

Mancı, E., & Günay, E. (2023). Physical activity in Turkish esports players: Age differences approach. *Journal of Sport Sciences Research, 8*(3), 763–774.

Mateo-Orcajada, A., Abenza-Cano, L., & Vaquero-Cristóbal, R. (2022). Analyzing the changes in the psychological profile of professional league of legends players during competition. *Computers in Human Behavior, 126*, Article 107030.

McLinton, S. S., & Pascale, S. J. (2024). Tilt in esports: Understanding the phenomenon in new digital contexts. *Computers in Human Behavior Reports, 14*, Article 100425.

Naragon-Gainey, K., McMahon, T. P., & Chacko, T. P. (2017). The structure of common emotion regulation strategies: A meta-analytic examination. *Psychological Bulletin, 143*(4), 384–427.

Nogueira, F. C. D. A., Bara, M. G., & Lourenço, L. M. (2019). Application of IZOF model for anxiety and self-efficacy in volleyball athletes: A case study. *Revista Brasileira de Medicina do Esporte, 25*, 338–343.

Poulus, D., Nicholson, M., Obine, E., Drew, M., Fisher, K., Vella, S., Seidler, Z., & Sharpe, B. T. (2026). Mental health and well-being in esports: A scoping review. *Applied Psychology, 75*(1), e70055.

Robazza, C., Bortoli, L., & Nougier, V. (2000). Performance emotions in an elite archer: A case study. *Journal of Sport Behavior, 23*(2).

Robazza, C., Pellizzari, M., & Hanin, Y. (2004). Emotion self-regulation and athletic performance: An application of the IZOF model. *Psychology of Sport and Exercise, 5*(4), 379–404.

Robazza, C. (2006). Emotion in sport: An IZOF perspective. In S. Hanton & S. D. Mellalieu (Eds.), *Literature reviews in sport psychology* (pp. 127–158). Nova Science.

Robazza, C., Pellizzari, M., Bertollo, M., & Hanin, Y. L. (2008). Functional impact of emotions on athletic performance: Comparing the IZOF model and the directional perception approach. *Journal of Sports Sciences, 26*(10), 1033–1047.

Ruiz, M. C., & Hanin, Y. L. (2004). Metaphoric description and individualized emotion profiling of performance states in top karate athletes. *Journal of Applied Sport Psychology, 16*(3), 258–273. https://doi.org/10.1080/10413200490498366

Ruiz, M. C., & Hanin, Y. L. (2014). Interactive effects of emotions on performance: An exploratory study in elite skeet shooters. *Revista De Psicología Del Deporte, 23*(2), 275–284.

Trotter, M. G., Obine, E. A. C., & Sharpe, B. T. (2023). Self-regulation, stress appraisal, and esport action performance. *Frontiers in Psychology, 14*, 1265778. https://doi.org/10.3389/fpsyg.2023.1265778

Türkay, S., Formosa, J., Adinolf, S., Cuthbert, R., & Altizer, R. (2020). See no evil, hear no evil, speak no evil: How collegiate players define, experience and cope with toxicity. In *Proceedings of the 2020 CHI Conference on Human Factors in Computing Systems* (pp. 1–13).

Wagner, M. G. (2006). On the scientific relevance of esports. In *Proceedings of the 2006 International Conference on Internet Computing and Conference on Computer Game Development* (pp. 437–440).

Woodcock, C., Cumming, J., Duda, J. L., & Sharp, L. A. (2012). Working within an Individual Zone of Optimal Functioning (IZOF) framework: Consultant practice and athlete reflections on refining emotion regulation skills. *Psychology of Sport and Exercise, 13*(3), 291–302.

World Health Organization. (2019). *International statistical classification of diseases and related health problems* (11th ed.). https://icd.who.int/

Wu, M., Lee, J. S., & Steinkuehler, C. (2021). Understanding tilt in esports: A study on young League of Legends players. In *Proceedings of the 2021 CHI Conference on Human Factors in Computing Systems* (pp. 1–9).

Chapter 5
Psychological Coaching in Esports: From Theory to Practice

Andrea Caputo, Giuseppe Vercelli, and Claudio Giovanni Cortese

5.1 Psychological Approach to Studying and Coaching Esports Players

Over the last decade, esports have progressively evolved from a niche activity into a highly structured and globally recognized competitive domain, attracting millions of followers and generating significant attention from both media and academia. Esports generally refer to the organized and competitive practice of specific video games, such as *League of Legends* or *Counter-Strike*, and can be understood as a hybrid phenomenon positioned between traditional sport, digital entertainment, and contemporary online culture (Pedraza-Ramirez et al., 2020). Similarities with traditional athletic performance are increasingly recognized, specifically regarding the mental performance, even if the formal recognition of esports as a "sport" remains debated (Leis & Lautenbach, 2020). Professional esports players are required to sustain high levels of concentration, make rapid decisions under intense time pressure, and coordinate effectively with teammates. In this regard, esports players' psychological demands closely recall those observed in many traditional high-performance sport contexts, particularly attentional control, communication, and performance consistency (Poulus et al., 2020).

A. Caputo (✉) · G. Vercelli · C. G. Cortese
Department of Psychology, University of Turin, Turin, Italy
e-mail: andrea.caputo@unito.it

G. Vercelli
e-mail: giuseppe.vercelli@unito.it

C. G. Cortese
e-mail: claudio.cortese@unito.it

G. Vercelli
Sport and Human Performance Psychology Center "Umbro Marcaccioli" (ISEF Foundation), Turin, Italy

S. Bekir (ed.), *The Psychology of Esports*, https://doi.org/10.1007/978-3-032-25090-2_5

Esports teams are structuring themselves in the same way as élite teams in other sports, also introducing multidisciplinary performance collaborators, such as psychologists (Watson et al., 2021). Then, it is not surprising that sport psychology has become a key component in this evolving ecosystem. Applied sport psychologists use psychological principles to help individuals in esports perform at a high level (Leis et al., 2025), with the same goal in helping traditional sports athletes: despite there are obvious differences as regards physical demands between esports and traditional sports, helping athletes integrate cognitive, emotional, tactical, and behavioral skills to enhance performance, while preserving well-being during training and competitions.

Interventions employed in sport psychology, including for example emotion regulation, attentional control, and communication skills training, have proven to be both applicable and effective in esports settings (Caputo et al., 2023). These strategies support players to cope with performance-related stress, sustain motivation, and coordinate within teams. This is supported by academic research on esports psychology, which is a growing field: empirical findings validate the application of these methods and support practitioners in overcoming skepticism (Leis et al., 2025).

5.1.1 Psychological Dimensions to Improve Esports Players

Competitive esports is characterized by complexity, rapid changes, and continuous performance monitoring. Players have to face psychological challenges due to game updates, online exposure, and time pressure, together with public criticism, team conflict, burnout, and job insecurity, i.e., common stressors for esports players (Leis et al., 2025). For these reasons, psychological support could be beneficial for players, coaches, and team staff.

A number of studies highlighted the mental abilities required for esports players to succeed. For example, Himmelstein et al. (2017) described eleven core psychological skills for élite performance in *League of Legends*, including present-moment focus, pre-performance routines, and the ability to adapt to competitive situations. The authors also stated that players develop these skills through activities like goal setting, feedback on performance, practice, and psychological training. In competitive play, the ability to maintain focus under pressure, manage emotional responses, and use adaptive coping strategies is essential, and this is why scholars and practitioners are increasingly recognizing psychological resilience and mental toughness as crucial for esports players.

5.1.2 Practical Approaches to Esports Coaching

Esports organizations are investing lot of money and resources in performance infrastructure, and there is also a growing interest in psychological interventions capable to help gamers dealing with the specific demands of competitive gaming. Thus, empirical research has begun to explore the effectiveness of some targeted psychological interventions or trainings; for example, mindset-based strategies (e.g., Sharpe et al., 2024) showed to be effective in promoting challenge appraisal, reducing anxiety, and fostering a performance-oriented mindset. Similarly, techniques based on imagery were useful in helping *League of Legends* players both manage performance anxiety and visualize success (Munroe-Chandler et al., 2023). These studies highlight the role of some key mental skills–e.g., focus, resilience, and self-regulation (Himmelsten et al., 2017)–in succeeding in competitive gaming, while acknowledging the potential of specific techniques to enhance coping and readiness.

Several psychological frameworks have also been proposed to conceptualize performance in esports. The Esports High-Performance Model (Poulus et al., 2025), for instance, describes three components influencing performance: training environment, interpersonal dynamics, and intrapersonal development. This model underscores the multidimensional nature of esports environment, and integrates psychological aspects within broader structural aspects. Other perspectives adopt different points of view: The Ecological Dynamics framework (Bubna et al., 2023) focuses on the continuous interaction between players and their environment, particularly related to skill acquisition, while a study by Papp et al. (2025) mapped the players' individual characteristics influencing performance, i.e., resilience, stress tolerance, adaptability, and goal-orientedness. Moreover, the recent review by Pedraza-Ramirez et al. (2025) highlights some other studies exploring theoretical frameworks of factors influencing performance enhancement in esports. For example, Bonilla et al. (2022) defined three macro-categories influencing esports performance, such as technical-tactical skills, psychological skills, and healthy habits. Among psychological skills, attentional control, emotional control, activation control, communication, team cohesion, thought control, goal control, and behavioral control emerged as factors influencing performance. Finally, Nagorsky and Wiemeyer (2020) referred to an integrate model where factors influencing esports performance (such as tactical-cognitive abilities, coordination skills, and social abilities) are affected by game competencies (such as cognitive, sensorimotor, and social competencies) and factors of sports performance (such as personality, conditioning, and psychic abilities).

However, many of these strategies often lack of an overarching conceptual framework that connects psychological skills with intervention practices, and, even if these theoretical models offer valuable insights, they often tend to focus on environmental conditions or isolated skills, making it difficult to structure psychological training into a systematic psychological training.

In this context, the S.F.E.R.A. model (Vercelli, 2005), widely used in Olympic contexts and recently adapted to the esports environment (Caputo et al., 2023), provides distinctive advantages integrating theory and practice within a single framework.

5.2 The S.F.E.R.A. Model

The S.F.E.R.A. model is a theoretical and practical framework introduced by Vercelli (2005) and widely adopted by the Italian National Olympic Committee (CONI), Olympic athletes, and élite professional sports teams across disciplines.[1] The model describes five core psychological components essential for achieving peak performance, namely Synchrony, (Points of) Strength, Energy, Rhythm, and Activation. Mental training structured with the S.F.E.R.A. framework has the goal to develop and find the balance of these components to support effective and consistent competitive functioning.

Synchrony refers to the player's ability to be fully immersed, both mentally and physically, in the present moment of performance. Players often describe this state as a sense of total alignment between thought and action, in which movements feel automatic and flow naturally, as if they were flowing without the presence of consciousness. This state can be trained through, for example, self-talk and mindful self-observation. Synchrony is expressed both internally, through the coordination of mental and bodily processes, and externally, through sustained attentional alignment with task demands.

(Points of) Strength highlights the importance for players to rely only one's resources during competitions. This means recognizing and recalling personal strengths, i.e., physical, technical, and psychological, that the player has fully developed and feels confident in. It is closely linked to the concept of self-efficacy. According to this factor, during performance, it is better to put aside attention to one's limitations, since the goal is to act on the basis of competence and certainty: one takes to the field with one's strengths. While in training there is time to recognize, challenge, and correct one's limitations, competition requires focusing exclusively on one's most established skills.

Energy, the third dimension, relates to the effective regulation of internal force. It refers not only to physical vigor, but also to players' emotional intensity; it is related to enthusiasm, readiness, assertiveness in competition, and the ability to influence teammates and opponents. Energy has to be appropriately regulated to support sustained performance avoiding excessive effort.

Rhythm refers to the ability to act with timing and elegance in movements, an internal sense of rhythm that allows for effective sequences of actions, contributing to both technical execution and psychological stability under pressure, supporting consistency throughout all phases of performance, thus contributing to the sense of "flow" in high-level performances.

Activation describes the player's motivation to perform at their best. It is based on setting personally meaningful goals, according to the well-known acronym S.M.A.R.T. (i.e., Specific, Measurable, Achievable, Relevant, and Time-bound). Players with high activation show a high level of motivation that drives them to make sacrifices in order to train and compete; also, they are able to convey their passion during the competition to spectators and teammates.

[1] https://www.psycosport.com/.

According to the S.F.E.R.A. model, optimal performance can be achieved when all five components are in balance. The player's mind and body have to work in unison, seeking to align conscious and unconscious processes to achieve a common goal. In this mental state, distractions and irrelevant thoughts are reduced, allowing the expression of internal resources that promote excellent performance.

It is now possible to understand the model's points of strength, lying in translating psychological principles into practical and performance-oriented activities, that can also be adapted to the specific psychological needs of esports context. S.F.E.R.A. focuses on a defined set of mental dimensions—i.e., Synchrony, Strengths, Energy, Rhythm, and Activation—that are directly trainable and closely linked to performance outcomes. This focus differentiates the model from broader high-performance or ecological frameworks, which typically embed psychological processes within wider social or environmental systems. S.F.E.R.A. is based on well-established psychological constructs reorganized into a sport-specific (and also "esports-specific") framework. For example, "Energy" mirrors vigor and dedication (two factors of the engagement dimension), while "Activation" is related to enjoyment in doing what players do, supporting motivation to train and the expression of pleasure during the excitement of a match.

The model provides empirical tools for assessment and monitoring: The e-S.F.E.R.A. Questionnaire has shown meaningful associations with flow, engagement, and performance indicators in esports players (Caputo et al., 2023), allowing practitioners to design evidence-based interventions. In contrast, other frameworks provide valuable conceptual insights without offering standardized instruments with predictive validity in competitive settings. Finally, the model integrates its five dimensions into a coherent framework of mental readiness: by jointly addressing synchronization between mind and body, mobilization of personal strengths, regulation of energy, alignment of rhythm with task demands, and optimal activation, S.F.E.R.A. captures the dynamic interplay of psychological mechanisms underlying performance. This holistic configuration supports peak performance for each player, recognizing their individual characteristics–which differ from one person to another–while other approaches often emphasize isolated constructs, such as resilience or coping strategies, or focus primarily on contextual moderators. In sum, the S.F.E.R.A. model seems to stand out thank to its theoretical integration, empirical validation, and holistic design, making it particularly suitable as a guiding framework for mental training interventions for esports performance optimization.

Over time, the S.F.E.R.A. model has been adapted to different contexts, with specific questionnaires created to assess its application in various sports and work environments, i.e., various types of "performance", including individual and team sports, both in training and competition, and it has been extended to the business (Cortese et al., 2018), teaching (Cortese & Emanuel, 2022), music (Mazzon et al., 2024), and now esports (Caputo et al., 2023).

5.2.1 *Empirical Evidence of the S.F.E.R.A. Model in Traditional Sports*

Several preliminary validations of the S.F.E.R.A. model have been conducted in traditional sports contexts. The first "S.F.E.R.A. Test" underwent psychometric testing with data collected from samples of players practicing basketball, soccer, volleyball, track and field, swimming, and martial arts. These studies confirmed the robustness of its five-factor structure, with results presented in international scientific contexts (e.g., Cortese et al., 2017; 2019a, 2019b) demonstrating the acceptable reliability and factorial validity of the model, and suggesting that this framework can effectively capture the psychological dimensions underlying performance in various competitive contexts. The S.F.E.R.A. framework has also been applied beyond sports, i.e., in managerial and educational contexts, further confirming its flexibility in assessing and improving human performance in different professional contexts (Cortese et al., 2018; Cortese & Emanuel, 2022).

Similarities between high-level performance in traditional sports and competitive gaming can be found. Esports players, like more traditional players, must sustain concentration, regulate activation, manage rhythm and energy, and align cognitive and bodily synchrony under conditions of high pressure and uncertainty. Such requirements mirror those found in sports such as basketball or football, where decision-making, reaction speed, and coordination are critical. Preliminary evidence supporting the effectiveness of the S.F.E.R.A. model in assessing and training these psychological mechanisms in traditional sports therefore provides a rationale for hypothesizing its usefulness in the field of esports. In this sense, the transferability of S.F.E.R.A. is supported both by the commonalities in cognitive-perceptual demands and by its initial applications in professional coaching contexts (e.g., with famous Italian Olympic players[2,3]).

Therefore, parallels with traditional sports performance and available preliminary evidence suggest that the S.F.E.R.A. model may represent a promising framework for assessing and optimizing psychological skills also in competitive gaming.

5.2.2 *Application to the Esports Context: The e-S.F.E.R.A. Questionnaire*

In 2023, the principles of the S.F.E.R.A. model were applied in the esports context through the development of a dedicated psychometric tool. The study (Caputo et al., 2023) validated a self-report questionnaire designed to assess key psychological dimensions relevant to optimizing mental performance in competitive gaming.

---

[2] https://paginedisport.net/2020/04/19/pagine-di-sport-intervista-daniele-molmenti-splendido-oro-nella-canoa-slalom-a-londra-2012/.

[3] https://raceskimagazine.it/sofia-goggia-la-forza-arrivare-al-successo/.

This effort led to the creation of the *e-S.F.E.R.A. Questionnaire*. Following, a brief description of the first study, regarding the validation of the e-S.F.E.R.A. Questionnaire.

The questionnaire's initial formulation was carried out by a full professor in applied psychology and a certified sport psychologist accredited by the International Olympic Committee. The tool was first developed in Italian and followed rigorous item-construction procedures, starting from 83 items in its very first version, which covered the five core dimensions of the model. In the subsequent phase, two experienced sport psychologists who regularly apply the S.F.E.R.A. model in their practice with players and managers were consulted to assess the content relevance of each item. Based on their evaluations, 23 items were removed, resulting in a more concise 60-item version. To enhance clarity and ensure the instrument's ecological validity, a pilot study was conducted with a small sample of former esports players and active competitive gamers; then, the research was extended to a larger sample of professional esports players. Some item wordings were refined based on their feedback, in order to improve clarity and the instrument's applicability across different gaming genres. The final version of the questionnaire asks participants to recall a recent competitive gaming experience. Respondents are asked to rate their agreement with a series of statements related to that performance, using a 5-point Likert scale ranging from 1 ("Completely disagree") to 5 ("Completely agree"). Statistical analyses conducted on the 60-item version helped to identify the most psychometrically valid items. As a result, the final version of the e-S.F.E.R.A. Questionnaire was reduced to 29 items (Table 5.1), a practical tool for psychological assessment and mental coaching in the esports domain. The detailed description of the questionnaire's validation process can be found in the study by Caputo et al. (2023).

When plotted on a radar chart, the scores offer a visual snapshot of the player's mental state during the specific competitive scenario they have been invited to reflected on. The so-called "S.F.E.R.A. radar" (Fig. 5.1) can be a useful tool for planning training sessions.

The radar representation does not describe players' psychological capacities in general terms, but reflects how these capacities were subjectively experienced and expressed in a specific competitive situation. Within the coaching context, this visualization can serve as a starting point for dialogue and reflection. By identifying the most fragile factor, the coach can start exploring patterns or situational triggers that may have influenced performance.

The pilot phase described above was conducted exclusively to refine the items and validate the e-S.F.E.R.A. Questionnaire (more details can be found in Caputo et al., 2023). By contrast, the experimental protocol presented in the following section was performed at a later stage and involved professional esports players. The questionnaire developed in the first study served as the foundation for designing the second study, which implements the training intervention described below.

Table 5.1 Items and sub-components of the e-S.F.E.R.A. questionnaire

Component	During the game that I thought about…
Synchrony	Thoughts and actions coincided
	I felt I had everything under control
	I had in mind all actions to be carried out "step by step"
	I could effortlessly perceive the signals coming from the game situation
	My thinking was completely focused on the action
Strength	I was aware of my strengths
	I knew I could perfectly perform every move
	I was afraid of not being able to tackle possible issues
	I knew exactly which skills to employ at different times
	I was afraid of breaking me down when faced with the first difficulties
	I felt that I could effectively deal with unexpected situations and problems
	I felt able to achieve the goals
Energy	I acted in a gritty way
	I wasn't able to let my energies flow
	I felt filled with grit for its entire duration
	I knew how to regulate my forces
	I felt determined
	I was able to regulate my energies to perform at my best
Rhythm	Thoughts, movements and commands came naturally to me
	I was awkward in my movements
	I moved with the right timing
	I dedicated the necessary time to each action
	I did everything at the appropriate time
	I was moving forward without indecision
	The rhythm of my actions was well suited to that situation
Activation	I couldn't wait to get started
	I felt that what I was doing had an important meaning for me
	I felt I could fulfil myself by doing that activity
	I felt proud of what I was doing
	I felt motivated to reach the goals that I had set

5.2.3 *Application to the Esports Context: A Training Protocol Based on e-S.F.E.R.A*

After the validation of the e-S.F.E.R.A. Questionnaire, research on the application of the e-S.F.E.R.A. model continued through an experimental protocol (explained below; Caputo et al., 2026). In particular, the protocol involved professional esports

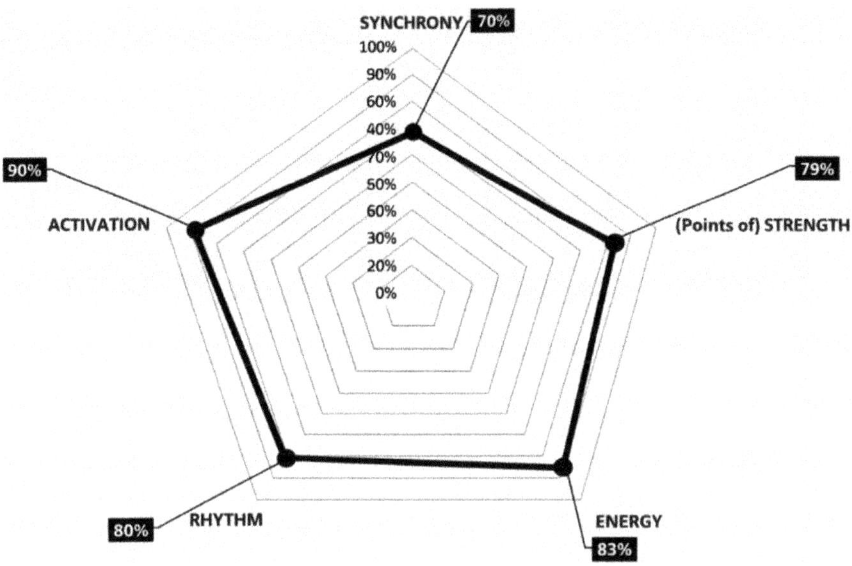

Fig. 5.1 Example of "e-S.F.E.R.A. radar"

players, meaning individuals under contract with professional teams or sports organizations, or those training to compete in tournaments with monetary prizes. Two groups were involved in the study, with the following characteristics:

Experimental Group: Professional players participated in a psychological training program based on the e-S.F.E.R.A. model. They completed a questionnaire at three time points: before the training (T0), after the first session (T1), and after the second session (T2).

Control Group: This group consisted of professional players who did not take part in the psychological training and were only asked to complete the same questionnaires at the corresponding time intervals as the experimental group.

The psychological training consisted of two sessions, each lasting between five days and two weeks. Each session included one exercise per e-S.F.E.R.A. factor, to be completed daily. Figure 5.2 provides an overview of the protocol.

The online survey, besides the e-S.F.E.R.A. dimensions, investigated also the engagement in playing esports and the satisfaction about player's performance. In total, two exercises were developed for each e-S.F.E.R.A. factor. These activities could involve physical or paper-and-pencil tasks. Each session included video-trainings presenting both the theoretical background of the e-S.F.E.R.A. factors and illustrations of the related technique. To monitor participation and engagement, each video concluded with a final reflection question accessed via a dedicated link. The study involved a total of 97 professional esports players, divided into an experimental group (n = 59) and a control group (n = 38). The sample is formed by 4.1% of women and 95.9% of men, with an average age of 27.22 years (*SD* = 7.76). Participants played the following titles: *Apex Legends* (n = 24; ranking from

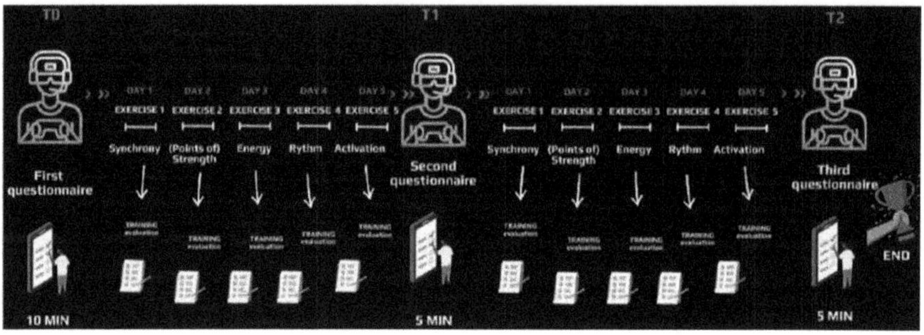

Fig. 5.2 Synthesis of the research protocol

"Master" to "Platinum"); *Assetto Corsa Competizione* (n = 4); *Brawl Stars* (n = 1; rank "Legendary"); *Call of Duty* (n = 27; ranking from "Gold" to "Iridescent"); *EA SPORTS FC 25* (n = 21; ranking from "Level 2 and 3 in Élite Division"); *Gran Turismo* (n = 1; rank "Class D"); *League of Legends* (n = 12; ranking from "Gold" to "Diamond"); *Rainbow Six Siege* (n = 2; ranking "Platinum" and "Diamond"); *Rocket League* (n = 2; rank "Diamond"); *Super Smash bros. Ultimate* (n = 1); *Tekken 8* (n = 1; rank "Flame Ruler"); *Valorant* (n = 1; rank "Immortal"). 23 players expressed no rank.

5.2.4 *Training Techniques*

Below is a brief overview of the exercises proposed for the training protocol for each of the S.F.E.R.A. factors.

Synchrony

- Exercise 1: Participants reflect on game or training situations where they felt "in sync" or "out of sync", identifying physical, mental, and behavioral indicators, emotions, and strategies used to (or that could have helped to) restore Synchrony. The goal is to increase awareness of signs that indicate alignment between body and mind.
- Exercise 2: Participants perform the typical actions they do while gaming (e.g., pressing buttons) very slowly, then analyze the micro-movements of this action, focusing on tactile sensations and step-by-step awareness. This attention aims to reconnect them to the present moment.

(Points of) Strength

- Exercise 1: The S.W.O.T. analysis helps participants assess personal strengths to recall while performing in esports, with the aim of fostering awareness and preparedness.

- Exercise 2: Participants analyze moments of a past competition, describing actions and outcomes. The sport psychologist guides reflection on the strengths that contributed to succeed.

Energy

- Exercise 1: A reflection exercise explores which aspects of participants' professional and personal lives contribute to increasing or decreasing their energy levels either during performance or in preparation for it. Participants describe factors that give them energy (e.g., socializing with friends) and those that drain their energy (e.g., fear of judgment, performing in front of a large audience). This activity encourages awareness of sources of energy.
- Exercise 2: Progressive muscle relaxation is used, which helps participants develop awareness of physical tension and then relaxation, promoting energy regulation.

Rhythm

- Exercise 1: Participants try out different speeds for performing a certain sport-specific action, from very slow to very fast, to identify their optimal personal pace for achieving efficient performance.
- Exercise 2: Breathing exercises characterized by rapid inhalation and slow, controlled exhalation aim to improve concentration and increase awareness of internal rhythm.

Activation

- Exercise 1: Participants complete a goal-setting activity, identifying specific, measurable goals (i.e., "s.m.a.r.t." goals), distinguishing among short-, medium-, and long-term objectives, and prioritizing performance-oriented targets (e.g., mastering specific technical skills).
- Exercise 2: A reflective exercise designed to assess participants' sense of control over performance-related goals. They evaluate the extent to which their actions are perceived as imposed (Duty), aligned with their knowledge (Competence), or self-directed (Desire/Agency), on a scale from 1 (not at all true) to 10 (completely true). Then, they answer further reflective questions such as "What do I want?", "Do I know what I want?", "Do I want what I know?", "What do I know?", aiming to enhance clarity and perceived control, key drivers of motivation in both training and competition.

5.2.5 Results

Repeated measures ANOVAs were performed to examine time × group interactions. Results showed significant interaction effects, with the experimental group showing greater improvements over time compared to the control group, particularly in performance satisfaction and perceived potential expression. Effect sizes (partial η^2) ranged from 0.04 to 0.12, indicating small to moderate effects according to Cohen's benchmarks (Cohen, 1988). Main results are presented in Table 5.2. Further empirical details are available in Caputo et al. (2026).

Note * Adapted from the Players' Subjective Performance Scale (Lee et al., 2023).

Repeated-measures ANOVAs both within- and between-subjects were conducted to assess changes across the three time points. Here, partial eta squared (η^2) was reported to indicate effect sizes, and 95% confidence intervals (CIs) were provided for each measurement. "Time" served as the within-subjects factor, while group assignment (experimental vs. control) was the between-subjects factor. Statistical significance was interpreted at $p < 0.05$.

Table 5.2 Results of repeated measures ANOVA.

Dimensions	item	F (Time×Group)	*p*-**value**	Partial η^2
Potential	How much do you feel you expressed your potential during your game performance?	7.583	< 0.001	0.074
Performance* (1)	Overall—To what extent are you satisfied with your gaming performance?	8.308	< 0.001	0.081
Performance* (2)	To what extent were your capabilities truly reflected?	10.666	< 0.001	0.101
Performance* (3)	To what extent are you satisfied with your functioning during the challenging moments?	9.542	< 0.001	0.091
Performance* mean	Mean	13.342	< 0.001	0.123
Performance ad hoc (1)	I was able to achieve the performance goals I set for myself	3.570	0.030	0.036
Performance ad hoc (2)	I was able to react appropriately to obstacles	5.310	0.006	0.053
Performance ad hoc (3)	I was able to manage my emotions during the game	3.713	0.026	0.038
Performance ad hoc mean	Mean	5.220	0.006	0.052
Engagement mean	Mean	7.872	0.006	0.077

5.2.6 Discussion

Psychological variables like performance satisfaction, perceived expression of potential, and engagement showed statistically significant improvements, offering preliminary empirical support for the model's applicability in this population. Repeated-measures ANOVAs revealed significant time × group interactions, indicating that the psychological training had a significant effect beyond mere exposure to competitive play. Only the experimental group, which took part in the e-S.F.E.R.A.-based exercises, showed consistent improvements across the evaluated domains.

Performance satisfaction and perceived expression of potential were the most influenced variables, crucial factors for professional esports players who deal with intense performance pressure. The improvement in engagement suggests that the intervention may have helped solicit a more intrinsic and focused form of motivation, in line with the model's emphasis on Activation. Mental preparedness and performance satisfaction seem to be enhanced by exercises that foster self-awareness, attentional anchoring, emotional regulation, and goal clarity. Interestingly, methods like breathing rhythm alignment, progressive muscle relaxation, and reflective thinking about in-game behaviors might have given players greater control over their internal states and external performance, inviting players to manage self-regulation and self-reflection.

However, the study is not exempt from limitations that have to be acknowledged. First, the sample was predominantly male (95.9%), limiting generalizability across genders. According to a Statista report, among Italian users of esports content, women account for 45% of gamers, but only 32% of esports viewers.[4] This trend is confirmed by a 2024 study by Deloitte and IIDEA.[5] Moreover, national awards for the best Italian esports players predominantly feature male players, reflecting a gender imbalance in professional recognition.[6] In terms of age, most Italian video gamers belong to the Millennial generation (25–44 years; 42%), followed by Generation Z (16–24 years; 19%). For example, the best Italian players voted in 2020 were born between 1993 and 2002. However, demographic data from scientific or official reports on Italian professional esports players are still lacking, including a clear operational definition of what constitutes a "professional" player in the national context—an understandable gap given that esports is still an emerging and progressively expanding phenomenon in Italy. Within this context, the gender and age distribution observed in the present sample is consistent with the current composition of the Italian esports landscape. At the same time, the sector continues to evolve and a number of campaigns are starting to appear to encourage diversity and inclusivity, like Women in Games, which promotes increased female involvement and representation in Italian gaming and esports. Furthermore, the effects shown in the study should be considered limited in time; although significant, the effects were small,

[4] https://www.statista.com/statistics/1616419/esports-fans-italy-gender/

[5] https://iideassociation.com/wpcontent/uploads/2024/11/2024-Italian-Esports-Report_Market-Streaming-Trends.pdf

[6] https://www.esportsmag.it/italian-esports-awards-ecco-le-nomination-per-il-best-italianplayer/

indicating the need for follow-up or further studies to obtain more robust and lasting results. Finally, the use of self-assessment measures may have introduced bias; for a more in-depth evaluation, future research could include behavioral observations or performance analyses.

5.3 Conclusion

Having explored this phenomenon at a more practical level, it is possible to conclude that these studies represent a promising step toward incorporating structured psychological training into professional esports environments. The e-S.F.E.R.A. model showed efficacy in improving professional players' perceived performance quality, potential expression, and engagement. These results provide support to the use of structured psychological protocols as an effective complement to technical training in esports. Future studies may explore the integration of physiological and biomechanical data; also, more research is needed to tailor psychological approaches to the specific features of each esports environment. A psychological perspective results necessary for effective coaching in esports, since high-level performance requires not only mechanics and tactics but also mindset, emotional resilience, and effective communication dynamics.

References

Bonilla, I., Chamarro, A., & Ventura, C. (2022). Psychological skills in esports: Qualitative study of individual and team players. *Aloma, 40*(1), 35–41. https://doi.org/10.51698/aloma.2022.40.1.36-41

Bubna, K., Trotter, M. G., Watson, M., & Polman, R. (2023). Coaching and talent development in esports: A theoretical framework and suggestions for future research. *Frontiers in Psychology, 14*, 1191801. https://doi.org/10.3389/fpsyg.2023.1191801

Caputo, A., Drivet, S., Sandretto, R., Vercelli, G., & Cortese, C. G. (2023). The e · S.F.E.R.A. Questionnaire: A new tool for sport psychologists working in mental training. *The Open Psychology Journal, 16*(1), 1–13. https://doi.org/10.2174/18743501-v16-230301-2022-105

Caputo, A., Vercelli, G., Cortese, C. G. (2026). Psychological training in esports: A research note on performance enhancement in professional esports athletes. International Journal of Sports Science & Coaching, 0(0), 1–9. https://doi.org/10.1177/17479541251407498

Cohen, J. (1988). *Statistical power analysis for the behavioral sciences* (2nd ed.). Erlbaum.

Cortese, C. G., Dolce, V., Borla Cart, V., D'Avino, M., & Vercelli, G. (2017). Psychometric properties of the S.F.E.R.A. Test: A first study on a sample of 153 athletes. In A. Lo Presti & P. Spagnoli (Eds.), *Italian Association of Psychology—XV National Congress of the Work and Organizational Psychology Section. Program of works and presented contributions* (Caserta, September 14–16, 2017) (p. 4). Italian Association of Psychology. ISBN 978–88–942913-0-8.

Cortese, C. G., Dolce, V., Borla Cart, V., Loretoni, I., & Vercelli, G. (2018). Psychometric properties of the SFERA business test: A first study on a sample of managers. *In* C. Consiglio, A. Callea, & M. L. Farnese *(Eds.), Italian Association of Psychology—XVI National Congress of the Work and Organizational Psychology Section. Program of works and presented contributions* (Rome, September 27–29, 2018) (pp. 110–111). Italian Association of Psychology.

Cortese, C. G., Dolce, V., Borla Cart, V., & Vercelli, G. (2019a, May 29–June 1). SFERA test: Preliminary validation with an athletes' *sample* [Poster presentation]. *XIX EAWOP Congress: Working for the Greater Good,*.

Cortese, C. G., Dolce, V., Bianciot, M., Borla Cart, V., & Vercelli, G. (2019b, September 26–28). SFERA Test: Preliminary validation on a sample of individual and team sport athletes [Poster presentation]. *XVII National Congress of the Work and Organizational Psychology Section of the Italian Association of Psychology: The future of work, the work of the future—Psychology to innovate, transform, and grow within organizations.*

Cortese, C. G., & Emanuel, F. (2022). The university lecturer: Teaching performance effectiveness and teaching self-efficacy. In *Training university teachers in teaching and assessment. In-depth topics and effectiveness of IRIDI programs* (pp. 26–45). FrancoAngeli.

Cottrell, C., McMillen, N., & Harris, B. S. (2019). Sport psychology in a virtual world: Considerations for practitioners working in esports. *Journal of Sport Psychology in Action, 10*(2), 73–81. https://doi.org/10.1080/21520704.2018.1518280

Himmelstein, D., Liu, Y., & Shapiro, J. L. (2017). An exploration of mental skills among competitive league of legends players. *International Journal of Gaming and Computer-Mediated Simulations, 9*(2), 1–21. https://doi.org/10.4018/IJGCMS.2017040101

Lee, S., Yun, H. J., Jeon, M., & Kang, M. (2023). Validating athletes' subjective performance scale: A Rasch model analysis. *International Journal of Applied Sports Sciences, 35*(2) https://doi.org/10.24985/ijass.2023.35.2.238

Leis, O., & Lautenbach, F. (2020). Psychological and physiological stress in non-competitive and competitive esports settings: A systematic review. *Psychology of Sport and Exercise, 51*, 101738. https://doi.org/10.1016/j.psychsport.2020.101738

Leis, O., Swettenham, L. D., & Sharpe, B. T. (2025). *Applied sport psychology in esports: Directions for future research and practical implications.* Under review.

Mazzon, L., Passarotto, E., Altenmüller, E., & Vercelli, G. (2024). Music performance anxiety and the Italian sport psychology SFERA model: An explorative study on 77 professional musicians. *Psychology of Music, 52*(3), 322–339. https://doi.org/10.1177/03057356231198239

Munroe-Chandler, K. J., Loughead, T. M., Zuluev, E. G., & Ely, F. O. (2023). An imagery-based intervention for managing anxiety in esports. *Journal of Imagery Research in Sport and Physical Activity, 18(s1), Article 20230005.* https://doi.org/10.1515/jirspa-2023-0005

Nagorsky, E., & Wiemeyer, J. (2020). The structure of performance and training in esports. PLoS One, 15(8), e0237584. https://doi.org/10.1371/journal.pone.0237584

Papp, D., Burján, R., & Csukonyi, C. (2025). Exploratory study of qualitative psychological factors influencing performance in esports. *Frontiers in Sports and Active Living, 7*, 1505409. https://doi.org/10.3389/fspor.2025.1505409

Pedraza-Ramirez, I., Musculus, L., Raab, M., & Laborde, S. (2020). Setting the scientific stage for esports psychology: A systematic review. *International Review of Sport and Exercise Psychology, 13*(1), 319–352. https://doi.org/10.1080/1750984X.2020.1723122

Pedraza-Ramirez, I., Sharpe, B., Behnke, M., Toth, A. J., & Poulus, D. R. (2025). The psychology of esports: Trends, challenges, and future directions. *Psychology of Sport and Exercise, 102967.* https://doi.org/10.1016/j.psychsport.2025.102967

Poulus, D., Coulter, T. J., Trotter, M. G., & Polman, R. (2020). Stress and coping in esports and the influence of mental toughness. *Frontiers in Psychology, 11*, 628. https://doi.org/10.3389/fpsyg.2020.00628

Poulus, D. R., Jackman, P. C., Fransen, J., Polman, R. C. J., & Bennett, K. J. M. (2025). An exploration of high-performance environments in esports: A preliminary model. *Journal of Sports Sciences, 43*(20), 2380–2403. https://doi.org/10.1080/02640414.2025.2533538

Sharpe, B. T., Leis, O., Moore, L., Sharpe, A. T. R., Seymour, S., Obine, E. A. C., & Poulus, D. R. (2024). Reappraisal and mindset interventions on pressurized esport performance. *Applied*

Psychology: An International Review. Advance online publication. https://doi.org/10.1111/apps.12544

Vercelli, G. (2005). *Vincere con la mente.* Ponte alle Grazie.

Watson, M., Abbott, C., & Pedraza-Ramirez, I. (2021). A parallel approach to performance and sport psychology work in esports teams. *International Journal of Esports, 1*(1) Retrieved from https://www.ijesports.org/article/52/html

Chapter 6
Psychological Recovery on Esports: Balancing Mental Load, Stress, and Performance

Şeval Kayğusuz

6.1 Introduction

With the increasing professionalization of its organizational structures, esports players have evolved into a performance domain characterized by high performance expectations. However, compared with traditional sports, the relatively lower physical load and the necessity for players to effectively manage substantial cognitive, emotional, and mental demands have become critical determinants of sustained performance. In esports players' performance, gameplay is not limited to mere device operation but also involves intense mental pressure and the requirement for accurate and rapid decision-making (Li et al., 2022). Moreover, competitive gaming is associated with high levels of arousal and stress (Forman et al., 2025). Schaaff et al. (2012) reported that high levels of stress and arousal directly influence mouse-click force. In efforts to enhance performance and refine their skills, esports players often engage in training for up to 8–12 hours per day and more than 30 hours per week; when such training loads are not supported by appropriate recovery practices, they have been shown to contribute not only to decrements in game-related performance but also to the development of spinal and musculoskeletal disorders (DiFrancisco-Donoghue et al., 2019; Forman et al., 2025; Leis & Lautenbach, 2020; Lindberg et al., 2020). Beyond these physical complaints, the esports environment is characterized by the presence of multiple stressors, including performance pressure, team dynamics, spectator expectations, social media, and challenges related to maintaining work–life balance (Leis et al., 2024; Poulus et al., 2021; Poulus & Polman, 2022). The effects of stress and stress-coping processes on esports players' performance and affective states have been demonstrated across numerous studies (Leis & Lautenbach, 2020). Empirical findings further indicate that these stressors are associated with increased symptoms of depression and anxiety, sleep disturbances, low mood,

Ş. Kayğusuz (✉)
Istanbul Gedik University, İstanbul, Türkiye
e-mail: seval.kaygusuz@gedik.edu.tr

S. Bekir (ed.), *The Psychology of Esports*, https://doi.org/10.1007/978-3-032-25090-2_6

and heightened stress levels among esports players (Birch et al., 2024; Gouttebarge et al., 2019; Monteiro Pereira et al., 2022; Nochaiwong et al., 2021). Considering such performance-impairing psychological factors, a notable gap is evident in the provision of athlete-specific, structured, and systematic psychological support interventions within the esports context (Poulus & Sharpe, 2025; Schary et al., 2022). Within this framework, given the intense stressors faced by esports players and the accompanying psychological challenges, psychological recovery should be conceptualized as a critical regulatory mechanism for both the maintenance of performance and the sustainability of psychological well-being.

6.1.1 Psychological Recovery on Sport

A player's ability to recover adequately is considered a determining factor in sporting success, health, and overall well-being (Heidari et al., 2022). Enhancing recovery has been shown to facilitate improvements in performance (Bishop et al., 2008). Recovery is defined as the replenishment of the resources players require to perform, unfolding over time as a multilevel process that operates both within and between individuals; moreover, it is a multidimensional process involving multiple systems (Kallus & Kellmann, 2016). Recent research has increasingly focused on how recovery should be conceptualized in order to achieve a balance between stress and recovery (Kellmann & Beckmann, 2022). In addition, it has been emphasized that recovery does not merely serve to offset imbalance but also functions as a preventive and protective approach by mitigating the negative effects of stress before they manifest. In this context, the use of psychological markers for the identification, monitoring, and prevention of overtraining syndrome in players, as well as their monitoring from a psychological recovery perspective, offers several advantages. These advantages were outlined by Kentta and Hassmen (1998) as follows.

1. Monitoring psychological changes in players is essential. Fluctuations in players' mood states tend to coincide with performance improvements and declines and are also reproducible over time.
2. It has been demonstrated that certain emotional states are sensitive to increases in training load, while others are more susceptible to overtraining syndrome.
3. It has been documented that variations in mood measurements frequently correlate with alterations in physiological symptoms.
4. The analysis of emotional responses to training loads has been identified as a significant potential preventative measure against overtraining syndrome.

During periods of intensive training and competitions, elite players are required to demonstrate cope with stress (Loch et al., 2019). Despite the pressure to which they are subjected, players are required to maintain their concentration, perceptual skills, and decision-making abilities during these periods, in order to perform at their optimal level (Nédélec et al., 2012). Players who face multi-dimensional stress factors specific to competitive, involving mental stress before, during and after competitions, experience mental fatigue and mental load (Balk & Englert, 2020; Loch et al., 2023; Nédélec et al., 2012). Mental fatigue is a psychobiological condition arising from cognitive activity, which is characterized by a sense of tiredness and reduced energy level (Boksem et al., 2006; Marcora et al., 2009). Consequently, impairments occur in executive functions (e.g. working memory or mental flexibility) and decision-making mechanisms (Loch et al., 2023). This situation, which has a detrimental effect on cognitive control, results in a lack of concentration, reduced alertness, and impaired attention (Carney et al., 2014). The competitive and collaborative nature of esports engenders psychological competencies, in addition to the mental skills required at a psychological level, akin to those observed in traditional sports (Murphy, 2009). However, the digital nature of esports introduces an additional layer of complexity that distinguishes it from traditional competitive environments. The intersection of competitive gaming, performance demands, and digital environments creates a context that differs from that of traditional sports in terms of affective state research (Trotter et al., 2023). This situation has led to several side effects, including prolonged screen exposure (Nicholson et al., 2024), irregular sleep patterns (Bonnar et al., 2022), intense online community interactions (Poulus et al., 2022), blurred boundaries between work and personal life in home spaces (Poulus et al., 2022), and career uncertainty leading to increased anxiety and burnout (Birch et al., 2024). Therefore, activities that require concentration, such as esports, can cause mental fatigue due to the specific mental demands they entail. The concept of mental recovery, a potential countermeasure to such situations, is attracting increasing attention in sports science research (Balk et al., 2019).

Mental recovery involves returning to baseline levels of mental ability, such as concentration and decision-making (Balk et al., 2017), replenishing necessary resources, resting the mind and coping with intrusive thoughts (Loch et al., 2023). The resources individuals utilize are related to their energy levels, which vary depending on their level of arousal. In this context, replenishing energy resources is one of the fundamental components of mental recovery and is directly related to the subjective feeling of vigour. Vigour refers to having a high level of energy and motivation to work hard, being resilient in the face of difficulties and having the ability to persevere despite obstacles. The restoration of these psychological resources depends on players being able to detach themselves from the demands of sport, both physically and mentally, during the recovery process. Therefore, to achieve psychological recovery, it is critical that players are able to physically and psychologically "detachment" from sports-related demands during the recovery phase (Eccles & Kazmier, 2019). Taking a break from or distancing oneself from sports-related demands is considered a main strategy and is referred to as detachment (Englert, 2016). Detachment is the state of withdrawing physically, cognitively and/or emotionally from the demands of sport. This allows players to recover their depleted physical and mental resources (Balk & Englert, 2020; Kellman & Günter, 2000). In sport, "detachment" refers to an individual feeling disconnected from the demands of training or competition (Balk et al., 2017).

The esports environment, in which digital toxicity and cyberbullying are highly prevalent, can give rise to conditions such as anxiety, social withdrawal, and loneliness among players (Leis et al., 2024; Trudgett-Klose & McLinton, 2024). The fact that the competition areas are located within the home environment blurs the distinction between privacy and competition, making recovery processes more difficult (Poulus et al., 2025). It has been observed that these stressors not only cause players to experience poor emotional states, but also make them more vulnerable (Poulus et al., 2026). In addition to the temporary suspension of sports-related demands and thoughts, as well as a general decrease in physical and cognitive activity, it is important for players to manage their emotions, thoughts and actions after a performance in order to optimize their recovery (Balk et al., 2017; Balk et al., 2020; Beckmann & Kellmann, 2004). This regulatory process aims not only to reduce negative psychological effects but also to facilitate players' reconstruction of positive psychological functioning and their attainment of a sustainable level of well-being. The concept of flourishing, which focuses on optimal mental functioning, encompasses individuals' emotional, psychological, and social well-being (Pankow et al., 2022; Pankow et al., 2023). Being filled with positive emotions and functioning flourishing psychologically and socially are fundamental characteristics of the concept of turning things around (Keyes, 2005).

The psychological aspect of recovery involves improving subjective feelings, encouraging relaxation and increasing well-being to re-establish a positive emotional state (Kellmann & Kallus, 1999). When designing any training program or seasonal plan, it should not be overlooked that players are able to achieve optimal performance only when they can effectively balance competitive or training-related stress with subsequent recovery (Jeffreys, 2005). If recovery efficiency can be improved and recovery processes in players can be systematically monitored, measured, and tracked, greater training volumes and enhanced performance outcomes may be achieved without exposure to the negative consequences of overtraining.

6.1.2 *Measuring Psychological Recovery*

In the context of resource depletion during the performance process and the integrated consideration of all relevant variables, monitoring changes in mood states reported through psychological assessments is regarded as a reliable indicator for identifying the underlying causes of prolonged fatigue associated with training or competition (Coutts et al., 2006; Coutts et al., 2007; Halson & Jeukendrup, 2004). Therefore, research suggests using psychometric self-report measures to monitor players' subjective experiences of recovery and stress throughout the training process (Kellmann, 2010; Kellmann et al., 2001). A review of the literature on measuring psychological recovery in sport reveals the existence of various scales, including the Sport Psychological Recovery Scale (SPRS), Total Quality Recovery (TQR), Daily Analysis of Life Demands for Athletes (DALDA), Acute Recovery and Stress Scale (ARSS), Short Recovery and Stress Scale (SRSS), Recovery Stress Questionnaire for Athletes (REST-Q Sport), and Profile of Mood States (POMS). Table 6.1 provides general information on self-report scales.

It has been demonstrated that a number of self-reporting tools related to psychological recovery in the field of sport can also be used by esports players. In this context, measuring psychological recovery in esports players can substantiate the results related to relieving the mental burden that arises after a competition. Consequently, the players' preparation for subsequent competitions can be meticulously planned to account for this recovery period. The monitoring of individual psychological recovery is an indispensable element in the planning of competition and training, and in the enhancement of performance.

6.2 Conclusion

Psychological recovery is defined as an individual's capacity to rebuild their emotional, cognitive and motivational resources after exposure to stressors. It is considered a fundamental mechanism in preventing negative outcomes such as performance decline, burnout and mental fatigue. In the context of esports, the high frequency of competitions, the continuous nature of the online competitive environment, and the constant evaluation of performance through instant feedback can make recovery processes difficult to achieve adequately. This situation can lead not only to a loss of performance but also to a deterioration in psychological well-being. The extant literature thoroughly examines the relationship between psychological recovery and performance, stress management, and post-injury adaptation processes in the traditional sports disciplines. However, research findings concerning the experience of this process by esports players are limited. However, the specific nature of esports, where mental strain takes precedence over physical fatigue, necessitates a re-examination of the concept of recovery. The significance of psychological recovery is manifest during periods of heightened mental fatigue, perceived stress, and emotional overload. This facilitates enhanced management of performance fluctuations and optimized utilization of cognitive resources, ensuring sustainable performance. This situation demonstrates that recovery is not a process limited solely to rest; it encompasses multidimensional psychological processes such as emotional regulation, cognitive restructuring and motivational renewal. The findings of the studies examined in this section largely coincide with those in traditional sports literature, which emphasizes the regulatory role of psychological recovery in the stress–performance relationship. However, it is indicated that within the context of esports, this relationship is shaped more by mental and emotional demands. In particular, the continuity of online competition, the instantaneous measurement of performance, and the intensity of social comparison stand out as specific factors that increase the need for recovery. In this context, the failure to incorporate recovery processes into esports may result in short-term performance declines and, over time, contribute to the development of

Table 6.1 Overview of different methods reported by players through self-reporting (adapted from Bestwick-Stevenson et al., 2022)

Measurement tools	Overwiev
Sport psychological recovery scale (SPRS)	This 20-item scale was developed by Kayğusuz and Karagözoğlu (2023) using a sample of Turkish players. This measure has been demonstrated to be both valid and reliable. The measure is designed to assess the extent to which players have recovered psychologically following periods of intensive training or competition. Sub-scales: Mental recovery, psychological detachment, energy and vigour, flourishing and total psychological recovery.
Total quality recovery (TQR)	It focuses on psychophysiological recovery. TQR'S objective is to differentiate between the cause and effect of stress, incorporating a consideration of both the source and magnitude of stress factors reflected in recovery.
Daily analysis of life demands for athletes (DALDA)	It is a measure that assesses a player's stress level and examines the factors causing this condition. It consists of two sections and 34 items. Section A examines nine sources of stress and section B examines 25 stress symptoms.
Acute recovery and stress scale (ARSS) Short recovery and stress scale (SRSS)	The ARSS, which is comprised of a series of 32 attributes, is designed to measure the physical, mental, emotional and general dimensions of an individual. The assessment of the balance between stress and recovery is facilitated by ARSS and its abbreviated version, SRSS.
Recovery stress questionnaire for athletes (REST-Q sport)	The stress and recovery scale for athletes, a tool developed by Kellmann and Kallus, offers a comprehensive evaluation of the sport-specific factors that influence a player's overall recovery-stress status. The scale under consideration comprises 76 items and 19 sub-dimensions, which are grouped under four dimensions. The statements address both sport-specific and non-sport-specific aspects of stress and recovery. Within the general stress dimension: General stress, emotional stress, social stress, conflicts/pressure, fatigue, lack of energy, physical complaints; within the general recovery dimension: Success, social recovery, physical recovery, Well-being and sleep quality; within the sport-specific stress dimension: Rest in sport, emotional exhaustion and injury; within the sport-specific recovery dimension: Fitness, personal success, self-efficacy and self-regulation sub-dimensions are included.
Profile of mood States (POMS)	The 65-item version addresses six dimensions of emotional state: Tension, depression, anger, vigour, fatigue, and confusion. A condensed version comprising 37 items is also available. It detects fluctuations in emotional states associated with training.

burnout and a decline in psychological well-being. Therefore, the role of psychological recovery in esports performance is a significant area of research, both in terms of supporting players' wellbeing and developing sustainable performance models.

When evaluated from an application perspective, these findings indicate the necessity of structured intervention and training programmes centred on psychological recovery for esports players. In the context of training and competition planning, the periodic monitoring of not only performance outcomes but also psychological load and recovery indicators can be regarded as a pivotal step in ensuring sustainable performance. Furthermore, it is imperative for coaches, sports psychologists and performance teams to develop holistic recovery models that take into account stressors specific to esports.

References

Balk, Y. A., De Jonge, J., Oerlemans, W. G. M., & Geurts, S. A. E. (2017). Testing the triple match principle among Dutch elite athletes: A day-level study on sport demands, detachment and recovery. *Psychology of Sport and Exercise, 33*, 7–17. https://doi.org/10.1016/j.psychsport.2017.07.006

Balk, Y. A., De Jonge, J., Oerlemans, W. G., & Geurts, S. A. (2019). Physical recovery, mental detachment and sleep as predictors of injury and mental energy. *Journal of Health Psychology, 24*(13), 1828–1838. https://doi.org/10.1177/1359105317705

Balk, Y. A., De Jonge, J., Oerlemans, W. G., & Geurts, S. A. (2020). "What a match!": The specific role of resources in the relation between demands and vigour in elite sport. *Applied Psychology, 69*(1), 120–147. https://doi.org/10.1111/apps.12188

Balk, Y. A., & Englert, C. (2020). Recovery self-regulation in sport: Theory, research, and practice. *International Journal of Sports Science and Coaching, 15*(2), 273–281. https://doi.org/10.1177/1747954119897528

Beckmann, J., & Kellmann, M. (2004). Self-regulation and recovery: Approaching an understanding of the process of recovery from stress. *Psychological Report, 95*(3 suppl), 1135–1153. https://doi.org/10.2466/pr0.95.3f.1135-1153

Bestwick-Stevenson, T., Toone, R., Neupert, E., Edwards, K., & Kluzek, S. (2022). Assessment of fatigue and recovery in sport: Narrative review. *International Journal of Sports Medicine, 43*(14), 1151–1162. https://doi.org/10.1055/a-1834-7177

Birch, P. D. J., Smith, M. J., Arumuham, A., de Gortari, A. O., & Sharpe, B. T. (2024). The prevalence of mentalill health in elite counter-strike athletes. *Journal of Electronic Gaming and Esports, 2*(1), 1–9. https://doi.org/10.1123/jege.2024-0006

Bishop, P. A., Jones, E., & Woods, A. K. (2008). Recovery from training: A brief review: Brief review. *The Journal of Strength & Conditioning Research, 22*(3), 1015–1024. https://doi.org/10.1519/JSC.0b013e31816eb518

Boksem, M. A. S., Meijman, T. F., & Lorist, M. M. (2006). Mental fatigue, motivation and action monitoring. *Biological Psychology, 72*(2), 123–132. https://doi.org/10.1016/j.biopsycho.2005.08.007

Bonnar, D., Lee, S., Roane, B. M., Blum, D. J., Kahn, M., Jang, E., Dunican, I. C., Gradisar, M., & Suh, S. (2022). Evaluation of a brief sleep intervention designed to improve the sleep, mood, and cognitive performance ofEsports athletes. *International Journal of Environmental Research and Public Health, 19*(7), 41–46. https://doi.org/10.3390/ijerph19074146

Carney, C. E., Moss, T. G., Lachowski, A. M., & Atwood, M. E. (2014). Understanding mental and physical fatigue complaints in those with depression and insomnia. *Behavioral Sleep Medicine, 12*(4), 272–289. https://doi.org/10.1080/15402002.2013.801345

Coutts, A. J., Slattery, K. M., & Wallace, L. K. (2007). Practical tests for monitoring performance, fatigue and recovery in triathletes. *Journal of Science and Medicine in Sport, 10*(6), 372–381. https://doi.org/10.1016/j.jsams.2007.02.007

Coutts, A. J., Wallace, L. K., & Slattery, K. M. (2006). Monitoring changes in performance, physiology, biochemistry, and psychology during overreaching and recovery in triathletes. *International Journal of Sports Medicine, 28*(2), 125–134. https://doi.org/10.1055/s-2006-924146

DiFrancisco-Donoghue, J., Balentine, J., Schmidt, G., & Zwibel, H. (2019). Managing the health of the eSport athlete: An integrated health management model. *BMJ Open Sport & Exercise Medicine, 5(1), Article e000467*. https://doi.org/10.1136/bmjsem-2018-000467

Eccles, D. W., & Kazmier, A. W. (2019). The psychology of rest in athletes: An empirical study and initial model. *Psychology of Sport and Exercise, 44*, 90–98. https://doi.org/10.1016/j.psychsport.2019.05.007

Englert, C. (2016). The strength model of self-control in sport and exercise psychology. *Frontiers in Psychology, 7*(314), 1–9. https://doi.org/10.3389/fpsyg.2016.00314

Forman, G. N., Beaudette, S. M., Gabriel, D. A., Sonne, M. W., Kociolek, A. M., & Holmes, M. W. (2025). Quantifying the physical demands of tactical first-person shooter gameplay: Muscle activity and movement characteristics during competitive Valorant. *Journal of Electronic Gaming and Esports, 3*(1) https://doi.org/10.1123/jege.2024-0040

Gouttebarge, V., Castaldelli-Maia, J. M., Gorczynski, P., Hainline, B., Hitchcock, M. E., Kerkhoffs, G. M., Rice, S. M., & Reardon, C. L. (2019). Occurrence of mental health symptoms and disorders in current and former elite athletes: A systematic review and metaanalysis. *British Journal of Sports Medicine, 53*(11), 700–706. https://doi.org/10.1136/bjsports-2019-100671

Halson, S. L., & Jeukendrup, A. E. (2004). Does overtraining exist? An analysis of overreaching and overtraining research. *Sports Medicine, 34*, 967–981.

Heidari, J., Jakowski, S., & Kellmann, M. (2022). The value of recovery-stress monitoring for athletes' Well-being. In M. Kellmann & J. Beckmann (Eds.), *Recovery and Well-being in sport and exercise* (pp. 3–16). Routledge.

Jeffreys, I. (2005). A multidimensional approach to enhancing recovery. *Strength & Conditioning Journal, 27*(5), 78–85.

Kallus, K. W., & Kellmann, M. (Eds.). (2016). *The recovery-stress questionnaires: User manual (p. 360)*. Pearson.

Kayğusuz, Ş., & Karagözoğlu, C. (2023). Sporda psikolojik toparlanma ölçeği (SPTÖ) geliştirme çalışması. *Journal of Sport Sciences Research, 8*(2), 157–174.

Kellmann, M. (2010). Preventing overtraining in athletes in high-intensity sports and stress/recovery monitoring. *Scandinavian Journal of Medicine & Science in Sports, 20*, 95–102. https://doi.org/10.1111/j.1600-0838.2010.01192.x

Kellmann, M., Altenburg, D., Lormes, W., & Steinacker, J. M. (2001). Assessing stress and recovery during preparation for the world championships in rowing. *The Sport Psychologist, 15*(2), 151–167. https://doi.org/10.1123/tsp.15.2.151

Kellmann, M., & Beckmann, J. (2022). *Recovery and Well-being in sport and exercise* (1st ed.). Routledge.

Kellmann, M., & Günther, K. D. (2000). Changes in stress and recovery in elite rowers during preparation for the Olympic games. *Medicine & Science in Sports & Exercise, 32*(3), 676–683.

Kellmann, M., & Kallus, K. W. (1999). Mood, recovery-stress state, and regeneration. In M. Lehhmann, C. Foster, U. Gastmann, H. Keizer, & J. M. Steinacker (Eds.), *Overload, performance incompetence, and regeneration in sport* (pp. 101–117). Kluwer Academic/Plenum Publishers.

Kentta, G., & Hassmen, P. (1998). Overtraining and recovery: A conceptual model. *Sports Medicine, 26*, 1–16.

Keyes, C. L. M. (2005). Mental illness and/or mental health? Investigating axioms of the complete state model of health. *Journal of Consulting and Clinical Psychology, 73*(3), 539–548. https://doi.org/10.1037/0022-006X.73.3.539

Leis, O., & Lautenbach, F. (2020). Psychological and physiological stress in non-competitive and competitive esports settings: A systematic review. *Psychology of Sport and Exercise, 51*, 101738. https://doi.org/10.1016/j.psychsport.2020.101738

Leis, O., Praisan, G., Pedraza-Ramirez, I., Sharpe, B. T., Laborde, S., & Lautenbach, F. (2024). Exploratory studyof psychophysiological stress in esports: Training and competition in professional league of legends. *Journal of Electronic Gaming and Esports, 2*(1), 1–13. https://doi.org/10.1123/jege.2024-0033

Li, G., Wang, M., Arippa, F., Barr, A., Rempel, D., Liu, Y., & Harris Adamson, C. (2022). Professional and high-level gamers: Differences in performance, muscle activity, and hand kinematics for different mice. *International Journal of Human–Computer Interaction,* 38(8), 691–706. https://doi.org/10.1080/10447318.2021.1960742.

Lindberg, L., Nielsen, S.B., Damgaard, M., Sloth, O.R., Rathleff, M.S., & Straszek, C.L. (2020). Musculoskeletal pain is common in competitive gaming: A cross-sectional study among Danish esports athletes. BMJ Open Sport & Exercise Medicine, 6(1), Article 000799. https://doi.org/10.1136/bmjsem-2020-000799.

Loch, F., Ferrauti, A., Meyer, T., Pfeiffer, M., & Kellmann, M. (2019). Resting the mind–a novel topic with scarce insights. Considering potential mental recovery strategies for short rest periods in sports. *Performance Enhancement & Health, 6*(3–4), 148–155. https://doi.org/10.1016/j.peh.2019.04.002

Loch, F., Ferrauti, A., Meyer, T., Pfeiffer, M., & Kellmann, M. (2023). Acute effects of mental recovery strategies in simulated air rifle competitions. *Frontiers in Sports and Active Living, 5*, 1087995. https://doi.org/10.3389/fspor.2023.1087995

Marcora, S. M., Staiano, W., & Manning, V. (2009). Mental fatigue impairs physical performance in humans. *Journal of Applied Physiology, 106*, 857–864. https://doi.org/10.1152/japplphysiol.91324.2008

Monteiro Pereira, A., Costa, J. A., Verhagen, E., Figueiredo, P., & Brito, J. (2022). Associations between esports participation and health: A scoping review. *Sports Medicine, 52*(9), 2039–2060. https://doi.org/10.1007/s40279-022-01684-1

Murphy, S. (2009). Video games, competition and exercise: A new opportunity for sport psychologists? *Sport Psychologist, 23*, 487–503. https://doi.org/10.1123/tsp.23.4.487

Nédélec, M., McCall, A., Carling, C., Legall, F., Berthoin, S., & Dupont, G. (2012). Recovery in soccer: Part I-post-match fatigue and time course of recovery. *Sports Medicine, 42*, 997–1015. https://doi.org/10.1007/BF03262308

Nicholson, M., Thompson, C., Poulus, D., Pavey, T., Robergs, R., Kelly, V., & McNulty, C. (2024). Physical activ-ity and self-determination towards exercise among esports athletes. *Sports Medicine Open, 10*(1), 40. https://doi.org/10.1186/s40798-024-00700-054

Nochaiwong, S., Ruengorn, C., Thavorn, K., Hutton, B., Awiphan, R., Phosuya, C., Ruanta, Y., Wongpakaran, N., & Wongpakaran, T. (2021). Global prevalence of mental health issues among the general population during the coronavirus disease-2019 pandemic: A systematic review and meta-analysis. Scientific Reports, *11*(1), Article 10173. https://doi.org/10.1038/s41598-021-89700-8.

Pankow, K., Mosewich, A. D., McHugh, T. L. F., & Holt, N. L. (2022). The role of mental health protection and promotion among flourishing Canadian university sport coaches. *Sport, Exercise, and Performance Psychology, 11*(1), 28–43. https://doi.org/10.1037/spy0000277

Pankow, K., Mosewich, A. D., McHugh, T. F., & Holt, N. L. (2023). A process map of flourishing between the coach and athlete in Canadian university sport. *Qualitative Research in Sport, Exercise and Health, 15*(3), 397–416. https://doi.org/10.1080/2159676X.2022.2127859

Poulus, D. R., Coulter, T. J., Trotter, M. G., & Polman, R. (2021). Longitudinal analysis of stressors, stress, coping and coping effectiveness in elite esports athletes. *Psychology of Sport and Exercise, 60, Article 102093.* https://doi.org/10.1016/j.psychsport.2021.102093

Poulus, D. R., Coulter, T. J., Trotter, M. G., & Polman, R. (2022). Longitudinal analysis of stressors, stress, coping and coping effectiveness in elite esports athletes. *Psychology of Sport and Exercise, 60*, 102093. https://doi.org/10.1016/j.psychsport.2021.102093

Poulus, D. R., Jackman, P. C., Fransen, J., Polman, R. C. J., & Bennett, K. J. M. (2025). An exploration of high-performance environments in esports: A preliminary model. *Journal of Sports Sciences, 43*(20), 2380–2403. https://doi.org/10.1080/02640414.2025.2533538

Poulus, D., Nicholson, M., Obine, E., Drew, M., Fisher, K., Vella, S., et al. (2026). Mental health and Well-being in esports: A scoping review. *Applied Psychology, 75*(1), e70055. https://doi.org/10.1111/apps.70055

Poulus, D., & Polman, R. (2022). Stress and coping in esports. In A. Tjønndal (Ed.), *Social issues in esports* (1st ed., pp. 83–100). Routledge. https://doi.org/10.4324/9781003258650-9

Poulus, D. R., & Sharpe, B. T. (2025). A protocol for international mental health guidelines for esports. *Journal of Electronic Gaming and Esports, 3*(1) https://doi.org/10.1123/jege.2024-0066

Schaaff, K., Degen, R., Adler, N., & Adam, M. T. P. (2012). Measuring affect using a standard mouse device. *Biomedical Engineering/Biomedizinische Technik, 57*, 761–764. https://doi.org/10.1515/bmt-2012-4013

Schary, D. P., Jenny, S. E., & Koshy, A. (2022). Leveling up esports health: Current status and call to action. International Journal of Esports, *3*(3), Article 70. https://www.ijesports.org/article/70/html.

Trotter, M. G., Obine, E. A. C., & Sharpe, B. T. (2023). Self-regulation, stress appraisal, and esport action performance. *Frontiers in Psychology, 14*, 1265778. https://doi.org/10.fpsyg.2023.1265778

Trudgett-Klose, L. H., & McLinton, S. S. (2024). “Pro gamers” & cyberbullying: Workplace bullying & sexual harassment in professional video gaming. *Entertainment Computing, 50*, 100702. https://doi.org/10.1016/j.entcom.2024.100702

Chapter 7
Cognitive Load and Attention in Esports

Serhat Yalçıner

7.1 Introduction

The origins of esports lie in the organization of video games, which gained popularity in the 1970s and 1980s, into competitions and tournaments (Baker, 2016). The rapid spread of technology and the intensive use of the internet in the fields of business, communication, and entertainment (Martynenko et al., 2021) paved the way for the emergence of electronic sports (esports). Since the 2010s, esports has become a major industry with million-dollar prize pools, sponsorships, media rights, and broadcasting platforms, creating a significant source of income for professional players and teams. Video games have become a professional field of expertise in this process (Faust et al., 2013). The popularity of these games, played and watched online, is rapidly increasing (Yalçıner & Kilci, 2023). Esports lies at the intersection of video games and traditional sports (Brown et al., 2018) and is defined as competitive events involving professional or amateur teams supported by companies, organized around different leagues or tournaments (Hamari & Sjöblom, 2017). Similar to traditional sports, it requires training, performance optimization, strategy, and team communication. With its global scale, media access, and large audience, it has become an interdisciplinary field of research (Scholz, 2019; Taylor, 2012). As the popularity of esports continues to grow rapidly, there is a need for numerous studies across various fields to gain insight into its diverse effects on humans.

Cognition is an important factor in performance in competitive environments (Thomas et al., 2019). Player performance in esports competitions is influenced by the effective management of cognitive processes such as processing high levels of visual and auditory information in a short time, demonstrating fast and accurate motor actions to make the right strategic decisions, and coordinating with team members. The related Cognitive Load Theory explains the positive and negative

S. Yalçıner (✉)
Department of Coaching Education, Balıkesir University, Balıkesir, Türkiye
e-mail: serhat.yalciner@balikesir.edu.tr

S. Bekir (ed.), *The Psychology of Esports*, https://doi.org/10.1007/978-3-032-25090-2_7

effects of cognitive load on performance by pointing to the capacity of working memory (Paas et al., 2003; Sweller, 1988). Players may need high cognitive skills to be successful in video games (Lee & Heeter, 2017). Furthermore, esports can contribute to the development of motor and cognitive skills (Pedraza-Ramirez et al., 2020). Most esports games require players to focus on multiple variables, manage them simultaneously, and push the limits of their cognitive capacity (Boot et al., 2008; Strobach & Schubert, 2021). Studies examining cognitive characteristics in esports have shown that professional players can process stimuli more quickly and accurately by executing their attentional processes more effectively (Green & Bavelier, 2003; Mishra et al., 2016), and that players of different game types, such as FPS and MOBA, exhibit higher cognitive skills than non-players in terms of cognitive flexibility, visual working memory, and attentional inhibition (Yalçıner, 2025).

The aim of this section is to adapt the theory of attention and cognitive load within the framework of cognitive psychology and learning sciences to the context of esports using a disciplinary approach and to establish a framework. The section will first address the cognitive demands of esports, cognitive load theory (Paas et al., 2003; Sweller, 1988) from an esports perspective, and attention. Subsequently, an assessment will be made on the relationship between attention and cognitive load in esports, and the section will conclude with the measurement of cognitive load and attention, along with recommendations.

7.2 Cognitive Demands for Esports

When viewed as a sport, traditional sports such as professional football focus on developing players' physical skills to enhance the appeal of the game, whereas esports focus on developing players' cognitive skills (Campbell et al., 2018; Himmelstein et al., 2017). Esports encompass a wide range of cognitive demands specific to the game, such as perception, attention, memory, planning, and decision-making, which are closely linked to physical coordination skills during gameplay (Bediou et al., 2018). As in traditional sports, systematic esports training benefits the development of motor, cognitive abilities, and skills characteristic of the game (Kane & Spradley, 2017). A review of the relevant literature reports that elite esports players and traditional players have similar levels of cognitive skills, such as sustained attention and the ability to make important decisions correctly under time pressure (Thiel & John, 2018). When comparing amateurism and professionalism, it has been reported that professional esports players have an advantage over amateur esports players in various cognitive skills (Miao et al., 2024). Furthermore, numerous studies have reported that esports games positively influence the development of various cognitive skills (Bediou et al., 2018; Hagiwara et al., 2020; Imanian et al., 2024; Kowal et al., 2018; Leong et al., 2022).

7.3 Cognitive Load Theory and Application to Esports

7.3.1 Cognitive Load Theory

Cognitive load refers to the capacity of mental resources used during a task. It is a particularly important concept in processes such as learning and problem-solving. Situations that complicate the task or distract attention increase the cognitive load on working memory. When working memory capacity is exceeded, task performance declines. Therefore, effective management of cognitive load plays a crucial role in the successful completion of a task. Cognitive Load Theory (CLT) explains learning and performance processes within the framework of the limited working memory capacity that humans possess (Paas et al., 2003; Sweller, 1988). According to the theory, there are three different types of load in the information processing process:

Intrinsic load: Cognitive load arising from the complexity of the task. The complexity of the task and the individual's level of knowledge about the subject determine the level of intrinsic load.

Extraneous load: Cognitive load arising from unnecessary stimuli outside the task. Isolating the task from extraneous stimuli reduces this load.

Germane load: This is the cognitive load that contributes to learning, skill development, and schema formation. It is the cognitive resources that enable the interpretation, conceptualization, and retention of information.

7.3.2 Cognitive Load Theory in Esports

Esports players must constantly update the important information necessary to progress in the game (Spence & Feng, 2010) and adapt their actions to constantly changing task conditions (Bavelier et al., 2012). Players need to have a high level of information processing and strategic planning skills to manage these variables and make effective decisions. In the context of esports, intrinsic load is related to the cognitive demands of the game and varies across different esports games (Dale et al., 2020). Working memory provides an esports player with a limited level of cognitive processing capacity. However, when long-term memory comes into play, it offers the possibility of greatly expanding this capacity. Schemas, which are formed as a result of learning and consist of numerous performance elements, are stored in long-term memory and become integrated into a single unit. When needed, they are transferred to short-term memory and used, contributing significantly to performance.

Let's explain with an example: A CS2 esports player, while advancing on the map during a match, has learned through previous experience and training where opponents may appear and advances while paying attention to these locations (schema in long-term memory). This positional knowledge helps the player focus their attention on potential positions in advance and increase their readiness level. When encountering an opponent, the player brings the schema formed in long-term memory which has become a single unit containing elements such as the hand (mouse) movement required to turn the crosshair toward the enemy, crosshair recoil control, crouching, moving left and right, and team communication codes into working memory and reflects it in their performance. This allows the player to focus on the performance components they have previously schematized and automated during the match, thereby reducing the load on their working memory. Working memory is only used to process information that arises spontaneously (previously unknown), such as positions where opponents may be encountered and the tactics employed by opponents. This reduces the cognitive load on working memory, and the key to gaining an advantage over opponents is having solid performance-related schemas and responding appropriately to spontaneous events.

7.3.3 How Does Cognitive Load Occur in Esports?

In esports games, intrinsic load stems from the inherent complexity of the game, such as understanding game dynamics and developing strategies against opponents. An example of intrinsic load is performing many different tasks simultaneously, such as map and environment control, team tactics and communication, position and crosshair controls. Extraneous load stems from unnecessary visual and auditory stimuli encountered outside the task itself that disrupt the focus of attention. Examples of extraneous load include unnecessary visual effects and animations, complex user interfaces, and exposure to environmental noise while experiencing intrinsic load. Germane load refers to the cognitive resources allocated to cognitive, motor, and strategic learning necessary to improve gaming skills and performance. Within the scope of germane load, learned information and various performance levels are examined to address deficiencies. For example, in a training session, different scenarios and strategies can be tested on the map to create various schemes, deficiencies in team communication can be addressed, and work can be planned to analyze and improve all in-game performance parameters.

7.3.4 The Role of Executive Functions in Cognitive Load

Executive functions enable the conscious organization of goal-directed behaviors (Nin et al., 2023). There is general agreement that there are three core executive functions: working memory, cognitive flexibility, and inhibition (Miyake et al., 2000). In esports, cognitive processes that play a significant role in maintaining long-term performance and achieving satisfactory results are primarily executive functions (Meeusen & Decroix, 2018; Tartar et al., 2019). Players need to have a high level of information processing and strategic planning skills to manage the in-game variables and make effective decisions. The relevant literature reports that playing video games at an amateur level provides individuals with cognitive advantages (Colzato et al.,

2010; Grushko et al., 2021), and that playing competitive esports games requires various advanced cognitive skills (Norman, 2011). In this context, regarding basic cognitive skills, it has been reported that advanced esports players have strengths in sustained attention, working memory, task-switching, and mental rotation (Kang et al., 2020; Li et al., 2020; Phillips & Green, 2023).

7.4 The Importance of Attention in Cognitive Load and Esports

Attention is a cognitive and behavioral process that allows for the selective processing or suppression of numerous sensory inputs from different areas (Treisman & Gelade, 1980). It is not possible to pay attention to all stimuli that enter sensory registration. Only those stimuli that are paid attention to are transferred to short-term memory. A 'selection' process must be carried out for the processing of perceived sensory inputs, and three fundamental operations are performed during this process. First, a decision is made about important information; second, focus is provided on important information; and finally, the focused information is sent to the processing stage (Yeşilyaprak, 2018). In this regard, individuals select specific stimuli that they consider important, ignoring other stimuli, and only the selected stimuli proceed to the processing stage (Senemoğlu, 2018).

The limited capacity of working memory means that only a limited amount of information can be processed at the same time (Sweller, 1988). If the countless stimuli encountered by players in esports (task difficulty, team communication, time pressure, map control, etc.) are not filtered correctly by attention, working memory becomes overloaded, and attention may be distracted. In this situation, attention is crucial for maintaining the level of cognitive load in working memory by prioritizing stimuli according to their importance and correctly managing which information to process and which to disregard. Advanced players automatically retrieve elements stored in their long-term memory (such as the opponent's possible position and location on the map) from their working memory when needed during a match, having previously learned and mastered them in relation to the game. This allows attention capacity to be shifted to various variables that occur spontaneously in the game and used more effectively. All these attention processes mentioned should be properly trained through consciously planned exercises and feedback and brought to a professional level.

7.5 Measuring Cognitive Load and Attention

Cognitive load and attention can be measured using various methods, including self-report scales (NASA-TLX), performance tests (Secondary Task Technique, Stroop Test, etc.), eye-tracking, electroencephalography (EEG), and functional near-infrared spectroscopy (fNIRS). The NASA-TLX (Task Load Index) self-report scale, developed by Hart and Staveland (1988) to measure six different types of loads, is also used in esports research (Lee et al., 2024; Orozco-Mora et al., 2024). One of the performance tests, the Secondary Task Technique, measures the cognitive load created by a task in an individual by observing their response to a secondary stimulus given while they are engaged in a task (Kerr, 1973). An increase in the response time and error rate to the secondary stimulus indicates that the primary task creates a high cognitive load in the individual. The Stroop Test (Stroop, 1935) is a typical attention/inhibition performance test that is also used in esports studies (Hagiwara et al., 2020). Eye-tracking devices are also used in esports research to track where the eye is looking and to monitor the pupil's movements in order to track the focus of attention (Mancini et al., 2022). Electroencephalography (EEG) is used in esports research to assess neural activity in the brain graphically and numerically to obtain information about attention levels (Ramyarangsi et al., 2024). fNIRS is used in esports studies to assess cognitive effort levels through oxygenation levels in brain regions during tasks (Mancı et al., 2024).

Each of these measurement methods can be utilized as a tool for determining the situation and gathering information to evaluate esports performance and develop appropriate interventions, taking into account the conditions of suitability and accessibility for the purpose. These measurements are crucial for esports coaches to identify the cognitive state of players and adjust training plans accordingly.

7.6 Conclusion

The section outlines a framework for understanding esports performance, focusing on cognitive load and attention. It is particularly important to use the specified measurement tools for diagnostic purposes. This enables players, coaches, and researchers to objectively recognize these processes, gain knowledge about them, and develop ideas about what needs to be done. When viewed from the perspective of cognitive load and attention, these factors emerge as important components that affect not only competition-specific performance but also the level of expertise. The most critical role of attention in performance is to ensure that working memory, which has limited capacity, is used as efficiently as possible. It achieves this by filtering out extraneous loads and supporting relevant loads. A thorough understanding and controlled use of the attention factor will enable the correct management of cognitive load. In this regard, it is important for esports coaches to analyze the cognitive skill levels of the players on their team and the cognitive demands of the esports game, and to incorporate appropriate cognitive exercises into their training plans in order to improve performance.

References

Baker, C. (2016). Stewart brand recalls first 'SpaceWar'video game tournament. *Rolling Stone, 25*(6).

Bavelier, D., Green C. S., Pouget, A., & Schrater, P. (2012). Brain plasticity through the life span: Learning to learn and action video games. *Annual Review of Neuroscience, 35*(1), 391–416. https://doi.org/10.1146/annurev-neuro-060909-152832

Bediou, B., Adams, D. M., Mayer, R. E., Tipton, E., Green, C. S., & Bavelier, D. (2018) Meta-analysis of action video game impact on perceptual attentional and cognitive skills. *Psychological Bulletin, 144*(1), 77–110. https://doi.org/10.1037/bul0000130

Boot, W. R., Kramer, A. F., Simons, D. J., Fabiani, M., & Gratton, G. (2008). The effects of video game playing on attention, memory, and executive control. *Acta Psychologica, 129*(3), 387–398. https://doi.org/10.1016/j.actpsy.2008.09.005

Brown, K. A., Billings, A. C., Murphy, B., & Puesan, L. (2018). Intersections of fandom in the age of interactive media: eSports fandom as a predictor of traditional sport fandom. *Communication & Sport, 6*(4), 418–435. https://doi.org/10.1177/2167479517727286

Campbell, M. J., Toth, A. J., Moran, A. P., Kowal, M., & Exton, C. (2018). eSports: A new window on neurocognitive expertise? *Progress in Brain Research, 240*, 161–174. https://doi.org/10.1016/bs.pbr.2018.09.006

Colzato, L. S., Van Leeuwen, P. J., Van Den Wildenberg, W., & Hommel, B. (2010). DOOM'D to switch: Superior cognitive flexibility in players of first person shooter games. *Frontiers in Psychology, 1*, 1515. https://doi.org/10.3389/fpsyg.2010.00008

Dale, G., Joessel, A., Bavelier, D., & Green, C. S. (2020). A new look at the cognitive neuroscience of video game play. *Annals of the New York Academy of Sciences, 1464*(1), 192–203. https://doi.org/10.1111/nyas.14295

Faust, K., Meyer, J., & Griffiths, M. D. (2013). Competitive and professional gaming: Discussing potential benefits of scientific study. *International Journal of Cyber Behavior, Psychology and Learning (IJCBPL), 3*(1), 67–77. https://doi.org/10.4018/ijcbpl.2013010106

Green, C. S., & Bavelier, D. (2003). Action video game modifies visual selective attention. *Nature, 423*(6939), 534–537. https://doi.org/10.1038/nature01647

Grushko, A., Morozova, O., Ostapchuk, M., & Korobeynikova, E. (2021). Perceptual-cognitive demands of esports and team sports: A comparative study. In *advances in cognitive research, artificial intelligence and neuroinformatics: Proceedings of the 9th international conference on cognitive sciences, Intercognsci-2020, October 10-16, 2020, Moscow, Russia 9* (pp. 36-43). Springer international publishing. https://doi.org/10.1007/978-3-030-71637-0_4

Hagiwara, G., Kawahara, I., & Kihara, S. (2020). An attempt to verify the positive effects of esports: Focusing on concentration and cognitive skill. *Journal of Japan Society of Sports Industry, 30*(3), 239–246. https://doi.org/10.5997/sposun.30.3_239

Hamari, J., & Sjöblom, M. (2017). What is eSports and why do people watch it? *Internet Research, 27*(2), 211–232. https://doi.org/10.1108/IntR-04-2016-0085

Hart, S. G., & Staveland, L. E. (1988). Development of NASA-TLX (task load index): Results of empirical and theoretical research. In *Advances in psychology* (Vol. 52, pp. 139–183). North-Holland. https://doi.org/10.1016/S0166-4115(08)62386-9

Himmelstein, D., Liu, Y., & Shapiro, J. L. (2017). An exploration of mental skills among competitive league of legend players. *International Journal of Gaming and Computer-Mediated Simulations (IJGCMS), 9*(2), 1–21. https://doi.org/10.4018/IJGCMS.2017040101

Imanian, M., Khatibi, A., Heydarinejad, S., Saemi, E., & Veisia, E. (2024). Effects of electronic sports on the cognitive skills of attention, working memory, and cognitive flexibility. https://doi.org/10.21203/rs.3.rs-3848418/v1.

Kane, D., & Spradley, B. D. (2017). Recognizing ESports as a sport. *The Sport Journal, 19*(05), 1–9.

Kang, J. O., Kang, K. D., Lee, J. W., Nam, J. J., & Han, D. H. (2020). Comparison of psychological and cognitive characteristics between professional internet game players and professional baseball players. *International Journal of Environmental Research and Public Health, 17*(13), 4797. https://doi.org/10.3390/ijerph17134797

Kerr, B. (1973). Processing demands during mental operations. *Memory & Cognition, 1*(4), 401–412.

Kowal, M., Toth, A. J., Exton, C., & Campbell, M. J. (2018). Different cognitive abilities displayed by action video gamers and non-gamers. *Computers in Human Behavior, 88*, 255–262. https://doi.org/10.1016/j.chb.2018.07.010

Lee, H., Lee, Y. E., Bowman, N. D., Yao, S., & Chen, S. (2024). Gaming on the go? Translation and validation of the video game demand scale to Korean. *International Journal of Human–Computer Interaction*, 40(22), 6984–6995. doi:https://doi.org/10.1080/10447318.2023.2260980.

Lee, Y. H., & Heeter, C. (2017). The effects of cognitive capacity and gaming expertise on attention and comprehension. *Journal of Computer Assisted Learning, 33*(5), 473–485. https://doi.org/10.1111/jcal.12193

Leong, A. Y. C., Yong, M. H., & Lin, M. H. (2022). The effect of strategy game types on inhibition. *Psychological Research, 86*(7), 2115–2127. https://doi.org/10.1007/s00426-021-01632-0

Li, X., Huang, L., Li, B., Wang, H., & Han, C. (2020). Time for a true display of skill: Top players in league of legends have better executive control. *Acta Psychologica, 204*, 103007. https://doi.org/10.1016/j.actpsy.2020.103007

Mancı, E., Gençtürk, U., Günay, E., Güdücü, Ç., Herold, F., & Bediz, C. Ş. (2024). The influence of acute sprint exercise on cognition, gaming performance, and cortical hemodynamics in esports players and age-matched controls. *Current Psychology, 43*(22), 19643–19654. https://doi.org/10.1007/s12144-024-05750-x

Mancini, M., Cherubino, P., Cartocci, G., Martinez, A., Di Flumeri, G., Petruzzellis, L., et al. (2022). Esports and visual attention: Evaluating in-game advertising through eye-tracking during the game viewing experience. *Brain Sciences, 12*(10), 1345. https://doi.org/10.3390/brainsci12101345

Martynenko, S. E., Godlevsky, P. P., Ganshina, G. V., Lobanova, E. V., Mikhaylovsky, M. N., & Prokopyev, A. I. (2021). Team esports as rehabilitation method in views of students with disabilities: Formation and development prospects. *Journal of Human Sport and Exercise, 16*(4proc), S1967–S1974. https://doi.org/10.14198/jhse.2021.16.Proc4.43

Meeusen, R., & Decroix, L. (2018). Nutritional supplements and the brain. *International Journal of Sport Nutrition and Exercise Metabolism, 28*(2), 200–211. Retrieved Jan 31, 2025, from. https://doi.org/10.1123/ijsnem.2017-0314

Miao, H., He, H., Hou, X., Wang, J., & Chi, L. (2024). Cognitive expertise in esport experts: A three-level model meta-analysis. *PeerJ, 12*, e17857. https://doi.org/10.7717/peerj.17857

Mishra, J., Anguera, J. A., & Gazzaley, A. (2016). Video games for neuro-cognitive optimization. *Neuron, 90*(2), 214–218. https://doi.org/10.1016/j.neuron.2016.04.010

Miyake, A., Friedman, N. P., Emerson, M. J., Witzki, A. H., Howerter, A., & Wager, T. D. (2000). The unity and diversity of executive functions and their contributions to complex "frontal lobe" tasks: A latent variable analysis. *Cognitive Psychology, 41*(1), 49–100. https://doi.org/10.1006/cogp.1999.0734

Nin, V., Delgado, H., Goldin, A. P., Fernández-Slezak, D., Belloli, L., & Carboni, A. (2023). A classroom-embedded video game intervention improves executive functions in kindergarteners. *Journal of Cognitive Enhancement, 7*(1), 19–38. https://doi.org/10.1007/s41465-023-00262-1

Norman, K. L. (2011). Assessing the components of skill necessary for playing video games. *Human-Computer Interaction Technical Report, 1*, 11–24.

Orozco-Mora, C. E., Fuentes-Aguilar, R. Q., & Hernández-Melgarejo, G. (2024). Dynamic difficulty adaptation based on stress detection for a virtual reality video game: A pilot study. *Electronics, 13*(12), 2324. https://doi.org/10.3390/electronics13122324

Paas, F., Renkl, A., & Sweller, J. (2003). Cognitive load theory and instructional design: Recent developments. *Educational Psychologist, 38*(1), 1–4. https://doi.org/10.1207/S15326985EP3801_1

Pedraza-Ramirez, I., Musculus, L., Raab, M., & Laborde, S. (2020). Setting the scientific stage for esports psychology: A systematic review. *International Review of Sport and Exercise Psychology, 13*(1), 319–352. https://doi.org/10.1080/1750984X.2020.1723122

Phillips, N., & Green, C. (2023). *Associations Between Cognitive Performance and Extreme Expertise in Different Competitive eSports. Proceedings of the Annual Meeting of the Cognitive Science Society*, 45.

Ramyarangsi, P., Bennett, S. J., Siripornpanich, V., Nanbancha, A., Pokaisasawan, A., Chatthong, W., & Ajjimaporn, A. (2024). EEG differences in competitive female gymnastics, soccer, and esports athletes between resting states with eyes closed and open. *Scientific Reports, 14*(1), 23317. https://doi.org/10.1038/s41598-024-74665-1

Scholz, T. M. (2019). *eSports is business: Management in the world of competitive gaming*. Springer.

Senemoğlu, N. (2018). Gelişim öğrenme ve öğretim: *Kuramdan uygulamaya* (26. Baskı). Ankara: Anı Yayıncılık, (s. 289).

Spence, I., & Feng, J. (2010). Video games and spatial cognition. *Review of General Psychology, 14*(2), 92–104. https://doi.org/10.1037/a0019491

Strobach, T., & Schubert, T. (2021). Video game training and effects on executive functions. *Cognitive training: An overview of features and applications, 229-241.* https://doi.org/10.1007/978-3-319-42662-4_11

Stroop, J. R. (1935). Studies of interference in serial verbal reactions. *Journal of Experimental Psychology, 18*(6), 643. https://doi.org/10.1037/h0054651

Sweller, J. (1988). Cognitive load during problem solving: Effects on learning. *Cognitive Science, 12*(2), 257–285. https://doi.org/10.1207/s15516709cog1202_4

Tartar, J. L., Kalman, D., & Hewlings, S. (2019). A prospective study evaluating the effects of a nutritional supplement intervention on cognition, mood states, and mental performance in video gamers. *Nutrients, 11*(10), 2326. https://doi.org/10.3390/nu11102326

Taylor, T. L. (2012). *Raising the stakes: E-sports and the professionalization of computer gaming*. Mit Press.

Thiel, A., & John, J. M. (2018). Is eSport a 'real'sport? Reflections on the spread of virtual competitions. *European Journal for Sport and Society, 15*(4), 311–315. https://doi.org/10.1080/16138171.2018.1559019

Thomas, C. J., Rothschild, J., Earnest, C. P., & Blaisdell, A. (2019). The effects of energy drink consumption on cognitive and physical performance in elite league of legends players. *Sports, 7*(9), 196. https://doi.org/10.3390/sports7090196

Treisman, A. M., & Gelade, G. (1980). A feature-integration theory of attention. *Cognitive Psychology, 12*(1), 97–136. https://doi.org/10.1016/0010-0285(80)90005-5

Yalçıner, S. (2025). *Espor Oyuncularının Yürütücü İşlev Düzeylerinin İncelenmesi*. (Doctoral dissertation,. Balıkesir University (Türkiye).

Yalçıner, S., & Kilci, A. K. (2023). Effect of pistol round and first kill on match outcome in the counter-strike: Global offensive major esports championships. *Aloma. Revista De Psicologia, Ciènces De l'Educació I De l'Esport, 41*(2), 21–25. https://doi.org/10.51698/aloma.2023.41.2.21-25

Yeşilyaprak, N. (2018). Eğitim Psikolojisi *Gelişim-Öğrenme-Öğretim* (21.Baskı). Öztürk B. ve Kısaç İ. (Ed), *Bilgiyi İşleme Modeli* içinde. : PEGEM Akademi, (s. 317–318).

Chapter 8
Reaction Time and Focus on Esports

Alp Kaan Kilci

8.1 Introduction

Reaction time is a critical skill in esports players performance, measured in milliseconds. The ability of players to swiftly perceive their opponents' movements, as well as in-game visual and auditory stimuli, and respond appropriately, is directly linked to success. Therefore, reaction time is considered an indicator of both technical skills and focus strategies (Cyma-Wejchenig et al., 2024). Research on amateur esports players indicates that, despite their low levels of physical activity, they demonstrate significantly faster reaction times in tests than non-players. This suggests that gaming practice can have a significant impact on cognitive speed and reaction time (Cyma-Wejchenig et al., 2024). Similarly, players who play digital games for more than 14 hours per week demonstrate significantly better visual and target-oriented reaction times than those who play for shorter periods. However, no significant difference was found between the two groups in terms of auditory reaction time. This indicates that esports particularly develop visual-spatial attention and targeting skills (Ersin et al., 2022). Reaction time performance is determined by playing time, focus, and visual attention strategies. Indeed, esports players with high skill levels have been found to exhibit greater variability and bimodal distribution in their visual fixation times, reflecting ambient (automatic) and focal (conscious) visual processing (Velichkovsky et al., 2019). This demonstrates that professional esports players can not only react faster but also direct their attention strategically between environmental and focused visual processing. Eye-tracking research on first-person shooter (FPS) games also confirms that reaction time and focus strategies are inextricably linked. Findings reveal that esports players' reaction times and accuracy of performance are strongly related to their eye movements. Players with a high skill level have been found to

A. K. Kilci (✉)
Department of Sport Management, Faculty of Sport Sciences, Balikesir University, Balıkesir, Turkey
e-mail: alpkaankilci@balikesir.edu.tr

S. Bekir (ed.), *The Psychology of Esports*, https://doi.org/10.1007/978-3-032-25090-2_8

have narrower horizontal gaze distribution, and these narrow gaze patterns are associated with faster and more accurate responses (Jeong et al., 2025). Therefore, focus must be considered not only in terms of reaction time, but also in conjunction with decision accuracy and visual strategy. Consequently, reaction time and focus are two critical, complementary cognitive performance indicators in esports. Game duration and practice enhance esports players' visual and target-directed reaction time skills. However, to reach a professional level, esports players must also consciously develop their visual focus strategies. Therefore, esports training should include exercises that increase reaction speed and optimise visual attention distribution to maximise performance (Cyma-Wejchenig et al., 2024; Ersin et al., 2022; Velichkovsky et al., 2019; Jeong et al., 2025). Reaction time and focus on esports have been observed to be influenced not only by natural talent and game practice, but also by various training methods. Technological tools create new opportunities to support esports players' cognitive and motor performance. Notably, virtual reality (VR)-based applications have gained increasing importance in esports training in recent years.

8.2 Reaction Time and VR

Virtual reality (VR)-based training has been found to significantly improve the reaction time (RT) and eye-hand coordination (EHC) of esports players. In research conducted by Lachowicz et al. (2024) on amateur esports players, the effects of short-term (8 days) and long-term (28 days) VR training sessions implemented through the Beat Saber game were compared. Short-term training sessions were found to particularly improve eye-hand coordination, while long-term training sessions produced stronger and more lasting effects on reaction time and motor timing. Furthermore, sustained improvements in eye-hand coordination observed in follow-up measurements suggest that VR-based training may induce neuroplastic changes resulting in long-term cognitive-motor development. Similarly, Rutkowski et al. (2021) demonstrated that short-term VR-based training increased reaction time and eye-hand coordination in young musicians. Meanwhile, Serweta-Pawlik et al. (2023) emphasised VR's ability to stimulate cognitive functions, and Szary et al. (2020) noted that increased physical exercise intensity in a VR environment contributes to improved attention and focus. These findings demonstrate that VR is a multidimensional tool that not only develops motor coordination and reaction speed, but also attention processes. The ability to strategically manage both reaction speed and attention focus enhances the educational value of VR applications. Pelosin et al. (2022) and Sokołowska (2023) have demonstrated that long-term VR and XR training powerfully affects cognitive flexibility and decision-making skills while supporting the development of reaction times. Furthermore, Gangemi et al. (2023) and Hwang et al. (2021) emphasise that VR-based cognitive-motor training can lead to lasting neural changes and sustainable performance improvements. This research shows that VR develops not only rapid reaction skills, but also attention control and decision-making accuracy, by exposing players to constantly changing and dynamic tasks. For professional esports players in particular, the ability to make decisions that require both speed and accuracy under high pressure makes these training methods even more important. VR games such as Beat Saber, which require a fast pace and intense focus, have been found to improve esports players' concentration while enhancing reaction time and supporting cognitive-motor integration. In this context, VR training can be considered an innovative tool that could provide professional teams with a strategic advantage, beyond improving individual performance. Findings on how VR-based training improves reaction time and focus skills clearly demonstrate the central role of this cognitive process in esports.

However, beyond technological developments, reaction time must be considered a fundamental component of human cognition. This is because even small advantages measured in milliseconds can directly impact players' performance and chances of success in the highly competitive esports environment.

8.3 Reaction Time in Esports

Reaction time is widely regarded as one of the most critical indicators of expertise in the domain of esports. As with players in 'catch-and-contact' sports such as tennis or baseball, who must demonstrate superior perceptual speed and rapid response skills (Mann et al., 2007; Voss et al., 2010), the same applies to esports players. A significant disparity in reaction time has been observed between elite-level players and novice and intermediate players. This discrepancy can be attributed not only to the development of motor skills but also to the enhanced efficiency of visual and cognitive processes. The findings of experimental research on fighting games have demonstrated that expert players exhibit a marked tendency to demonstrate significantly superior performance in relation to simple reaction time tasks. The findings of Phillips and Green (2023) indicate a close relationship between rapid information processing capacity and competitive success. This advantage, measured in milliseconds rather than seconds, manifests concretely in players' abilities to anticipate opponents' moves, select the appropriate response, and translate this to the motor level. Consequently, reaction time is regarded not solely as a metric of speed in esports, but also as an indicator of cognitive efficiency. Research examining the performance of action video game players also supports this view. Research by Green and Bavelier (2003) and Bediou et al. (2018, 2023) has demonstrated that these players exhibit considerable advantages in visual-spatial attention and reaction speed. This finding suggests that long-term gaming practice exerts enduring effects on neurocognitive functions, indicating that reaction time is not merely an innate capacity but a skill that can be cultivated through systematic experience and deliberate practice.

The advent of reaction time as a foundational cognitive element in esports performance underscores the significance of both the capacity for expeditious response and the ability to maintain this response throughout the duration of the game. In order for the decisions made by players within milliseconds to be meaningful, it is essential that this level of attention is maintained at a high level for extended periods.

8.3.1 Sustained Attention in Esports

Beyond reaction speed, the ability to sustain attention over extended periods is a critical component of high-level esports performance. The finding is further supported by the observation that fighting game experts exhibit faster and more accurate responses in sustained attention tasks compared to novice and intermediate players. This finding suggests that expert players are capable of maintaining a higher level of alertness within a dynamic and constantly changing competitive environment (Phillips & Green, 2024).

In traditional sports, it is also known that expert players can adjust their areas of attention according to the specific requirements of their discipline (Hüttermann et al., 2014). A similar phenomenon has been observed in the domain of esports, where the capacity to maintain concentration under conditions of incessant and rapidly evolving sensory input has been identified as a critical factor. The capacity to sustain concentration is widely regarded as a pivotal element in the ability to foresee opponents' strategic intentions, formulate effective counter-manoeuvres in response to the evolving circumstances, and disseminate these processes over the course of the game.

Sustained attention is a cornerstone of high performance in esports; however, this skill is utilised in a distinct manner in each game type. The cognitive strategies and forms of focus required for different esports disciplines are diverse, with each type shaping reaction time and attention processes in a distinct manner.

8.4 Cognitive Demands across Game-Genres

The cognitive demands imposed by different types of esports vary significantly in terms of reaction time and attention. In the context of fighting games, players are required to rapidly discern their opponents' movements, formulate swift decisions, and devise suitable counter-moves. Conversely, rhythm games demand superior motor timing, rhythmic accuracy, and impeccable execution of repetitive sequences. Consequently, fighting games demand elevated levels of alertness and the capacity to respond expeditiously to constantly shifting circumstances. Conversely, rhythm games assess players' timing sensitivity, motor control, and the capacity to sustain attention (Tanaka et al., 2013; Phillips & Green, 2023).

It has been demonstrated that individuals with expertise in rhythm games exhibit superior performance not only in rhythmic coordination skills but also in specific response selection tasks. This finding suggests the existence of a degree of overlap in cognitive skills across different genres, indicating the possibility of transferability.

In summary, the two distinct facets of cognitive performance are supported by the integration of two distinct yet interconnected facets of gaming: the rapid decision-making and environmental awareness aspects of fighting games, and the attention intensity and motor coordination requirements of rhythm games. Consequently, each game type functions as a training ground that fosters the development of players' cognitive capacities through its distinct demands.

The fact that different esports genres present distinct cognitive demands is important for understanding how expertise is shaped. However, irrespective of the differences between genres, the impact of expertise levels on cognitive processes should be evaluated from a more holistic perspective.

8.5 Expertise and Cognition

The impact of esports expertise on cognitive performance is not uniform across all cognitive domains. Research findings indicate that expert players exhibit marked superiority, particularly with regard to reaction time and attention control. This finding indicates that mastery in esports provides the greatest advantage in the processes of rapid information processing, accurate perception of stimuli, and developing appropriate motor responses. In highly competitive environments, such skills have been shown to have a direct impact on performance (Phillips & Green, 2024).

In contrast, no significant differences were observed between expert and novice players in more general cognitive abilities such as fluid intelligence or working memory. This finding indicates that esports expertise may foster the development of processes related to the competitive demands of the game, with a comparatively limited impact on general cognitive capacities. Consequently, reaction time and attention emerge as the most reliable cognitive indicators of high performance in esports, while more general cognitive abilities remain secondary in explaining the level of expertise.

The efficacy of expertise level in enhancing reaction time and attention control has been demonstrated. However, a comprehensive understanding of these effects necessitates an examination of the relationship between different game types and cognitive processes. Extended assessments, informed by parallel findings, demonstrate that cognitive performance in esports cannot be adequately explained by a single dimension alone.

8.6 Neurocognitive Performance in Esport: Reaction and Attention

It is evident that reaction time and attention are among the most critical determinants of esports performance. The capacity to formulate swift resolutions and react promptly to unanticipated stimuli confers upon elite esports players a substantial competitive edge. Research has demonstrated that experts in fighting games exhibit superior reaction time capabilities in comparison to novice players in fundamental reaction time tasks. The findings indicate that elite players' rapid information processing capabilities are underpinned by cognitive foundations. Moreover, empirical evidence from studies demonstrating that individuals who engage in playing action video games demonstrate superior performance in visual selective attention and reaction speed. The present study hypothesises that cognitive speed is a key factor in achieving superiority in both offensive and defensive strategies.

In addition to instantaneous reaction speed, the capacity to sustain attention over time is also critical for ensuring sustainable performance. The finding that fighting game experts respond more quickly and accurately in tasks requiring sustained attention suggests that they maintain a higher level of alertness in competitive environments. This finding aligns with the conclusions of research that has demonstrated the capacity of expert players in conventional sports to adapt their focus of attention in a manner that is discipline-specific (Hüttermann et al., 2014). In the domain of esports, the capacity to maintain concentration in the face of constantly evolving stimuli is not merely a cognitive ability, but also a potential source of strategic advantage.

Cross-genre comparisons are indicative of the diversity of esports in terms of cognitive demands. The genre of fighting games requires players to instantly perceive opponents' moves and develop quick responses. By contrast, rhythm games rely on motor timing, rhythmic accuracy, and flawless execution of repetitive sequences. It is noteworthy that individuals with expertise in rhythm games exhibit superior performance not only in terms of rhythmic accuracy but also in selective response tasks. This finding suggests that cognitive skills partially overlap across different genres, and that players' genre-specific experiences also influence their overall cognitive profiles.

It has also been observed that esports expertise creates limited but powerful effects in cognitive domains. Research findings indicate that expert players exhibit marked superiority in reaction time and attention control, yet no substantial discrepancy is observed in more general cognitive abilities such as fluid intelligence or working memory (Phillips & Green, 2023). Consequently, the cognitive effects of expertise are more pronounced in game-specific processes. In this context, reaction time and attention are considered the most reliable indicators for predicting high performance in esports.

From an academic and practical perspective, these findings offer important implications. As posited by Bowman et al. (2018), reaction time and attention measurements have been demonstrated to be effective predictive variables in identifying elite players. Furthermore, training programmes have the capacity to incorporate exercises with a focus on attention development, rhythm-based applications, and reaction time acceleration protocols. Consequently, future research endeavours must integrate laboratory tests with in-game performance data to achieve higher ecological validity, a critical requirement.

The findings concerning reaction time, attention, and expertise provide significant insights into the cognitive aspects of esports. However, it is insufficient to evaluate these processes solely through behavioural outputs. Neurophysiological measurements, particularly those revealing the brain's reflections of attention and focus processes, enable a more detailed understanding of the mechanisms underlying esports performance.

8.7 Neurophysiological Insights in Esport

The evolution of esports has been such that it has become a significant component of the competitive sports ecosystem, a development that has been noted by Wagner (2006). While physical prowess is paramount in conventional sporting activities, cognitive abilities, particularly those pertaining to attention and reaction time, emerge as pivotal factors in the realm of esports (Campbell et al., 2018; Himmelstein et al., 2017). Research indicates that the impact of esports extends beyond the conventional negative aspects (e.g., aggression, screen time) (Ferguson, 2007; Swing et al., 2010), encompassing developmental benefits for cognitive processes such as attention and executive function (Bediou et al., 2018).

In this context, a research study conducted by Hagiwara et al. (2020) evaluated cognitive skills and attention levels using electroencephalography (EEG) and the Stroop Test on 20 male university students who were members of an esports club. The participants' baseline electroencephalogram (EEG) measurements were obtained, their executive functions were assessed using the Stroop Test, and then they were requested to participate in a Mario Kart game to evaluate their attention levels during and after the game. The Stroop Test response times were found to be significantly reduced after the game (congruent task: 14.68 ± 2.25 sec to 13.02 ± 1.59 sec; incongruent task: 17.16 ± 2.36 sec to 13.94 ± 1.39 sec; $p < 0.001$). The findings of this study suggest that racing-type games may have a positive effect on the enhancement of executive functions.

The EEG recordings are of particular interest with regard to attention processes. The power ratios of the beta wave ($M = 40.85$, $SD = 9.67$) and SMR wave ($M = 61.33$, $SD = 4.77$) recorded from the frontal lobe during gameplay were found to be significantly higher than in the baseline condition (beta: $M = 16.29$, $SD = 9.95$; SMR: $M = 42.62$, $SD = 8.96$) ($p < 0.001$). This increase indicates that selective attention and focus are intensely activated during gameplay (Hagiwara et al., 2020). In a similar insight, Lim et al. (2019) also reported an increase in beta and SMR waves during gaming in esports players. The findings of the present study suggest that esports activities serve a function that optimises not only reaction time but also attention processes.

This neurophysiological evidence is consistent with previous behavioural findings. Green and Bavelier (2003) discovered that action games enhance selective attention skills, while Anguera et al. (2013) demonstrated that digital games increase cognitive control even in older adults. The extant literature suggests that esports have the capacity to support attention and executive function across different age groups and game types.

It is widely acknowledged that electronic sports exert a considerable influence on factors such as reaction time and levels of attention. These cognitive contributions have been demonstrated to enhance both individual performance and the appeal of esports for spectators (Toth et al., 2019). It is suggested that the scope of esports‘cognitive contributions may be more comprehensively revealed by future research using different age groups and game types, as well as neurophysiological measurements.

Furthermore, electroencephalography (EEG) and attention-based findings demonstrate that esports influence not only individual cognitive processes but also game-specific performance profiles. Consequently, an examination of reaction time as a multifaceted variable, considering its variation across diverse esports genres, is imperative to achieve a comprehensive understanding of the cognitive architecture of this domain.

8.8 Reaction Time and Focus in Game-Genres

Reaction time is a critical factor in determining performance in both traditional sports and esports. It is evident that discrepancies of a millisecond can exert a direct influence on the outcome of a competition, potentially determining victory or defeat. The rapidly expanding esports industry, which generated $1.1 billion in revenue and attracted a global audience of nearly 495 million in 2020, demands that players be not only physically fit but also cognitively prepared (Newzoo, 2020). In a variety of game types, including multiplayer online battle arenas (MOBA), first-person shooter games (FPS), fighting games, and sports simulations, players are required to respond to visual and auditory stimuli in a timely manner, make optimal decisions, and manage multiple tasks concurrently (Bányai et al., 2019; Kowal et al., 2018). In this respect, esports bears a resemblance to traditional sports such as short-distance running or team sports in terms of the need for quick reactions (Dykiert et al., 2012; Hüttermann et al., 2019).

A comparison of studies reveals that professional and amateur esports players exhibit comparable reaction times to those observed in traditional players. Research utilising the Vienna Test System revealed no substantial disparities in simple visual, auditory, and selective reaction times between professional esports players, amateur players, and traditional players; all groups exhibited performance levels that exceeded the standard population average (Bickmann et al., 2021). This finding suggests that both sports and esports may play a similar role in enhancing reaction time. The strong correlation between motor reaction times and general reaction times indicates that perceptual processes and motor skills function as an inseparable entity under high pressure (Zwierko et al., 2010). However, it has been demonstrated that differences between game genres have a significant impact on reaction time and focus. In the study conducted by Bickmann et al. (2021), it was observed that sports simulation players demonstrated faster responses compared to those playing MOBA games, particularly in auditory and selective reaction tests. In contrast, FPS players exhibited the fastest reaction times in visual and selective reaction tests. These findings are consistent with research showing that action-based video games improve attention management, visual search, perceptual-motor coordination, and selective attention skills (Green & Bavelier, 2003; Schubert et al., 2015; Wu & Spence, 2013). The rapid responses of sports simulation players may stem from the structured and dynamic nature of these games, while the relatively slower responses of MOBA players are associated with differences in attention strategies (Deleuze et al., 2017; Dale et al., 2020).

The findings of this study indicate that performance level and focus skills appear to be more decisive factors in reaction time performance than simply game duration or years of experience. Indeed, the finding that high-level MOBA players demonstrate superior performance in cognitive control tests, while exhibiting no difference in terms of game duration, lends further support to this hypothesis (Li et al., 2020). This finding indicates that not only does the duration of practice influence performance, but also the development of attention, focus, and executive functions. In addition, it has been established that elite players in traditional sports demonstrate a superior level of attention and perceptual skills (Voss et al., 2010).

The findings indicate that esports players and traditional players exhibit comparable reaction times, yet distinct cognitive profiles emerge due to varied game-specific attention strategies. The findings of this study offer valuable insights into the selection of talent, the planning of training programmes, and the development of player development programmes in the context of esports. In a manner analogous to the utilisation of mental training in conventional sports to enhance attention and focus, it is asserted that cognitive training protocols can also be employed in esports to augment reaction speed, attention control, and decision-making flexibility (Pedraza-Ramirez et al., 2020). Consequently, in the domain of esports, which is undergoing rapid professionalisation, a comprehensive understanding of the scientific foundations of reaction time and focus processes has become imperative for enhancing both player performance and the efficacy of coaching practices. A comparison of different game types reveal that reaction time and focus strategies manifest in different forms, not only within the context of esports, but also when contrasted with traditional sports. Such comparisons provide a critical framework for understanding how cognitive-motor skills adapt to the nature of the sport.

8.9 Reaction and Focus Strategies: Esports Vs Traditional Sports

Reaction time and focus are among the fundamental cognitive-motor skills that determine performance in both esports and traditional sports. Esports players have been shown to rely heavily on hand-eye coordination to respond quickly and accurately to visual and auditory stimuli. In contrast, traditional players often have to effectively use both hand-eye and hand-foot coordination. This discrepancy also impacts the areas of focus: in esports, the ability to respond within milliseconds to stimuli appearing in the centre and periphery of the screen is paramount, while in traditional sports, players must be able to utilise central and peripheral visual information concurrently within a broad field of view (Mańkowska et al., 2015; Schwab & Memmert, 2012).

A comparative study reveals notable parallels and distinctions between esports players and university players with regard to reaction time and environmental perception. However, university players demonstrated faster foot-based reactions compared to professional esports players. This finding suggests that the dynamic nature of traditional sports develops lower extremity coordination, while esports reinforce hand-eye-based rapid responses. Prolonged screen tracking requires esports players to constantly use their peripheral visual perception, while attention distribution and refocusing between multiple focal points in moving field conditions are decisive in the cognitive strategies of traditional players (Ando et al., 2001; Bickmann et al., 2021). There is a direct correlation between peripheral vision and reaction times, and the capacity for focus. It has been established that elite players are able to predict their opponents' movements and the general progression of the game by employing their peripheral vision in a more efficient manner (Vaeyens et al., 2007; Ghasemi et al., 2009). It has been demonstrated that professional esports players are capable of tracking multiple stimuli concurrently in a virtual environment, with the capacity to rapidly shift their focus in order to make decisions. This process has been demonstrated to exhibit cognitive flexibility and the potency of selective attention mechanisms (Green & Bavelier, 2003, 2006). However, there are differences in attention strategies between esports and traditional sports. In esports, focus is directed towards rapid stimulus detection on the screen and motor response generation (Kim et al., 2022). In traditional sports, focus relies more on broader environmental perception and multi-motor coordination. The concept of focus encompasses not only attention span but also the capacity to select the correct response.

8.10 Caffeine and Esports Performance

Caffeine is widely acknowledged as one of the most effective ergogenic aids in the domain of sports, yet its effects in the context of esports are only beginning to be explored through research (Rogers et al., 2024). In the specific case of first-person shooter (FPS) games, reaction time and focus have been identified as key cognitive indicators that directly influence player success. Recent research has demonstrated that both low (1 mg·kg^{-1} BW) and moderate (3 mg·kg^{-1} BW) doses of caffeine intake accelerate reaction time and increase focus levels. The aforementioned effects contribute to esports players' ability to make faster and more accurate decisions in competitive environments characterised by intense cognitive demands.

The stimulatory properties of caffeine on the central nervous system, in addition to its inhibitory effect on adenosine receptors, are the mechanisms through which its effect of shortening reaction time is achieved. This biological mechanism has been demonstrated to enhance attention and alertness, thereby facilitating a more expeditious response to environmental stimuli (McLellan et al., 2016). In accordance with the findings of Rogers et al. (2024), esports players who consumed caffeine exhibited significantly faster response times in both psychometric tests and tasks simulating FPS games. This finding indicates that caffeine can enhance reflex speed, a critical component of success in esports.

In the domain of esports, the ability to respond swiftly is of paramount importance. In addition, the capacity to sustain concentration is a pivotal skill. Research has demonstrated that caffeine intake enhances accuracy, particularly in 'reactive tracking' tasks. The execution of such tasks necessitates the player to sustain uninterrupted concentration, thereby offering a genuine and quantifiable assessment of in-game focus. The extant literature provides robust evidence that caffeine exerts a positive effect on attention, alertness, and cognitive performance (Calvo et al., 2021; Crawford et al., 2017). It can thus be concluded that caffeine not only supports quick reflexes but also provides esports players with a cognitive advantage in terms of focus and accuracy.

The role of caffeine in enhancing reaction time and focus in esports underscores the significance of cognitive processes for optimal performance. However, it is imperative to consider cognitive speed and reaction time not only in the context of esports, but also in comparison to traditional sports. Such comparisons provide an important framework for understanding the cognitive foundations of expertise across different sports.

8.11 Esports, Cognition, and Health

The global expansion of esports has been rapid, metamorphosing from a competitive sport to a significant domain for investigating cognitive performance (Franks et al., 2022; Chikish et al., 2019). It is evident that a combination of technical abilities and cognitive processes, including attention, perception, decision-making, and reaction time, play a pivotal role in determining players' performance. Research has demonstrated a direct correlation between rapid decision-making and strategic thinking abilities, on the one hand, and focus levels and reaction speed, on the other (Martin-Niedecken & Schättin, 2020).

Research indicates that esports players typically exhibit reduced levels of physical activity, yet they demonstrate superior performance in terms of game-specific reaction times (Rudolf et al., 2020; Giakoni-Ramírez et al., 2022; Trotter et al., 2020). A study undertaken by Cyma-Wejchenig et al. (2024) discovered that amateur esports players exhibited superior reaction times in comparison to non-players. However, this was accompanied by a tendency towards lower levels of physical activity. This finding indicates that while esports may enhance mental agility, they also carry potential health risks associated with a sedentary lifestyle.

The relationship between reaction time and physical activity is a complex one. Leisure activities centred on enjoyment have been shown to enhance reaction time, while this relationship is less pronounced in the context of work or regular sports-based activities. Cyma-Wejchenig et al. (2024) also identified a positive correlation between leisure activities and reaction time, thereby emphasising the cognitive benefits of pleasure-based activities. This finding suggests that esports practice alone is not sufficient and that supporting it with different types of activities may be more sustainable in terms of performance and health.

Conversely, it has been established that extended periods of gaming can enhance concentration skills; however, they concomitantly carry potential risks to physical health. Players who allocate more than six hours daily to screen-based activities are more prone to encountering neck, back, and joint discomfort. Ergonomic seating arrangements, regular stretching, and appropriate training programmes have been demonstrated to play an important role in reducing these risks (DiFrancisco-Donoghue et al., 2019. Consequently, in addition to the cognitive advantages of esports, health management must also be an integral component of training programmes.

The findings indicate that esports players exhibit superior reaction time and focus levels in comparison to traditional players. However, the sustainability of these advantages is only possible by balancing the risks posed by physical inactivity and a sedentary lifestyle. Consequently, future research should concentrate on integrating physical exercises into esports training programmes in a manner that preserves reaction time and attention levels (Erickson et al., 2019; Zhang et al., 2023).

8.12 Conclusion

In conclusion, it is evident that reaction time and concentration skills play a pivotal role in determining esports performance. The importance of reaction advantages, measured in milliseconds, cannot be overstated in either the realm of technical skills or that of strategic decision-making. Indeed, such advantages are pivotal in the pursuit of in-game superiority. In particular, advanced visual-spatial attention and the capacity for rapid, target-oriented responses enable players to anticipate their opponents' moves and respond appropriately. In this context, reaction time is regarded as an indicator not only of motor speed but also of cognitive activity and perceptual selectivity. In a similar manner, focus has been demonstrated to directly influence performance, not only through short-term concentration but also through the ability to sustain attention over extended periods.

Research has demonstrated that professional gamers have developed more flexible strategies, not only in terms of quick response, but also in consciously distributing and refocusing their attention. This finding indicates that focus cannot be regarded as a standalone entity, but rather as a complementary process to reaction time. An analysis of various game genres reveal that while fast reaction and visual focus are more prevalent in first-person shooter (FPS) and fighting games, long-term attention and strategic focus skills are emphasised in multiplayer online battle arena (MOBA) games. Consequently, the collaborative cultivation of focus capacity and reaction time engenders a framework that fosters both the player's immediate reflex performance and their long-term strategic decision-making capabilities.

In view of these findings, it is hypothesised that esports training programmes should encompass not only technical skills but also cognitive exercises that facilitate the reduction of reaction time and enhance concentration capacity. Virtual reality applications, rhythm-based training, and attention development protocols are considered important tools in this context. It is important to note that cognitive advantages are not sustainable without physical health support. Consequently, it can be argued that the most critical step for the future, both academically and practically, is to support reaction time and concentration skills with holistic training approaches to achieve the highest level of success in esports.

References

Ando, S., Kida, N., & Oda, S. (2001). Central and peripheral visual reaction time of soccer players and nonathletes. *Perceptual and Motor Skills, 92*(3), 786–794. https://doi.org/10.2466/pms.2001.92.3.786

Anguera, J. A., Boccanfuso, J., Rintoul, J. L., Al-Hashimi, O., Faraji, F., Janowich, J., Kong, E., Larraburo, Y., Rolle, C., Johnston, E., et al. (2013). Video game training enhances cognitive control in older adults. Nature, 501(7465), 97–101. doi:https://doi.org/10.1038/nature12486.

Bányai, F., Griffiths, M. D., Király, O., & Demetrovics, Z. (2019). The psychology of esports: A systematic literature review. *Journal of Gambling Studies, 35*(2), 351–365. https://doi.org/10.1007/s10899-018-9763-1

Bediou, B., Adams, D. M., Mayer, R. E., Tipton, E., Green, C. S., & Bavelier, D. (2018). Meta-analysis of action video game impact on perceptual, attentional, and cognitive skills. *Psychological Bulletin, 144*(1), 77–110. https://doi.org/10.1037/bul0000130

Bediou, B., Rodgers, M. A., Tipton, E., Mayer, R. E., Green, C. S., & Bavelier, D. (2023). Effects of action video game play on cognitive skills: A meta-analysis. *Technology, Mind, and Behavior, 4*(1). https://doi.org/10.1037/tmb0000102.supp

Bickmann, K., Wechsler, K., Rudolf, C., Tholl, C., Froböse, I., & Grieben, C. (2021). Comparison of reaction time between esports players of different genres and sportsmen. *International Journal of Esports Research, 1*(1), 1–16. https://doi.org/10.1093/ijesr/1.1.1

Bowman, N. D., Wasserman, J., & Banks, J. (2018). Development of the video game demand scale. In *Video games* (pp. 208–233). Routledge. https://doi.org/10.4324/9781351235266-13

Calvo, J. L., Fei, X., Domínguez, R., & Pareja-Galeano, H. (2021). Caffeine and cognitive functions in sports: A systematic review and meta-analysis. *Nutrients, 13*(3), 868. https://doi.org/10.3390/nu13030868

Campbell, M. J., Toth, A. J., Moran, A. P., Kowal, M., & Exton, C. (2018). Esports: A new window on neurocognitive expertise? *Progress in Brain Research, 240*, 161–174. https://doi.org/10.1016/bs.pbr.2018.09.006

Chikish, Y., Carreras-Simó, M., & Garci, J. (2019). eSports: A new era for the sports industry and a new impulse for the research in sports (and) economics? In *Sports (and) economics* (pp. 477–508). FUNCAS.

Crawford, C., Teo, L., Lafferty, L., Drake, A., Bingham, J. J., Gallon, M. D., et al. (2017). Caffeine to optimize cognitive function for military mission-readiness: A systematic review and recommendations for the field. *Nutrition Reviews, 75*(6), 17–35. https://doi.org/10.1093/nutrit/nux007

Cyma-Wejchenig, M., Maciaszek, J., Ciążyńska, J., & Stemplewski, R. (2024). The level of physical activity, E-game-specific reaction time, and self-evaluated health and injuries' occurrence in non-professional Esports players. *Electronics, 13*(12), 2328. https://doi.org/10.3390/electronics13122328

Dale, G., Joessel, A., Bavelier, D., & Green, C. S. (2020). A new look at the cognitive neuroscience of video game play. *Annals of the New York Academy of Sciences, 1464*(1), 192–203. https://doi.org/10.1111/nyas.14295

Deleuze, J., Christiaens, M., Nuyens, F., & Billieux, J. (2017). Shoot at first sight! First person shooter players display reduced reaction time and compromised inhibitory control in comparison to other video game players. *Computers in Human Behavior, 72*, 570–576. https://doi.org/10.1016/j.chb.2017.02.027

DiFrancisco-Donoghue, J., Balentine, J., Schmidt, G., & Zwibel, H. (2019). Managing the health of the esport athlete: An integrated health management model. *BMJ Open Sport & Exercise Medicine, 5*(1), e000467. https://doi.org/10.1136/bmjsem-2018-000467

Dykiert, D., Der, G., Starr, J. M., & Deary, I. J. (2012). Age differences in intra-individual variability in simple and choice reaction time: Systematic review and meta-analysis. *PLoS One, 7*(10), e45759. https://doi.org/10.1371/journal.pone.0045759

Erickson, K. I., Hillman, C., Stillman, C. M., Ballard, R. M., Bloodgood, B., Conroy, D. E., Macko, R., Marquez, D. X., Petruzzello, S. J., & Powell, K. E. (2019). Physical activity, cognition, and brain outcomes: A review of the 2018 physical activity guidelines. *Medicine & Science in Sports & Exercise, 51*(6), 1242–1251. https://doi.org/10.1249/MSS.0000000000001936

Ersin, A., Tezeren, H. C., Pekyavas, N. O., Asal, B., Atabey, A., Diri, A., & Gonen, İ. (2022). The relationship between reaction time and gaming time in e-sports players. *Kinesiology, 54*(1), 36–42.

Ferguson, C. J. (2007). The good, the bad and the ugly: A meta-analytic review of positive and negative effects of violent video games. *Psychiatric Quarterly, 78*(4), 309–316. https://doi.org/10.1007/s11126-007-9056-9

Franks, R. R., King, D., Bodine, W., Chisari, E., Heller, A., Jamal, F., IV, Luksch, J., Quinn, K., Singh, R., & Solomon, M. (2022). AOASM position statement on esports, active video gaming, and the role of the sports medicine physician. *Clinical Journal of Sport Medicine, 32*(1), e221–e229. https://doi.org/10.1097/JSM.0000000000001017

Gangemi, A., De Luca, R., Fabio, R. A., Lauria, P., & Rifici, C. (2023). Effects of virtual reality cognitive training on neuroplasticity: A quasi-randomized clinical trial in patients with stroke. *Biomedicine, 11*(11), 3225. https://doi.org/10.3390/biomedicines11113225

Ghasemi, A., Momeni, M., Rezaee, M., & Gholami, A. (2009). The difference in visual skills between expert versus novice soccer referees. *Journal of Human Kinetics, 22*, 15–20. https://doi.org/10.2478/v10078-009-0021-6

Giakoni-Ramírez, F., Merellano-Navarro, E., & Duclos-Bastías, D. (2022). Professional esports players: Motivation and physical activity levels. *International Journal of Environmental Research and Public Health, 19*(4), 2256. https://doi.org/10.3390/ijerph19042256

Green, C. S., & Bavelier, D. (2003). Action video game modifies visual selective attention. *Nature, 423*(6939), 534–537. https://doi.org/10.1038/nature01647

Green, C. S., & Bavelier, D. (2006). Effect of action video games on the spatial distribution of visuospatial attention. *Journal of Experimental Psychology: Human Perception and Performance, 32*(6), 1465–1478. https://doi.org/10.1037/0096-1523.32.6.1465

Hagiwara, G., Kawahara, I., & Kihara, S. (2020). An attempt to verify the positive effects of esports: Focusing on concentration and cognitive skill. *Journal of Japan Society of Sports Industry, 30*(3), 239–246.

Himmelstein, D., et al. (2017). An exploration of mental skills among competitive league of legends players. *International Journal of Gaming and Computer-Mediated Simulations, 9*(2), 1–21. https://doi.org/10.4018/IJGCMS.2017040101

Hüttermann, S., Ford, P. R., Williams, A. M., Varga, M., & Smeeton, N. J. (2019). Attention, perception, and action in a simulated decision-making task. *Journal of Sport & Exercise Psychology, 41*(4), 230–241. https://doi.org/10.1123/jsep.2018-0177

Hüttermann, S., Memmert, D., & Simons, D. J. (2014). The size and shape of the attentional "spotlight" varies with differences in sports expertise. *Journal of Experimental Psychology: Applied, 20*(2), 147–157. https://doi.org/10.1037/xap0000012

Hwang, N. K., Choi, J. B., Choi, D. K., Park, J. M., & Hong, C. W. (2021). Effects of semi-immersive virtual reality-based cognitive training combined with locomotor activity on cognitive function and gait ability in community-dwelling individuals. *Healthcare, 9*(7), 814. https://doi.org/10.3390/healthcare9070814

Jeong, I., Nobuto, T., Kaneko, N., Kato, T., & Nakazawa, K. (2025). High-skilled first-person shooter game players have superior situation-based gaze control abilities: Perspectives from the actual and controlled gaming environment. *Journal of Electronic Gaming and Esports, 3*(1).

Kim, H., Kim, S., & Wu, J. (2022). Perceptual-motor abilities of professional esports gamers and amateurs. *Journal of Electronic Gaming and Esports, 1*(1). https://doi.org/10.1123/jege.2022-0001

Kowal, M., Toth, A. J., Exton, C., & Campbell, M. J. (2018). Different cognitive abilities displayed by action video gamers and non-gamers. *Computers in Human Behavior, 88*, 255–262. https://doi.org/10.1016/j.chb.2018.07.010

Lachowicz, M., Serweta-Pawlik, A., Konopka-Lachowicz, A., Jamro, D., & Żurek, G. (2024). Amplifying cognitive functions in amateur esports athletes: The impact of short-term virtual reality training on reaction time, motor time, and eye–hand coordination. *Brain Sciences, 14*(9), 1104. https://doi.org/10.3390/brainsci14091104

Li, X., Huang, L., Li, B., Wang, H., & Han, C. (2020). Time for a true display of skill: Top players in league of legends have better executive control. *Acta Psychologica, 204*, 103007. https://doi.org/10.1016/j.actpsy.2020.103007

Lim, S., Yeo, M., & Yoon, G. (2019). Comparison between concentration and immersion based on EEG analysis. *Sensors, 19*(7), 1669. https://doi.org/10.3390/s19071669

Mańkowska, M., Poliszczuk, T., Poliszczuk, D., & Johne, M. (2015). Visual perception and its effect on reaction time and time-movement anticipation in elite female basketball players. *Polish Journal of Sport and Tourism, 22*(1), 3–8. https://doi.org/10.1515/pjst-2015-0001

Mann, D. T., Williams, A. M., Ward, P., & Janelle, C. M. (2007). Perceptual-cognitive expertise in sport: A meta-analysis. *Journal of Sport and Exercise Psychology, 29*(4), 457–478. https://doi.org/10.1123/jsep.29.4.457

Martin-Niedecken, A. L., & Schättin, A. (2020). Let the body'n'brain games begin: Toward innovative training approaches in esports athletes. *Frontiers in Psychology, 11*, 138. https://doi.org/10.3389/fpsyg.2020.00138

McLellan, T. M., Caldwell, J. A., & Lieberman, H. R. (2016). A review of caffeine's effects on cognitive, physical and occupational performance. *Neuroscience & Biobehavioral Reviews, 71*, 294–312. https://doi.org/10.1016/j.neubiorev.2016.09.001

Newzoo. (2020). Newzoo global esports market report 2020: Light version. https://newzoo.com/insights/trend-reports/newzoo-global-esports-market-report-2020-light-version/

Pedraza-Ramirez, I., Musculus, L., Raab, M., & Laborde, S. (2020). Setting the scientific stage for esports psychology: A systematic review. *International Review of Sport and Exercise Psychology, 13*(1), 319–352. https://doi.org/10.1080/1750984X.2020.1723122

Pelosin, E., Ponte, C., & Putzolu, M. (2022). Motor–cognitive treadmill training with virtual reality in Parkinson's disease: The effect of training duration. *Frontiers in Aging Neuroscience, 13*, 753381. https://doi.org/10.3389/fnagi.2021.753381

Phillips, N., & Green, C. S. (2023). Associations between cognitive performance and extreme expertise in different competitive esports. *Cognitive Science, 6*(1), 1–15. https://doi.org/10.1111/cogs.13290

Rogers, E. J., Trotter, M. G., Johnson, D., Desbrow, B., & King, N. (2024). Kovaak's aim trainer as a reliable metrics platform for assessing shooting proficiency in esports players: A pilot study. *Frontiers in Sports and Active Living, 6*, 1309991. https://doi.org/10.3389/fspor.2024.1309991

Rudolf, K., Bickmann, P., Froböse, I., Tholl, C., Wechsler, K., & Grieben, C. (2020). Demographics and health behavior of video game and esports players in Germany: The esports study 2019. *International Journal of Environmental Research and Public Health, 17*(6), 1870. https://doi.org/10.3390/ijerph17061870

Rutkowski, S., Adamczyk, M., Pastuła, A., Gos, E., Luque-Moreno, C., & Rutkowska, A. (2021). Training using a commercial immersive virtual reality system on hand–eye coordination and reaction time in young musicians: A pilot study. *International Journal of Environmental Research and Public Health, 18*(3), 1297. https://doi.org/10.3390/ijerph18031297

Schubert, T., Finke, K., Redel, P., Kluckow, S., Müller, H., & Strobach, T. (2015). Video game experience and its influence on visual attention parameters: An investigation using the framework of the theory of visual attention (TVA). *Acta Psychologica, 157*, 200–214. https://doi.org/10.1016/j.actpsy.2015.03.005

Schwab, S., & Memmert, D. (2012). The impact of a sports vision training program in youth field hockey players. *Journal of Sports Science and Medicine, 11*(4), 624–631.

Serweta-Pawlik, A., Lachowicz, M., Żurek, A., Rosen, B., & Żurek, G. (2023). Evaluating the effectiveness of visuospatial memory stimulation using virtual reality in head and neck cancer patients—Pilot study. *Cancers, 15*(6), 1639. https://doi.org/10.3390/cancers15061639

Sokołowska, B. (2023). Impact of virtual reality cognitive and motor exercises on brain health. *International Journal of Environmental Research and Public Health, 20*(5), 4150. https://doi.org/10.3390/ijerph20054150

Swing, E. L., Gentile, D. A., Anderson, C. A., & Walsh, D. A. (2010). Television and video game exposure and the development of attention problems. *Pediatrics, 126*(2), 214–221.

Szary, P., Kiper, P., Buchta, K., Bedrunka, D., Zabłotni, S., Rutkowska, A., Szczepańska-Gieracha, J., & Rutkowski, S. (2020). Investigating exercise intensity in virtual reality among healthy volunteers. *Human Movement, 21*(2), 54–60. https://doi.org/10.5114/hm.2020.93016

Tanaka, S., Ikeda, H., Kasahara, K., Kato, R., Tsubomi, H., Sugawara, S. K., Mori, M., Hanakawa, T., Sadato, N., Honda, M., & Watanabe, K. (2013). Larger right posterior parietal volume in action video game experts: A behavioral and voxel-based morphometry (VBM) study. *PLoS One, 8*(6), e66998. https://doi.org/10.1371/journal.pone.0066998

Toth, A. J., Kowal, M., & Campbell, M. J. (2019). The color–word Stroop task does not differentiate cognitive inhibition ability among esports gamers of varying expertise. *Frontiers in Psychology, 10*, 2852. https://doi.org/10.3389/fpsyg.2019.02852

Trotter, M. G., Coulter, T. J., Davis, P. A., Poulus, D. R., & Polman, R. (2020). The association between esports participation, health and physical activity behaviour. *International Journal of Environmental Research and Public Health, 17*(20), 7329. https://doi.org/10.3390/ijerph17207329

Vaeyens, R., Lenoir, M., Williams, A. M., Mazyn, L., & Philippaerts, R. M. (2007). The effects of task constraints on visual search behavior and decision-making skill in youth soccer players. *Journal of Sport and Exercise Psychology, 29*(2), 147–169. https://doi.org/10.1123/jsep.29.2.147

Velichkovsky, B. B., Khromov, N., Korotin, A., Burnaev, E., & Somov, A. (2019, August). Visual fixations duration as an indicator of skill level in esports. In *IFIP conference on human-computer interaction* (pp. 397–405). Springer International Publishing.

Voss, M. W., Kramer, A. F., Basak, C., Prakash, R. S., & Roberts, B. (2010). Are expert athletes 'expert' in the cognitive laboratory? A meta-analytic review of cognition and sport expertise. *Applied Cognitive Psychology, 24*(6), 812–826. https://doi.org/10.1002/acp.1588

Wagner, M. G. (2006). On the scientific relevance of esports. *International Conference on Internet Computing*, 437–442.

Wu, S., & Spence, I. (2013). Playing shooter and driving videogames improves top-down guidance in visual search. *Attention, Perception, & Psychophysics, 75*(4), 673–686. https://doi.org/10.3758/s13414-013-0440-2

Zhang, W., Wang, X., Li, X., Yan, H., Song, Y., Li, X., Zhang, W., & Ma, G. (2023). Effects of acute moderate-intensity aerobic exercise on cognitive function in e-athletes: A randomized controlled trial. *Medicine, 102*(45), e35108. https://doi.org/10.1097/MD.0000000000035108

Zwierko, T., Osinski, W., Lubinski, W., Czepita, D., & Florkiewicz, B. (2010). Speed of visual sensorimotor processes and conductivity of visual pathway in volleyball players. *Journal of Human Kinetics, 23*, 21–27. https://doi.org/10.2478/v10078-010-0002-

Chapter 9
Physical Activity in Esports

Fatih Sülün and Ahmet Vatansever

9.1 The Rise of Esports and the Problem of Physical Inactivity

Emerging in the early 1990s, esports gained popularity over the following decade alongside a significant increase in its player base (Jonasson & Thiborg, 2010). Esports is viewed as a competitive sport where players compete against each other in a virtual environment using their physical and mental skills (IESF, 2021). It has continued its rapid expansion through the hosting of numerous professional events worldwide, such as the League of Legends Championship Series (LCS), and has been embraced as a cultural phenomenon by many countries such as the USA, South Korea, and the United Kingdom (Pedraza et al., 2020). The France Esports Association underscored the significance of the player base by stating that 9.4 million players and viewers are associated with esports in France alone (Rodrigues-Vion et al., 2023).

Prolonged sedentary behavior is known to be associated with and lead to numerous chronic health issues (Bailey et al., 2019; Patterson et al., 2018). Meta-analyses have reported that extended periods of inactivity, such as television viewing and daily sitting habits, increase the risk of cardiovascular diseases and type II diabetes (Wilmot et al., 2012; Biswas et al., 2015). Current research indicates that the time esports players spend in front of a computer or console ranges from 5.5 to 11 hours, raising concerns about player health due to this prolonged inactivity (Yin et al., 2020; Bayrakdar et al., 2020; Rudolf et al., 2020). Similarly, another study found that esports players who spending up to 10 hours in front of a screen suffer from eye strain, as well as back, neck, and wrist pain (Di Francisco-Donoghue et al., 2019).

F. Sülün (✉)
Department of Sports Science, Trakya University, Edirne, Turkey
e-mail: fatihsulun@trakya.edu.tr

A. Vatansever
Independent Researcher, İstanbul, Turkey

S. Bekir (ed.), *The Psychology of Esports*, https://doi.org/10.1007/978-3-032-25090-2_9

The increasing digitalization of society and the widespread adoption of esports, coupled with the emergence of sedentary lifestyles, underscore the growing importance of this issue. Research has reported that individuals with high video game addiction are associated with irregular sleep patterns and abdominal obesity. Due to its cardiometabolic risk, the type of abdominal obesity is a cause for concern for these individuals (Turel et al., 2016; Bastien et al., 2014; Cameron et al., 2012).

Esports players' prolonged sitting in front of consoles or computers, combined with the specific positioning of equipment such as monitors, keyboards, and mice, causes the body to deviate from its natural posture. Consequently, excessive strain on the neck and back muscles, along with abnormal muscle contractions, leads to fatigue and muscular pain. This condition impairs the function of spinal support, increasing mechanical stress on discs and ligaments, and predisposes players to musculoskeletal disorders (Waongenngarm et al., 2020). Additionally, health issues caused by inactivity and obesity emerge as significant risk factors (Aksakallı, 2024).

As esports has gained popularity, the relationship between esports and health has become a focal point in scientific literature. Research has analyzed various health parameters of esports players, including anthropometric characteristics, body composition, physical activity habits, musculoskeletal issues, and sleep patterns (Tang et al., 2023). Integrating physical activity into the daily routines of esports players plays a critical role in both preventing and addressing health risks. Furthermore, regular physical activity has the potential to enhance the gaming performance of esports players by mitigating fatigue and muscle pain (Gram et al., 2014).

9.2 The Effect of Physical Activity on Esports Performance

In recent studies on esports, the relationship between physical activity and gaming performance has emerged as a significant research topic. The potential for physical activities and specific exercise protocols to enhance both the motor capacity and gaming performance of esports players has become a focal point for academics and esports professionals alike. Although esports players do not directly exhibit gross motor skills they utilize cognitive skills such as hand-eye coordination and reaction speed, in addition to focus, attention, and tactical or strategic thinking (Goulart et al., 2023; Hallman & Giel, 2018). Furthermore, similar to disciplines such as archery and shooting esports involving fine motor skills including the hand, wrist, and fingers (Funk et al., 2018).

It is essential for esports players to design training programs that incorporate the physical, mental, and cognitive skills used in gaming performance. Integrating these elements into training programs has the potential to enhance cognitive performance, including decision-making, information processing and the reduction of stress and anxiety (Mendoza et al., 2021; Wattanapisit et al., 2020). In a study on esports players, Şengül (2023) examined the effects of an exercise intervention on LOL performance. This controlled experimental study implemented a 15-min intervention program including movements such as jogging, jumping jacks, step touches, good mornings and knee ups prior to competition, reporting higher in-game performance and cognitive test scores in the exercise group. Similarly, another study conducted with professional esports players found that an eight-week exercise intervention improved both cognitive endurance and physical performance (Sanz-Matesanz et al., 2024). A systematic review by Lam et al. (2020), which included six studies, reached significant conclusions regarding the lifestyle, general health, and physical activity habits of esports players. The study reported that while the majority of esports players met the World Health Organization (WHO) physical activity recommendations, prolonged inactivity, sleep disorders, and poor nutritional habits could negatively affect health and gaming performance. Additionally, it was noted that esports players are prone to musculoskeletal disorders.

Due to the nature of esports, prolonged sitting, intense screen time, and extended periods of inactivity emerge as significant factors threatening the health of players. Indeed, Di Francisco-Donoghue et al. (2019) reported in their study that professional esports players play for 25 hours per week, a figure that rises to 14 hours per day during competition periods. In a systematic review by McNulty et al. (2023) involving 12 studies, it was concluded that esports players who exercise regularly exhibit shorter reaction times and higher attention scores; consequently, the integration of exercise into the training programs of professional esports teams was recommended. Another recent study conducted on esports players found a significant correlation between cardiorespiratory fitness levels and reaction time (Dykstra et al., 2021). This result indicates that esports players with higher cardiorespiratory fitness can achieve faster and more accurate reaction times. A study by De Las Heras et al. (2020) on professional esports players examined the impact of a 15-minute high-intensity interval training (HIIT) session performed prior to gaming, on subsequent performance. The implemented 15-minute exercise protocol resulted in a 9% increase in eliminating in-game targets and a 75% increase in strike accuracy.

Another dimension emphasizing the importance of physical activity in esports players is musculoskeletal health. In a field study conducted in Denmark, physical activity opportunities were offered to esports clubs, and 84% of the esports players participated. It was reported that esports players who engaged in physical activity experienced less neck, shoulder, and lower-back pain (Pedersen et al., 2023). In another recent study, esports players in an eight-week intervention program achieved an increase of approximately 1 kg in muscle mass and a 63% to 105% improvement in compound exercise performance such as bench press, squat, and deadlift (Dichiara et al., 2024). These findings demonstrate that physical activity both reduces health risks and significantly enhances physical fitness.

Physical activity exerts powerful effects not only on physical but also on cognitive performance. The literature reports improvements of 65% in attention, 29% in memory, 38% in information processing speed, and 25% in task switching following regular exercise (Ludyga et al., 2020). Beyond cognitive benefits, physical activity is a potent supporter of psychological well-being. It has been established that regular exercise reduces levels of the stress hormone cortisol while increasing the secretion of serotonin and dopamine, thereby alleviating symptoms of anxiety and depression

(Lubans et al., 2016). Given that esports players must perform under high pressure and stress during tournaments, these effects are crucial for maintaining concentration and motivation. Furthermore, even short-term interventions aimed at in-game performance are noteworthy. It was revealed that players who took a six-minute walking break during 2 h of gameplay showed a significant improvement in executive functions compared to those who took only a resting break (Trotter et al., 2020). This finding suggests that even brief bouts of physical activity can contribute to the cognitive functions of esports players.

Considering existing research and the inactivity issues faced by esports players, it is evident that physical activity enhances reaction speed, hand-eye coordination, and cognitive abilities, while reducing stress and anxiety levels to boost in-game performance. Taking their lifestyles into account it is vital for esports players to integrate physical activity into their training programs to maintain health and optimize their performance. All these findings demonstrate that physical activity plays a critical role in esports, not only in preventing health problems but also in enhancing cognitive functions increasing psychological resilience and supporting gaming performance. Consequently, it is essential for esports organizations to design multidisciplinary health programs and mandate exercise-oriented support processes to contribute to the positioning of esports as a sustainable sports discipline.

9.3 Healthy Lifestyle Strategies for Esports Players

Today, esports stands out not only for digital gaming performance but also for a structure that requires a lifestyle routine similar to that of professional players. Players' hours-long training sessions, travel schedules, competitive pressure, and digital screen exposure necessitate healthy living strategies beyond performance alone. In this context, achieving sustainable success for esports players is directly linked not only to in-game skills but also to regular physical activity, healthy nutrition, ergonomics, and psychological resilience (Di Francisco-Donoghue et al., 2019). A sedentary lifestyle causes esports players to develop a risk profile regarding musculoskeletal health. Therefore, regular and structured exercise programs are vital not only for injury prevention but also for enhancing cognitive functions and reaction speed (Basso & Suzuki, 2017).

Nutrition is another critical element for esports players. During prolonged gaming sessions, inadequate nutrition and irregular eating habits increase the risk of obesity and lead to metabolic disorders (Trotter et al., 2020). For optimal performance, it is recommended to adopt nutritional strategies rich in omega-3 fatty acids, B vitamins, and antioxidants that support cognitive functions, alongside adequate energy intake (Walsh, 2019). Furthermore, as dehydration negatively impacts both physical endurance and cognitive performance, hydration strategies for esports players are of great importance (Judelson et al., 2007). Ultimately, the physiological support provided by nutrition and hydration can only be processed by the body, allowing for full recovery, through a regular sleep regimen.

In this context, a consistent sleep pattern emerges as an integral part of sustainable performance strategies for esports players. Nighttime tournaments and extended gaming hours cause disruptions to the circadian rhythm, which negatively impact both cognitive performance and the immune system (Köller et al., 2021). Research indicates that seven to nine hours of quality sleep per day enhances decision-making processes, accelerates learning and improves reaction times (Fullagar et al., 2015). Therefore, maintaining a regular sleep schedule is of critical importance not only for overall health but also for in-game performance.

Alongside cognitive and biological processes, managing the physical loads placed on esports players requires as much attention as sleep and nutrition. Due to the prolonged sitting positions of esports players, ergonomic adjustments hold a significant place in healthy lifestyle strategies. Proper seating posture, wrist supports, monitor alignment, and lighting adjustments play a critical role in preventing musculoskeletal issues (DiFrancisco-Donoghue et al., 2019). Furthermore, taking regular breaks for short walks has been shown to support executive functions (Trotter et al., 2020). The long and intensive training periods of esports players expose them to various physical ailments, primarily musculoskeletal injuries resulting largely from a sedentary lifestyle, incorrect posture, and repetitive movements (Chan et al., 2022). Injuries to the hand and wrist, in particular, are highly prevalent among esports players due to gaming sessions involving hundreds of repeated commands per minute, often leading to serious injuries that require physiotherapeutic intervention (Lepp et al., 2023). Research indicates that a lack of regular physical activity not only adversely affects musculoskeletal health but can also have indirect effects on the general health status and body composition of esports players. For instance, prolonged inactivity can increase the risk of metabolic syndrome, predisposing players to weight gain, which further elevates injury risk by increasing the biomechanical load on the joints (Monteiro et al., 2022). Therefore, to protect the health of esports players and ensure sustainable performance, it is of critical importance to include them in holistic health programs that encompass regular physical exercise and posture training alongside ergonomic adjustments.

Another common issue among esports players is high stress levels. It is well documented that players in professional leagues face intense competitive pressure, performance anxiety, and societal expectations. In this regard, regular physical activity serves as a powerful supporter of not only physical but also psychological well-being. By increasing serotonin and dopamine levels, exercise reduces anxiety and facilitates stress management (Lubans et al., 2016). Additionally, there is evidence that mindfulness-based practices improve attentional control and enhance psychological resilience in esports players (Noetel et al., 2019).

9.4 Conclusion

The findings presented in this chapter demonstrate that physical activity, nutrition, sleep, ergonomics, and psychological resilience strategies play a critical role for esports players, not only for health but also for the sustainability of performance. The literature strongly indicates that regular exercise supports musculoskeletal health, enhances cognitive functions and improves psychological well-being. Similarly, healthy eating habits, adequate hydration, adherence to sleep hygiene and ergonomic adjustments are key factors that determine the long-term performance and career longevity of esports players.

Current literature relies heavily on cross-sectional studies or short-term interventions, which limits our understanding of the long-term effects. Future research should consider the following:

- Longitudinal studies can be conducted to examine the long-term effects of physical activity and healthy lifestyle strategies.
- Cross-cultural comparisons can analyze the lifestyle strategies of esports players across different geographical regions.
- Psychological skills training programs (e.g., mental training, stress management, and motivation enhancement) can be experimentally tested on esports players.
- Qualitative research can provide a more in-depth understanding of players' subjective experiences.

In conclusion, it is evident that physical activity, sleep, nutrition, and psychological resilience strategies play a critical role for esports players, not only for health but also for performance sustainability. Broadly considered, healthy lifestyle strategies, have been shown to increase motivation, facilitate stress management, and strengthen mental toughness in esports players. The structural integration of these strategies by esports clubs, federations, and coaches within multidisciplinary frameworks will contribute to the positioning of esports as a sustainable sports discipline.

References

Aksakallı, O. (2024). Çocuklarda direnç antrenmanı. In Z. Göktaş & D. S. Yılmaz (Eds.), *Teori ve uygulamada spor bilimleri 2* (p. s. 25–48). Duvar Yayınları.

Bailey, D. P., Hewson, D. J., Champion, R. B., & Sayegh, S. M. (2019). Sitting time and risk of cardiovascular disease and diabetes: A systematic review and meta-analysis. *American Journal of Public Health, 109*(9), 1237–1245. https://doi.org/10.2105/AJPH.2019.305215

Bastien, M., Poirier, P., Lemieux, I., & Després, J. P. (2014). Overview of epidemiology and contribution of obesity to cardiovascular disease. *Progress in Cardiovascular Diseases, 56*(4), 369–381. https://doi.org/10.1016/j.pcad.2013.08.001

Bayrakdar, A., Yildiz, Y., & Bayraktar, I. (2020). Do e-athletes move? A study on physical activity level and body composition in elite e-sports. *Physical Education of Students, 24*(5), 259–264. https://doi.org/10.15561/20755279.2020.0501

Biswas, A., Oh, P. I., Faulkner, G. E., Bajaj, R. R., Silver, M. A., Mitchell, M. S., & Alter, D. A. (2015). Sedentary time and its association with risk for disease incidence, mortality, and hospitalization in adults: A systematic review and meta-analysis. *Annals of Internal Medicine, 162*(2), 123–132. https://doi.org/10.7326/M14-1651

Cameron, A. J., Magliano, D. J., Shaw, J. E., Zimmet, P. Z., Carstensen, B., Alberti, K. G. M., & Söderberg, S. (2012). The influence of hip circumference on the relationship between abdominal obesity and mortality. *International Journal of Epidemiology, 41*(2), 484–494. https://doi.org/10.1093/ije/dyr212

Chan, G., Huo, Y., Kelly, S., Leung, J., Tisdale, C., & Gullo, M. (2022). The impact of eSports and online video gaming on lifestyle behaviours in youth: A systematic review. *Computers in Human Behavior, 126*, 106974.

de Las Heras, B. M., Li, D., & Kachurin, A. (2020). The impact of a short high-intensity interval training on esports performance. *International Journal of Exercise Science, 13*(6), 1621.

Dichiara, A., Bruno, C., Esposito, F., & Raiola, G. (2024). The impact of an exercise training program on physical fitness and health in esport players: A pilot study. *Applied Sciences, 14*(7), 2845. https://doi.org/10.3309/app14072845

DiFrancisco-Donoghue, J., Balentine, J., Schmidt, G., & Zwibel, H. (2019). Managing the health of the eSport athlete: An integrated health management model. *BMJ Open Sport & Exercise Medicine, 5*(1), e000467. https://doi.org/10.1136/bmjsem-2018-000467

Dykstra, T. M., Hovanec, D. P., Shrier, I., & Ross, R. (2021). Cardiorespiratory fitness and reaction time in esports players. *Medicine & Science in Sports & Exercise, 53*(8S), 21. https://doi.org/10.1249/01.mss.0000761109.84379.8e

Fullagar, H. H. K., Skorski, S., Duffield, R., Hammes, D., Coutts, A. J., & Meyer, T. (2015). Sleep and athletic performance: The effects of sleep loss on exercise performance, and physiological and cognitive responses to exercise. *Sports Medicine, 45*(2), 161–186. https://doi.org/10.1007/s40279-014-0260-0

Funk, D. C., Pizzo, A. D., & Baker, B. J. (2018). eSport management: Embracing eSport education and research opportunities. *Sport Management Review, 21*(1), 7–13. https://doi.org/10.1016/j.smr.2017.07.003

Goulart, J. B., Aitken, L. S., Siddiqui, S., Cuevas, M., Cardenas, J., Beathard, K. M., & Riechman, S. E. (2023). Nutrition, lifestyle, and cognitive performance in esport athletes. *Frontiers in Nutrition, 10*, 1120303. https://doi.org/10.3389/fnut.2023.1120303

Gram, B., Andersen, C., Zebis, M. K., Bredahl, T., Pedersen, M. T., Mortensen, O. S., & Sjøgaard, G. (2014). Effect of training supervision on effectiveness of strength training for reducing neck/shoulder pain and headache in office workers: Cluster randomized controlled trial. *BioMed Research International, 2014*, Art 693013. doi:https://doi.org/10.1155/2014/693013.

Hallmann, K., & Giel, T. (2018). eSports–competitive sports or recreational activity? *Sport Management Review, 21*(1), 14–20. https://doi.org/10.1016/j.smr.2017.07.011

International Esports Federation. (2021). Esports - True sports? https://iesf.org/esports.

Jonasson, K., & Thiborg, J. (2010). Electronic sport and its impact on future sport. *Sport in Society, 13*(2), 287–299. https://doi.org/10.1080/17430430903522996

Judelson, D. A., Maresh, C. M., Anderson, J. M., Armstrong, L. E., Casa, D. J., Kraemer, W. J., Volek, J. S., & Sebastianelli, W. J. (2007). Hydration and muscular performance: Does fluid balance affect strength, power and high-intensity endurance? *Sports Medicine, 37*(10), 907–921. https://doi.org/10.2165/00007256-200737100-00006

Köller, A., Rothschild, J., & Sadeh, A. (2021). Sleep patterns and health outcomes in competitive esports players: A review. *Current Sleep Medicine Reports, 7*(3), 102–110. https://doi.org/10.1007/s40675-021-00209-0

Lam, M. Y., Cen, Y., Am-Earc, A., & Chung, J. W. (2020). Esports athletes' lifestyle behaviors, physical activity habits, and overall health and wellbeing: A systematic review. *Physical Therapy Reviews, 25*(5–6), 449–461. https://doi.org/10.1080/10833196.2020.1843335

Lepp, A., Dowdell, B., Yim, B., & Barkley, J. E. (2023). Esports gamers, recreational gamers, and the active couch potato lifestyle. *American Journal of Lifestyle Medicine, 15598276231184159.*

Lubans, D. R., Richards, J., Hillman, C. H., Faulkner, G., Beauchamp, M. R., Nilsson, M., Kelly, P., Smith, J. J., Raine, L. B., & Biddle, S. J. H. (2016). Physical activity for cognitive and mental health in youth: A systematic review of mechanisms. *Preventive Medicine, 92*, 139–150. https://doi.org/10.1016/j.ypmed.2016.07.019

Ludyga, S., Gerber, M., Pühse, U., Looser, V. N., & Kamijo, K. (2020). Systematic review and meta-analysis investigating moderators of long-term effects of exercise on cognition in healthy individuals. *Nature Human Behaviour, 4*(6), 603–612. https://doi.org/10.1038/s41562-2020-0851-8

McNulty, C., Jenny, S. E., Leis, O., Poulus, D., Sondergeld, P., & Nicholson, M. (2023). Physical exercise and performance in esports players: An initial systematic review. *Journal of Electronic Gaming and Esports, 1*(1). https://doi.org/10.1123/jege.2022-0010

Mendoza, G., Clemente-Suárez, V. J., Alvero-Cruz, J. R., Rivilla, I., García-Romero, J., Fernández-Navas, M., & Jiménez, M. (2021). The role of experience, perceived match importance, and anxiety on cortisol response in an official esports competition. *International Journal of Environmental Research and Public Health, 18*(6), 2893. https://doi.org/10.3390/ijerph18062893

Monteiro Pereira, A., Costa, J. A., Verhagen, E., Figueiredo, P., & Brito, J. (2022). Associations between esports participation and health: A scoping review. *Sports Medicine, 52*(9), 2039–2060.

Noetel, M., Ciarrochi, J., Van Zanden, B., & Lonsdale, C. (2019). Mindfulness and acceptance approaches to sporting performance enhancement: A systematic review. *International Review of Sport and Exercise Psychology, 12*(1), 139–175. https://doi.org/10.1080/1750984X.2017.1387803

Patterson, R., McNamara, E., Tainio, M., de Sá, T. H., Smith, A. D., Sharp, S. J., & Woodcock, J. (2018). Sedentary behaviour and risk of all-cause, cardiovascular and cancer mortality, and incident type 2 diabetes: A systematic review and dose response meta-analysis. *European Journal of Epidemiology, 33*(9), 811–829. https://doi.org/10.1007/s10654-018-0380-1

Pedersen, T., Helge, J. W., & Dall, P. M. (2023). Physical activity behavior and musculoskeletal pain among young esports players: A cross-sectional study. *Journal of Electronic Gaming and Esports, 2*(1), 1–12. https://doi.org/10.1123/jege.2023-0017

Pedraza-Ramirez, I., Musculus, L., Raab, M., & Laborde, S. (2020). Setting the scientific stage for esports psychology: A systematic review. *International Review of Sport and Exercise Psychology, 13*(1), 319–352. https://doi.org/10.1080/1750984X.2020.1733122

Rodrigues-Vion, J. N., Baliros-Bonnel, M., Rodrigues-Vion, F., Assadan, S., & Attoh-Mensah, E. (2023). Training, lifestyle and physiological conditions and performance in esports: A review. *Sports Medicine-Open, 9*(1), 1–17. https://doi.org/10.1186/s40798-023-00620-6

Rudolf, K., Bickmann, P., Froböse, I., Tholl, C., Wechsler, K., & Grieben, C. (2020). Demographics and health behavior of video game and esports players in Germany: The esports study 2019. *International Journal of Environmental Research and Public Health, 17*(6), 1870. https://doi.org/10.3390/ijerph17061870

Sanz-Matesanz, M., García-García, J., Barba-Moreno, L., & Ayllón-Ronco, F. (2024). Effects of an 8-week physical training intervention on cognitive endurance and physical performance in professional esports players. *Journal of Sport and Health Science. Advance online publication.* https://doi.org/10.1016/j.jshs.2024.03.003

Şengül, A. (2023). Mücadeleci bir espor oyunu öncesi yapılan fiziksel aktivitenin espor performansını belirleyen parametreler üzerine etkisi [Yüksek Lisans Tezi, Marmara Üniversitesi].

Tang, D., Sum, K. W. R., Ma, R., & Ho, W. K. (2023). Beyond the screen: Do esports participants really have more physical health problems? *Sustainability, 15*(23), 16391. https://doi.org/10.3390/su152316391

Trotter, M. G., Coulter, T. J., Davis, P. A., Poulus, D. R., & Polman, R. (2020). The association between esports participation, health and physical activity behaviour. *International Journal of Environmental Research and Public Health, 17*(19), 7329. https://doi.org/10.3390/ijerph17197329

Turel, O., Romashkin, A., & Morrison, K. M. (2016). Health outcomes of information system use lifestyles among adolescents: Videogame addiction, sleep curtailment and cardio-metabolic deficiencies. *PLoS One, 11*(5), e0154764. https://doi.org/10.1371/journal.pone.0154764

Walsh, N. P. (2019). Nutrition and athlete immune health: New perspectives on an old paradigm. *Sports Medicine, 49*(S2), 153–168. https://doi.org/10.1007/s40279-019-01160-3

Waongenngarm, P., van der Beek, A. J., Akkarakittichoke, N., & Janwantanakul, P. (2020). Perceived musculoskeletal discomfort and its association with postural shifts during 4-h prolonged sitting in office workers. *Applied Ergonomics, 89*, 103225. https://doi.org/10.1016/j.apergo.2020.103225

Wattanapisit, A., Wattanapisit, S., & Wongsiri, S. (2020). Public health perspectives on eSports. *Public Health Reports, 135*(3), 295–298. https://doi.org/10.1177/0033354920912125

Wilmot, E. G., Edwardson, C. L., Achana, F. A., Davies, M. J., Gorely, T., Gray, L. J., et al. (2012). Sedentary time in adults and the association with diabetes, cardiovascular disease and death: Systematic review and meta-analysis. *Diabetologia, 55*(11), 2895–2905. https://doi.org/10.1007/s00125-012-2677-z

Yin, K., Zi, Y., Zhuang, W., Gao, Y., Tong, Y., Song, L., & Liu, Y. (2020). Linking esports to health risks and benefits: Current knowledge and future research needs. *Journal of Sport and Health Science, 9*(6), 485–488. https://doi.org/10.1016/j.jshs.2020.05.003

Chapter 10
Esports Players and Health: A Medical Perspective

Yasin Atay and Burak Bezirganoğlu

10.1 Introduction

Esports have grown rapidly in recent years and have become a prominent field of competition. As the industry becomes more professionalized, both the number of participants and the amount of research focusing on health-related issues have increased significantly (Monteiro Pereira et al., 2022). Esports are no longer viewed solely as a form of entertainment. With their structured organization, economic influence, and social impact, they are increasingly regarded as a legitimate form of sport (Jenny et al., 2017). This evolution has brought new questions and concerns regarding the health of those involved in competitive gaming. Unlike traditional sports, esports come with distinct health risks, including prolonged sitting, repetitive movements, extended screen exposure, psychological stress, and irregular daily routines (Mondal & Nithish, 2024).

Although esports players typically engage in low levels of physical activity, they are subject to significant cognitive, reflexive, and psychomotor demands (Ketelhut & Nigg, 2024). This combination creates a unique health profile that sets them apart from other athletic populations. As a result, the concept of esports medicine has begun to emerge, although it remains relatively underrepresented in the broader sports medicine literature (Monteiro Pereira et al., 2022). Addressing the health needs of esports players requires the integration of multiple disciplines, including sports medicine, physiotherapy, ergonomics, nutrition, sleep science, and psychology

Y. Atay (✉)
Atatürk City Hospital, Sports Medicine Unit, Balıkesir, Turkey
e-mail: yasinatay@istanbul.edu.tr

B. Bezirganoğlu
Speciality Registrar in General Practice, Oxford, UK

S. Bekir (ed.), *The Psychology of Esports*,
https://doi.org/10.1007/978-3-032-25090-2_10

(Mondal & Nithish, 2024). In this context, esports medicine may be defined as a multidisciplinary field focused on the prevention, diagnosis, management, and performance optimization of health conditions arising from competitive digital gaming (Emara et al., 2020).

Recent studies have highlighted a number of common health issues among professional esports players. These include carpal tunnel syndrome, eye strain, shoulder and neck pain, sleep disturbances, anxiety, and burnout (DiFrancisco-Donoghue et al., 2019; Mondal & Nithish, 2024). For example, the comprehensive review conducted by Pereira et al. (2022) found that regular participation in competitive gaming is not simply associated with low physical activity, as often assumed, but rather with high levels of sedentary behavior. Importantly, this sedentary pattern may negatively affect musculoskeletal health regardless of overall physical activity levels (Monteiro Pereira et al., 2022). Similarly, Franks et al. (2022) emphasized the need for regular health screenings for esports players and recommended that healthcare professionals working in this field receive specialized training to address the unique risks associated with esports (Franks et al., 2022).

Evaluating esports from a health perspective is essential not only for the well-being of individual players but also for informing health policies across a broader range of stakeholders, including federations, team managers, coaches, and sponsors (Mondal & Nithish, 2024; Monteiro Pereira et al., 2022). The high level of competition in the esports industry can sometimes lead players toward unhealthy lifestyle habits (Kelly & Leung, 2021). This is especially concerning among younger individuals, who may face increased risks related to excessive screen time, sleep disturbances, and social isolation (Lee et al., 2020).

This book chapter aims to examine the physiological, neurocognitive, and systemic impacts of esports through a review of current scientific literature, while offering practical strategies for physicians and healthcare professionals. As the chapter progresses, it will focus both on identifying key health issues and on developing evidence-based preventive approaches. Ultimately, the goal is to support the long-term health and sustainable participation of individuals involved in esports.

10.2 Health-Related Physiological and Cognitive Stressors in Esports

Esports may seem to require little physical effort, but at the professional level, it involves significant cognitive and physiological strain as athletes face a state of psychological tension that results in autonomic nervous system alteration (Leis & Lautenbach, 2020; Sousa et al., 2020). Players must process information quickly, make rapid decisions, maintain sustained attention, and coordinate visual and motor functions simultaneously to analyze various stimuli for coordinated actions (Jenny et al., 2017; Sousa et al., 2020). These mental demands increase further in competitive environments where time pressure is constant and players are exposed to intense performance pressures (Leis & Lautenbach, 2020; Machado et al., 2025; Trotter et al., 2023). In such settings where every second matters, mental performance can decline, leading to cognitive fatigue, reduced inhibitory control, and significant decision making errors (Imanian et al., 2025).

A primary source of cognitive stress in esports is mental fatigue, resulting from the requirement for prolonged focus and rapid decision-making (Koshy et al., 2020; Machado et al., 2025). To improve their competitive skills, players often engage in intensive training sessions that typically last between 5.5 and 10 hours daily (Lindberg et al., 2020). During these sessions, the substantial cognitive workload required for information processing and visual-spatial skills can place an excessive demand on executive functions, particularly inhibition and flexibility, which potentially leads to mental fatigue and burnout (Franks et al., 2022). Consequently, empirical evidence indicates that this state of cognitive fatigue leads to a measurable loss of accuracy and increased impulsivity, as the brain's capacity to maintain inhibitory control significantly diminishes over the course of a continuous session (Sousa et al., 2020).

The autonomic nervous system, which plays a key role in stress regulation, shows noticeable changes in physiological markers such as heart rate, respiratory rate, and minute ventilation under pressure during esports activities (Koshy et al., 2020; Machado et al., 2025). In their 2025 study, Machado et al. observed a significant decrease in heart rate variability (HRV) and an increase in stress responses among professional players during high stakes playoff matches, indicating greater sympathetic activation (Machado et al., 2025). These findings suggest that esports players experience stress-related physiological reactions similar to those seen in traditional sports competitors, as tournament conditions produce a psychological state of tension that results in autonomic nervous system alteration (Ahn & Kim, 2024; Machado et al., 2025; Sousa et al., 2020).

Prolonged screen exposure and late-night training sessions significantly affect sleep quality and duration, particularly when combined with competitive cognitive stress (Klier et al., 2022; Lee et al., 2020). Research by Lee et al. (2020) indicates that professional esports players exhibit a severely delayed sleep phase compared to non-athletes, with training schedules frequently extending into the early morning hours (Lee et al., 2020). Furthermore, Klier et al. (2022) experimentally demonstrated that even a single evening of excessive gaming significantly reduces total sleep time compared to non-gaming conditions, largely due to heightened stress levels and delayed bedtimes (Klier et al., 2022).

Disrupted sleep patterns interfere with both mental and physical recovery, as sleep is regarded as the single most effective recovery strategy available to elite athletes (Halson, 2008). These disturbances result in lower sleep quality and reduced feelings of refreshment upon awakening, which compromise performance capacity the following day (Lee et al., 2020). Ultimately, sleep deprivation is linked to slower reaction times and reduced concentration, resulting in a significant increase in attention lapses that can increase error rates and the risk of injury (Halson, 2008; Smithies et al., 2024). This state of cognitive fatigue causes a loss of accuracy and increased impulsivity as the brain's inhibitory control diminishes over the course of a session (Sousa et al., 2020).

In conclusion, recognizing and managing the cognitive and physiological stress factors faced by esports players is essential for both protecting their health and ensuring sustained performance. Identifying these stressors early and addressing them with appropriate strategies is necessary for players to maintain a healthy and lasting professional career.

10.3 Musculoskeletal and Systemic Health Problems in Esports Players

Professional esports does not involve the high impact collisions or full body movements characteristic of traditional sports, yet it imposes consistent and localized strain on specific body regions over extended periods (Lindberg et al., 2020; Monteiro Pereira et al., 2022). The most frequently affected areas are the hands, wrists, forearms, neck, and upper back (DiFrancisco-Donoghue et al., 2019; Lindberg et al., 2020). These regions are subjected to repetitive micro-movements reaching 500–600 actions per minute, long durations of static posture, and often inadequate ergonomic setups (Emara et al., 2020). Over time, these conditions can lead to the development of musculoskeletal disorders such as carpal tunnel syndrome and tendinitis, including De Quervain tenosynovitis (Mondal & Nithish, 2024). Furthermore, athletes are prone to upper trapezius tension associated with upper crossed syndrome and chronic pain in the cervical and thoracic spine due to prolonged aberrant posturing (Emara et al., 2020; Franks et al., 2022).

Many players fail to recognize or report early signs of physical discomfort, often dismissing pain or stiffness as a normal part of the gaming experience (DiFrancisco-Donoghue et al., 2019; Madden & Harteveld, 2021). Neglecting symptoms to avoid taking time away from play may lead to worsening conditions that force extended breaks from competitive play (Ahn & Kim, 2024). Unlike traditional athletes who undergo routine medical evaluations, esports players often lack structured health monitoring systems, resulting in delayed identification of musculoskeletal issues (Ahn & Kim, 2024; Mondal & Nithish, 2024). Postural imbalances from prolonged sitting result in uneven muscular development, joint stiffness, and compromised spinal alignment (Mondal & Nithish, 2024). These imbalances can reduce reaction time and fine motor control, which is critical as elite performance hinges on millisecond decisions and rapid actions (Szot et al., 2022). Research confirms that while players may maintain speed during long sessions, they often experience a significant decline in accuracy and inhibitory control (Smithies et al., 2024; Sousa et al., 2020).

Evidence from current literature supports the widespread prevalence of these musculoskeletal issues in the competitive gaming community (DiFrancisco-Donoghue et al., 2019; Monteiro Pereira et al., 2022). A comprehensive scoping review by Pereira et al. (2022) identified that physical complaints are common among players, specifically noting high frequencies of pain in the back, neck, and shoulder regions. However, many athletes currently adopt a reactive approach, dismissing early signs of discomfort and seeking medical attention or implementing recovery exercises only after pain begins to disrupt their training or ability to compete (Monteiro Pereira et al., 2022). Franks et al. (2022) emphasized that these injury risks can be significantly mitigated through proactive clinical interventions, including detailed ergonomic assessments of gaming stations, regular posture evaluations, and the implementation of individualized stretching and strengthening routines (Franks et al., 2022).

Creating an environment where musculoskeletal health is prioritized requires active cooperation between players, coaches, and healthcare professionals (DiFrancisco-Donoghue et al., 2019). Preventive strategies such as equipment adjustments, scheduled movement breaks, targeted physiotherapy, and ergonomic training sessions are not merely supportive tools but necessary elements of long-term player development (Emara et al., 2020). Without such measures, physical strain and repetitive microtrauma can quietly accumulate, threatening the athlete's well-being and the sustainability of their career (DiFrancisco-Donoghue et al., 2019; Emara et al., 2020). Long-term success in esports depends not only on cognitive ability and technical skill but also on physical resilience, as evidenced by research from Trotter et al. (2020) showing that the highest ranked players are often more physically active (Trotter et al., 2020). Furthermore, Yamagata et al. (2022) highlights that as professional gaming evolves into a lifelong career, medical awareness and prevention should mirror this growth to safeguard athletes from devastating health outcomes (Yamagata et al., 2022). By integrating musculoskeletal care into daily routines and building structured medical oversight into the industry, the field can move toward a healthier and more sustainable model for professional competition (DiFrancisco-Donoghue et al., 2019).

10.4 Health Risk Factors Specific to Esports Participation

Esports players are exposed to a broad spectrum of health risks that differ substantially from those typically seen in traditional sports. While the absence of physical collisions might suggest a lower risk profile, the reality is more complex. The primary challenges arise not from bodily contact, but from the physical and mental demands associated with prolonged screen use, extended periods of sitting, repetitive hand and wrist movements, and sustained cognitive effort. These factors contribute to a distinct and multifaceted health profile that requires targeted medical and preventative attention (Franks et al., 2022; Madden & Harteveld, 2021).

One of the most pressing concerns is the sedentary nature of the activity (Lindberg et al., 2020). Professional esports players frequently train or compete for 5.5–10 h a day, often without sufficient physical or mental breaks (DiFrancisco-Donoghue et al., 2019; Lindberg et al., 2020). The sustained seated posture and lack of movement can lead to musculoskeletal issues, including lower back pain, shoulder tension, and stiffness in the neck and hips. Over time, this immobility contributes to muscle imbalances and postural dysfunctions, increasing the likelihood of chronic pain or injury. In addition, prolonged inactivity is associated with reduced cardiovascular fitness and impaired glucose metabolism (Lam et al., 2022). Several studies have noted that esports players may be at greater risk for developing obesity, insulin resistance, or other metabolic syndromes due to low daily energy expenditure, irregular meal patterns, and high-calorie diets dominated by convenience foods (Arslan et al., 2024).

Visual strain is another prominent health concern. Players are required to maintain constant focus on fast-moving digital environments, often under poor lighting conditions and for extended durations (Palanichamy et al., 2020). This leads to digital eye strain, which can manifest as dry eyes, blurry vision, eye fatigue, headaches, and light sensitivity. These symptoms are exacerbated when players do not take visual breaks or fail to follow ergonomic screen placement guidelines (Mondal & Nithish, 2024; Palanichamy et al., 2020). The blue light emitted by gaming monitors and mobile devices is also known to interfere with melatonin production, contributing to circadian rhythm disruption and making it harder to initiate or maintain restful sleep (Alam et al., 2024).

Mental and emotional well-being is equally vulnerable in the esports setting. Players must consistently perform under pressure, often in front of live audiences, online followers, and team stakeholders (Lee et al., 2020; Madden & Harteveld, 2021). This public exposure and constant performance evaluation can foster a state of chronic stress. The intense competitive atmosphere, high personal expectations, and lack of psychological support can lead to emotional fatigue, irritability, mood swings, and even symptoms of anxiety or depression. Burnout is increasingly recognized among professional gamers, particularly those without access to mental health resources or adequate recovery time between tournaments and training cycles (Ahn & Kim, 2024).

Nutrition and hydration are frequently neglected during long sessions. It is common for players to skip balanced meals in favor of fast snacks, sugary drinks, or high-caffeine beverages to maintain alertness (Arslan et al., 2024; Szot et al., 2022). These habits, when repeated over time, can impair concentration, contribute to fatigue, and impact gastrointestinal health. Inadequate hydration can lead to headaches, muscle cramps, and reduced physical and cognitive performance (McCartney et al., 2017). Poor dietary patterns combined with sedentary behavior may further aggravate long-term health outcomes, increasing the risk of preventable chronic diseases (McCartney et al., 2017; Szot et al., 2022). Another emerging concern in esports is the potential misuse of stimulants and performance-enhancing substances (Yamagata et al., 2022). The pressure to maintain sustained attention and rapid reaction times may increase reliance on high doses of caffeine, energy drinks, or even prescription stimulants, raising ethical, regulatory, and health-related questions within competitive gaming environments (Szot et al., 2022; Yamagata et al., 2022).

Social isolation and poor life balance represent critical health risks for athletes in the professional gaming environment. Many players, particularly those aged 14–24, dedicate an average of six to thirteen hours per day to training, competition, and content creation, frequently at the expense of academic progress and meaningful real-life relationships. This intense digital immersion can lead to reduced exposure to real-world social norms and empathy skills, resulting in social withdrawal and the development of "shallow" virtual friendships that may reinforce feelings of social anxiety and isolation (Madden & Harteveld, 2021). Furthermore, a lack of structured daily routines, compounded by grueling training schedules that often extend from midnight until dawn, contributes to significant circadian phase delays, emotional instability, and an increased susceptibility to Internet Gaming Disorder (IGD) and insomnia (Lee et al., 2020; Solmaz et al., 2025).

These health risks often emerge gradually and may remain unnoticed until they begin to affect performance or quality of life. For this reason, the esports community must adopt a more holistic approach to athlete care. This approach should extend beyond injury management to include the promotion of physical activity, balanced nutrition, mental health support, sleep hygiene, and effective time management. Teams, organizations, and healthcare professionals involved in esports should emphasize early education, conduct regular health assessments, and implement multidisciplinary strategies to support the long-term well-being and career sustainability of players (DiFrancisco-Donoghue et al., 2019; Franks et al., 2022).

10.5 Preventive and Protective Strategies in Esports Medicine

As esports continues to expand and gain recognition as a legitimate form of competitive activity, the importance of preventive health strategies has become increasingly evident. While traditional sports benefit from long-established medical frameworks, the field of esports medicine is still emerging and requires tailored approaches that reflect the unique characteristics of gaming culture and practice.

One of the foundational elements of prevention is increasing awareness and education. Players, coaches, and team staff need to be informed about the potential health consequences of prolonged gameplay, including issues related to posture, screen time, sleep quality, nutrition, and mental health. Educational initiatives that integrate this information into team routines, such as onboarding sessions, informational materials, or regular health briefings, can help instill healthy habits from an early stage (Franks et al., 2022). When players understand the risks and recognize early warning signs, they are more likely to take responsibility for their well-being and seek appropriate support before problems become severe (Madden & Harteveld, 2021).

Ergonomics plays a central role in the physical health of esports players, as appropriate evaluation and individualized workstation fitting can reduce injury risk and physical strain (Franks et al., 2022). Prolonged gaming in static seated positions may lead to musculoskeletal problems, particularly affecting the wrists, neck, shoulders, and back (Emara et al., 2020; Franks et al., 2022). Ensuring that each player's setup includes an ergonomic chair, properly positioned monitors (ideally 5–6 in.

below the horizontal line of vision), and supportive peripherals can meaningfully decrease mechanical stress (Franks et al., 2022; Mondal & Nithish, 2024). When combined with maintenance of a neutral spine posture, these measures also contribute to reducing the incidence of tension-type headaches and visual strain (Emara et al., 2020; Mondal & Nithish, 2024).

The integration of regular physical activity into daily routines serves as a critical mechanism for injury prevention and the enhancement of overall health among esports players (Gaasedal et al., 2024; Kari et al., 2021). While competitive gaming does not inherently require intense physical exertion, the sedentary nature of the activity is a documented risk factor for muscular imbalances, impaired blood circulation, and a decline in cardiovascular fitness (Emara et al., 2020; Franks et al., 2022). Engaging in even modest levels of exercise such as stretching, light strength training, or aerobic activity has been shown to improve postural stability, heighten mental alertness, and assist in stress regulation by attenuating the adverse physiological and psychological impacts of prolonged gaming (Gaasedal et al., 2024).

Another key pillar of prevention in esports is sleep hygiene (Bonnar et al., 2019). Irregular training and match schedules, particularly scrims extending late into the night, can severely disrupt circadian rhythms and impair sleep quality (Klier et al., 2022; Solmaz et al., 2025). This is often exacerbated by a gaming culture that prioritizes grinding and late-night play, leading to a circadian phase delay where athletes struggle to initiate sleep at normal hours. Addressing these issues involves promoting consistent sleep and wake times and establishing a dedicated wind-down time to reduce cognitive and physiological arousal before bed (Bonnar et al., 2019). Key strategies include limiting screen exposure at least 30 minutes before sleep, utilizing blue light filtering tools or glasses, managing caffeine intake, and creating environments conducive to rest by removing electronic devices from the sleeping area (Smithies et al., 2024). High-quality sleep is essential as it not only enhances cognitive performance and reaction speed, which is critical for tasks like rapid mouse-click precision, but also supports emotional regulation and immune function by preventing the inflammatory cascades associated with sleep deprivation (Żerek & Sitarek, 2024).

Mental health is a foundational component of sustainable participation and long-term career success in the professional gaming environment (Trotter et al., 2021). Esports players are frequently vulnerable to chronic stress and anxiety due to intense performance pressure, public evaluation from spectators and social media, and a relative lack of social engagement outside of digital spaces (Madden & Harteveld, 2021; Smith et al., 2019). The competitive atmosphere, combined with high internal expectations and interpersonal conflicts, particularly during team feedback sessions, can lead to emotional exhaustion and burnout (Ahn & Kim, 2024; Smith et al., 2019). Establishing access to formalized psychological support through mental coaches or counselors is critical, especially as evidence indicates that esports players often receive significantly less social support compared to traditional athletes (Madden & Harteveld, 2021; Trotter et al., 2021). Furthermore, the integration of mindfulness practices, self-regulation training, and structured downtime enables players to manage psychological demands more effectively by shifting from maladaptive avoidance coping toward more constructive, problem-focused strategies (Smith et al., 2019).

Nutrition and hydration are frequently overlooked in gaming contexts but remain essential for maintaining optimal performance and overall well-being (Ribeiro et al., 2021). Prolonged gaming sessions can disrupt normal eating habits, leading to skipped meals, particularly breakfast, or an increased reliance on fast food and energy drinks (Arslan et al., 2024; Ribeiro et al., 2021). Encouraging balanced meals, healthy snacks, and adequate fluid intake throughout the day can enhance focus, energy levels, and metabolic health while mitigating the risk of cognitive fatigue. Consulting with sports nutritionists to design simple and sustainable dietary plans may further enhance players' readiness and career resilience (Ribeiro et al., 2021).

Creating a culture of health and prevention in esports requires coordinated efforts from individuals, teams, and organizations. Health education, ergonomic adjustments, physical conditioning, psychological support, and structured routines all contribute to long-term sustainability in professional gaming. By proactively addressing these areas, the esports community can help ensure that athletes maintain both high performance and a high quality of life throughout their careers.

10.6 Future Directions in Esports Medicine

Esports medicine is still in its formative years but continues to evolve rapidly in response to the growing recognition of esports as a serious competitive domain (Franks et al., 2022). As the field matures, future directions must address both the gaps in current research and the practical needs of players, teams, and healthcare professionals who support them (Monteiro Pereira et al., 2022). This evolving discipline requires not only the adaptation of knowledge from traditional sports medicine but also the development of new frameworks tailored to the specific demands of digital performance and cognitive endurance (Bonnar et al., 2019; Franks et al., 2022).

One of the most critical steps forward is the creation of standardized health guidelines for esports players, as current research highlights a significant and unmet need for clinical practice protocols in the industry (DiFrancisco-Donoghue et al., 2019; Gaasedal et al., 2024). At present, there is no universally accepted protocol for injury prevention, health monitoring, or performance optimization in gaming, with existing recommendations often being sporadic and largely adapted from office work standards. Developing evidence-based best practices for posture, screen time limits, hydration, sleep routines, and mental health support would provide consistent care standards, moving beyond simple hazard management toward performance optimization (Emara et al., 2020). These guidelines should be endorsed by professional organizations and international governing bodies to encourage widespread implementation and ensure the long-term sustainability of players' careers (Franks et al., 2022; Mondal & Nithish, 2024).

Another promising area is the integration of interdisciplinary medical teams within esports organizations (DiFrancisco-Donoghue et al., 2019; Emara et al., 2020). Similar to traditional sports clubs that employ physiotherapists, psychologists, nutritionists, and performance coaches, esports teams should incorporate healthcare professionals with specialized knowledge of the gaming environment. These professionals can conduct regular screenings, manage acute health problems, and design personalized plans for performance enhancement and recovery (DiFrancisco-Donoghue et al., 2019; Franks et al., 2022). Having medical staff embedded in team structures may also reduce the stigma around seeking help, particularly for mental health challenges (Madden & Harteveld, 2021).

Technology itself will also shape the future of esports medicine. Wearable devices that monitor posture, eye strain, heart rate variability, and sleep quality are becoming increasingly accessible and accurate (Georgiou et al., 2018; Kwasnicki et al., 2018; Simpson et al., 2019). These tools offer real-time feedback that can help players adjust their behaviors proactively. Additionally, digital platforms for remote health tracking, virtual consultations, and personalized wellness programs will likely play a larger role in making healthcare more accessible for players regardless of location (Franks et al., 2022; Madden & Harteveld, 2021).

Education is a fundamental requirement for the future of this field, and it is recommended that esports medicine be integrated into clinical and allied health curricula to prepare future healthcare professionals (DiFrancisco-Donoghue et al., 2019; Franks et al., 2022). Specialized research centers, certifications, and academic conferences will contribute to building a robust knowledge base specifically focused on digital performance and cognitive endurance (Franks et al., 2022). Additionally, educational outreach directed at amateur and youth level players can instill preventive habits like ergonomics and sleep hygiene before health issues arise (Bonnar et al., 2019; Klier et al., 2022). As the industry becomes more competitive and commercialized, the need for long-term athlete development models that follow structured progression pathways, similar to those in traditional sports, continues to grow (Bonnar et al., 2019). These models should encompass age appropriate training volumes, psychological support during transition periods, and health literacy education that evolves alongside competitive experience (Bonnar et al., 2019; Solmaz et al., 2025).

Finally, more robust and diverse research is needed to guide future decisions. Longitudinal studies that examine health trajectories in esports players over time will be essential in understanding risks, outcomes, and effective interventions. Studies that explore differences in health needs based on game genre, age group, gender, and playing level can further refine personalized care approaches. It is important to acknowledge that much of the existing literature in this field is based on cross-sectional designs, self-reported measures, and relatively small or homogeneous samples, which limits causal inference and generalizability (Lindberg et al., 2020; Madden & Harteveld, 2021).

In summary, the future of esports medicine lies in collaboration, innovation, and a commitment to holistic care. By combining insights from science, technology, and clinical practice, stakeholders can build a medical ecosystem that not only supports high performance but also prioritizes long-term health, sustainability, and well-being for everyone involved in the esports world.

References

Ahn, H., & Kim, I. (2024). *An exploratory study on the conceptualization of burnout among the professional esports athletes: Focused on league of legends champions Korea league*. Healthcare.

Alam, M., Abbas, K., Sharf, Y., & Khan, S. (2024). Impacts of blue light exposure from electronic devices on circadian rhythm and sleep disruption in adolescent and young adult students. *Chronobiology in Medicine, 6*(1), 10–14.

Arslan, S., Atan, R. M., Sahin, N., & Ergul, Y. (2024). Evaluation of night eating syndrome and food addiction in esports players. *European Journal of Nutrition, 63*(5), 1695–1704.

Bonnar, D., Lee, S., Gradisar, M., & Suh, S. (2019). Risk factors and sleep intervention considerations in esports: A review and practical guide. *Sleep Medicine Research, 10*(2), 59–66.

DiFrancisco-Donoghue, J., Balentine, J., Schmidt, G., & Zwibel, H. (2019). Managing the health of the eSport athlete: An integrated health management model. *BMJ Open Sport & Exercise Medicine, 5*(1).

Emara, A. K., Ng, M. K., Cruickshank, J. A., Kampert, M. W., Piuzzi, N. S., Schaffer, J. L., & King, D. (2020). Gamer's health guide: Optimizing performance, recognizing hazards, and promoting wellness in esports. *Current Sports Medicine Reports, 19*(12), 537–545.

Franks, R. R., King, D., Bodine, W., Chisari, E., Heller, A., Jamal, F., IV, Luksch, J., Quinn, K., Singh, R., & Solomon, M. (2022). AOASM position statement on esports, active video gaming, and the role of the sports medicine physician. *Clinical Journal of Sport Medicine, 32*(3), e221–e229.

Gaasedal, J., Thøgersen, M. R., Straszek, C. L., & Guldager, J. D. (2024). Young danish esports players physical health, and their opportunities and wishes for physical activity from their esports club: A cross-sectional study. *Journal of Electronic Gaming and Esports, 2*(1).

Georgiou, K., Larentzakis, A. V., Khamis, N. N., Alsuhaibani, G. I., Alaska, Y. A., & Giallafos, E. J. (2018). Can wearable devices accurately measure heart rate variability? *A systematic review. Folia medica, 60*(1), 7–20.

Halson, S. L. (2008). Nutrition, sleep and recovery. *European Journal of Sport Science, 8*(2), 119–126.

Imanian, M., Khatibi, A., Dhamala, M., Moheb, E., Heydarinejad, S., Veisia, E., & Saemi, E. (2025). Verify the effects of esports on cognitive skill: Focusing on decision making. *BMC Sports Science, Medicine and Rehabilitation, 17*(1), 195.

Jenny, S. E., Manning, R. D., Keiper, M. C., & Olrich, T. W. (2017). Virtual (ly) athletes: Where eSports fit within the definition of "sport". *Quest, 69*(1), 1–18.

Kari, T., Siutila, M., & Karhulahti, V.-M. (2021). An extended study on training and physical exercise in esports. In *Research anthology on business strategies, health factors, and ethical implications in sports and eSports* (pp. 716–733). IGI Global Scientific Publishing.

Kelly, S., & Leung, J. (2021). The new frontier of esports and gaming: A scoping meta-review of health impacts and research agenda. Frontiers in sports and active Living, 3, 640362. In.

Ketelhut, S., & Nigg, C. R. (2024). Heartbeats and high scores: Esports triggers cardiovascular and autonomic stress response. *Frontiers in Sports and Active Living, 6*, 1380903.

Klier, K., Seiler, K., & Wagner, M. (2022). Influence of esports on sleep and stress. *Zeitschrift für. Sportpsychologie*.

Koshy, A., Cironis, L., McVey, M., Sousa, A., Ahmad, S. L., Hassan, T., Yuen, K., Douris, P. C., Zwibel, H., & DiFrancisco-Donoghue, J. (2020). An observation of common physiological parameters during esports activity. *International Journal of Esports, 1*(1).

Kwasnicki, R. M., Cross, G. W., Geoghegan, L., Zhang, Z., Reilly, P., Darzi, A., Yang, G. Z., & Emery, R. (2018). A lightweight sensing platform for monitoring sleep quality and posture: A simulated validation study. *European Journal of Medical Research, 23*(1), 28.

Lam, W., Chen, B., Liu, R., Cheung, J., & Wong, D. (2022). Spine posture, mobility, and stability of top mobile esports athletes: A case series. Biology, 11 (5), 737. In.

Lee, S., Bonnar, D., Kim, Y., Lee, Y., Lee, S., Gradisar, M., & Suh, S. (2020). Sleep characteristics and risk factors of Korean esports athletes: An exploratory study. *Sleep Medicine Research, 11*(2), 77–87.

Leis, O., & Lautenbach, F. (2020). Psychological and physiological stress in non-competitive and competitive esports settings: A systematic review. *Psychology of Sport and Exercise, 51*, 101738.

Lindberg, L., Nielsen, S. B., Damgaard, M., Sloth, O. R., Rathleff, M. S., & Straszek, C. L. (2020). Musculoskeletal pain is common in competitive gaming: A cross-sectional study among Danish esports athletes. *BMJ Open Sport & Exercise Medicine, 6*(1), 000799.

Machado, S., & de Oliveira Sant'Ana, L., Cid, L., Teixeira, D. S., Nardi, A. E., Travassos, B., & Monteiro, D. (2025). Effects of a playoff match on competitive anxiety and autonomic regulation in professional esports players. *Clinical Practice and Epidemiology in Mental Health: CP & EMH, 21*, e17450179293069.

Madden, D., & Harteveld, C. (2021). "Constant pressure of having to perform": Exploring player health concerns in esports. Proceedings of the 2021 CHI conference on human factors in computing systems,

McCartney, D., Desbrow, B., & Irwin, C. (2017). The effect of fluid intake following dehydration on subsequent athletic and cognitive performance: A systematic review and meta-analysis. *Sports Medicine-Open, 3*(1), 13.

Mondal, R., & Nithish, G. (2024). Integrated analysis of health dynamics in esports: Injury profiles, intervention strategies, and health optimization protocols. *International Journal of Community Medicine and Public Health, 11*(6), 2484–2499.

Monteiro Pereira, A., Costa, J. A., Verhagen, E., Figueiredo, P., & Brito, J. (2022). Associations between esports participation and health: A scoping review. *Sports Medicine, 52*(9), 2039–2060.

Palanichamy, T., Sharma, M. K., Sahu, M., & Kanchana, D. (2020). Influence of Esports on stress: A systematic review. *Industrial Psychiatry Journal, 29*(2), 191–199.

Ribeiro, F. J., Viana, V. M., Borges, N. P., & Teixeira, V. H. (2021). The emergence of eSports nutrition: A review. *Central European Journal of Sport Sciences and Medicine, 33*(1), 81–95.

Simpson, L., Maharaj, M. M., & Mobbs, R. J. (2019). The role of wearables in spinal posture analysis: A systematic review. *BMC Musculoskeletal Disorders, 20*(1), 55.

Smith, M. J., Birch, P. D., & Bright, D. (2019). Identifying stressors and coping strategies of elite esports competitors. *International Journal of Gaming and Computer-Mediated Simulations (IJGCMS), 11*(2), 22–39.

Smithies, T. D., Toth, A. J., & Campbell, M. J. (2024). The effect of Total sleep deprivation on the cognitive and in-game performance of rocket league Esport players. *Nature and Science of Sleep*, 2183–2204.

Solmaz, S., İnan, M., & Şahin, M. Y. (2025). The moderating effects of physical activity on social anxiety and sleep disturbance: Managing gaming disorder in young e-sports players. *Frontiers in Public Health, 13*, 1544044.

Sousa, A., Ahmad, S. L., Hassan, T., Yuen, K., Douris, P., Zwibel, H., & DiFrancisco-Donoghue, J. (2020). Physiological and cognitive functions following a discrete session of competitive esports gaming. *Frontiers in Psychology, 11*, 1030.

Szot, M., Karpęcka-Gałka, E., Dróżdż, R., & Frączek, B. (2022). Can nutrients and dietary supplements potentially improve cognitive performance also in esports?. Healthcare,

Trotter, M. G., Coulter, T. J., Davis, P. A., Poulus, D. R., & Polman, R. (2020). The association between esports participation, health and physical activity behaviour. *International Journal of Environmental Research and Public Health, 17*(19), 7329.

Trotter, M. G., Coulter, T. J., Davis, P. A., Poulus, D. R., & Polman, R. (2021). Social support, self-regulation, and psychological skill use in e-athletes. *Frontiers in Psychology, 12*, 722030.

Trotter, M. G., Obine, E. A., & Sharpe, B. T. (2023). Self-regulation, stress appraisal, and esport action performance. *Frontiers in Psychology, 14*, 1265778.

Yamagata, K., Yamagata, L. M., & Abela, M. (2022). A review article of the cardiovascular sequalae in esport athletes: A cause for concern? *Hellenic Journal of Cardiology, 68*, 40–45.

Żerek, M., & Sitarek, G. (2024). Sleep quality and immune function: Implications for overall health–A literature review. *Journal of Education, Health and Sport, 75*, 56048–56048.

Chapter 11
(Illicit) Performance Optimization and Ethics

Maximilian A. Friehs

11.1 The Quest for the Competitive Edge

Players play to have fun. In a competitive setting, and likely in general, winning a match against the opponent(s) enhances the experience. So why not try to win? Why not try to gain an advantage over the other team or player? When a player desperately wants to beat the opponent they may search for methods to enhance their performance. Consequently they may train more efficiently (Johanson et al., 2019) or live more healthily (McNulty et al., 2023) as any other player would. However, they may also want to take pharmaceuticals or drugs to be more alert or stimulate their brain with electricity. But now we have to ask the question: are all of those methods created equal? And if they are not; what makes them different and are they potentially problematic? When asking what is permissible and what is not, many people and esports agencies would agree that a healthy lifestyle coupled with effective training, as long as it does not become a soul- and body-destroying grind, is the best way to enhance performance. Conversely, there is agreement that any changes on the software or hardware level (e.g., aim-bots) are not fair and should not be permitted in competitive settings. While Valve-Anti-Cheat software in Counter Strike: Global Offensive (or CS:GO for short/CS2) has been banning people regularly since its inception, in 2014, several professional players were banned for using aim-bots. Furthermore, even though they knew it was a bug and most likely against the rules, in 2020 several CS:GO coaches and teams were penalized for misuse of a free cam that allowed team coaches to see parts of the map they normally would not see and

M. A. Friehs (✉)
Psychology of Conflict Risk and Safety, University of Twente, Enschede, Netherlands
e-mail: m.a.friehs@utwente.nl

Secondary: Visiting Research Fellow, School of Psychology, University College Dublin, Dublin, Ireland

S. Bekir (ed.), *The Psychology of Esports*,
https://doi.org/10.1007/978-3-032-25090-2_11

gather information about enemy movements.[1] While in the aforementioned examples, people can quickly come to clear-cut judgments, there are some instances where a lengthier discussion seems warranted. Two of those potential enhancement methods are pharmacological enhancements (i.e., misusing pharmaceuticals and drugs beyond the intended therapeutic use) and modern consumer-grade non-invasive brain stimulation devices (via for example transcranial direct current stimulation). Although typically pharmaceutical enhancements beyond the therapeutic use is what would be considered "doping", the question arises if other forms of performance optimization are doping as well and where the line can be drawn.

11.1.1 Pharmacological Enhancement

Pharmacological enhancement has been an issue across most sports and has also made its way into esports. In 2015, for example a professional CS:GO/CS2 player, called "Semphis", admitted that he and his team were using prescription medication (specifically the drug Adderall which is usually prescribed to treat attention deficit disorders).[2] Although at the time it was treated as an isolated incident, before and after, across many esports (e.g., World of Warcraft and Overwatch) people were (ab)using pharmaceuticals. When this issue first arose in esports there were no rules and regulations in place yet and every tournament organizer followed their own slightly different ruleset. However, following a community outcry, the Electronic Sports League and others introduced anti-doping policies in esports in line with the regulations put forward by the World Anti-Doping Agency (WADA). The WADA has a strict no-pharmaceuticals policy but allows them to be used if medically necessary: the so-called "therapeutic use exemption" (TUE). Thus, for example while pharmaceuticals such as certain beta-blockers may be allowed for players that are diagnosed with heightened blood pressure, a sports shooter taking beta blockers to slow down their heart rate without a diagnosis will have an unfair advantage. Although in theory, the "therapeutic use exemption" should only affect people that actually need a certain pharmaceutical to overcome a limitation, in reality, people will find a way to gain access to that exemption via illegitimate means (e.g., bribery, forgery) or circumvent the drug-screening process (Dimeo, 2016; Dimeo & Taylor, 2013; Henning & Dimeo, 2015). Thus a harder regulatory stance may be taken, but that may also lead to wrongful denial of medication. Drug testing in esports is still in its infancy and organizations such as the Esports Integrity Commission (ESIC), have compiled a list of prohibited (and mainly stimulating) substances. Importantly, linking it to the TUE, many of the prohibited substances are prescription medications. This therapeutic use

[1] For more examples of banned players in CS:GO refer to the liquipedia page. See for example: https://liquipedia.net/counterstrike/Banned_Players/Other.

[2] For the original interview see https://www.youtube.com/watch?v=XFMY5RQxCpw or as reported at https://www.vice.com/en/article/counter-strike-esports-pro-we-were-all-on-adderall/ or https://www.bbc.com/news/technology-33650486.

clause is not without flaw, as there is evidence that prescriptions for enhancement rather than treatment can be easy to obtain (Grant et al., 2018; Kudlow et al., 2013; Petersen et al., 2015).

Although pharmaceuticals are undoubtably used and a problem, there is little evidence that they actually work reliably across individuals to enhance performance. As Roberts and colleagues put it in their review on cognitive enhancement in healthy adults "there is a user perception that these drugs are effective cognitive enhancers, but this is not supported by the evidence so far". (Roberts et al., 2020). Potentially one of the more convincing studies that do not support the claim that methylphenidate nor modafinil enhance performance was published by Franke et al. (2017). The authors analyzed 3059 chess games and the pharmaceuticals could only enhance performance under specific circumstances and when players were under no time pressure. Since most esports require split-second decision making it is doubtful that the aforementioned pharmaceuticals could be consistently useful for esports players. Thus the same may be true for more physical as well as more cognitive sports (such as esports players): the health-risk of performance enhancing drugs may likely outweigh the benefits (Momaya et al., 2015; Warrier et al., 2024).

11.1.2 Non-Invasive Brain Stimulation

Non-invasive brain stimulation (NIBS) uses external methods like magnetic pulses or electrical currents to modulate brain activity without surgery or incision. Common NIBS techniques include Transcranial Magnetic Stimulation (TMS) and Transcranial Electrical Stimulation (tES), which use magnetic fields or weak electrical currents to alter the excitability of specific brain regions. Generally speaking, although these methods are promising ways to study the basics of cognition (Friehs et al., 2021; He et al., 2024), human language (Floel, 2012; Hartwigsen, 2015; Klaus & Schutter, 2018) and even advance our treatment and understanding of certain illnesses (Liang et al., 2023; Obeso et al., 2016; Yang et al., 2020), they are inherently variable and inconsistent on an individual level (Bergmann & Hartwigsen, 2020). Put differently: even when researchers in the lab try to control for all intervening factors in the lab, there is no guarantee that the same stimulation procedure in two people will result in the same outcome, or that the same procedure applied multiple times to the same person will result in the same outcome. When considering any form of NIBS as a potential enhancement methods in esports this is problematic because of the inherently complexity of not only (most of) the games but also the competitive environment (especially in offline on-stage tournaments). Although there is some evidence to suggest that some forms of NIBS, under specific circumstances, for specific games (or game-like tasks), can enhance performance or alleviate stress, the overall pattern of results across literature is inconsistent (Friehs et al., 2020a; Friehs et al., 2020b; Friehs et al., 2022b; Haccou et al., 2025; Machado et al., 2019; Machado et al., 2022; Sharpe et al., 2025; Toth et al., 2021). Generally speaking one could argue that, the simpler the action required in the game and the more clearly the neurophysiological processes involved are known, the more effective brain stimulation could be in enhancing performance or training effects (Zhuang et al., 2020).

For the sake of argument we may now consider that a form of NIBS is effective and somewhat reliable in the future. Similar to taking pharmaceuticals without medical supervision, applying an electric current or magnetic field to the brain can be dangerous. In research or medical settings the amount of charge applied to the brain is tightly controlled to stay within safety limits. However, since some of the brain stimulation devices (e.g., transcranial direct current simulation) are easy to build at home and commercial products aimed at self-enhancement exist, the safety limits cannot be guaranteed. Furthermore, if any from of NIBS would be reliably effective and enhance player performance beyond what is deemed fair by regulators, controlling for it would be almost impossible. While the WADA requires players to have a biological passport in which key biological variables (e.g., hormone levels) are tracked across time, the inclusion of a brain state criterium is not feasible. If a player has taken a certain drug before a competition, this can be detected in blood or urine samples. However, in order to detect enhancement via NIBS, a constant monitoring of players and their brain states would be required. Furthermore, on a fundamental level, one has to ask whether or not a player that is enhanced by NIBS during their training is still an authentic player and how much that training assistance differs from employing specialized coaches to improve performance. Thus the potential application of NIBS outside of the controlled clinical or research use raises many ethical as well as legal questions (Au, 2022; Greenbaum, 2025).

11.2 Ethical and Regulatory Considerations

In the eyes of agencies such as the WADA or ESIC cheating undermines the "spirit of the sport". However what is cheating and who decides this? Esports here is also a special case because there is not only ESIC or a specific tournament organizer like ESL that has an impact, but also, unlike other sports like chess or basketball, the game that is being played in esports is actually directly owned and developed by a company with a financial motive; or put differently: nobody owns basketball but Riot Games owns League of Legends. In any case, to protect the sport and the health of the players, some regulatory lines must be drawn between ethical performance enhancement and illegal doping. With that being said, research has uncovered that a complex interaction of micro, meso and macro level factors contribute to whether a player decides to dope or not (Blank et al., 2016; Ntoumanis et al., 2014). For example the personal beliefs and attitudes of a player as well as their ultimate goal in sports influence the decision to dope (or not) as much as the culture and the social norms in the sport.

If a specific performance enhancement method is banned then it also needs to be controlled for and tested, and while testing for some things (e.g., manipulations of software or hardware) is comparatively simple, the testing for the (ab)use of pharmaceuticals is difficult. Consequently the number of detected users is likely to be much lower compared to the actual prevalence (De Hon et al., 2015). Furthermore, is it ethical when only a portion of the players have access to legitimate performance enhancement due to, for example, high-costs? Especially because esports and games in general attract such a large variety of players, a one-size-fits-all approach may inevitably fail. Esports is an inclusive space where the initial barriers for participation are low and physiological disparities do not matter. Other "mind sports" such as chess are similar to esports in this regard. The International Chess Federation (FIDE) generally follows WADA guidelines but stresses the importance for of certain stimulants and monitors the players' intake of other non-prohibited substances (e.g., caffeine). Similar to a judge or a jury in court-cases, regulators in esports need to decide how to treat players under investigation and who has the burden of proof and if the player is presumes guilty or innocent from the start.

Furthermore, esports, like any higher sport with a large revenue associated to it, is impacted by sponsors that want to turn a profit. For example, the gaming and esports market is heavily targeted by energy drink companies, such as "Red Bull". Although in isolation this may not be problematic, the heightened consumption of energy drinks may not only be problematic for health reasons but potentially undermines anti-doping policies in general (Frias, 2022; Holden et al., 2019; Wall Tweedie, 2022). Similarly, nootropic manufacturers (e.g., LevlUp) or brain stimulation companies (e.g., Halo) may soon start sponsoring esports teams to increase their public exposure and increase profits. All of these potential enhancers have an inherent health risk associated with them, with no guarantee to actually enhance performance in an individual. So the question needs to be asked whether or not a "potential" enhancer should be regulated or not, and what regulations should apply for "potentially" unhealthy substances. Given that esports itself as well as its regulation is de-centralized and driven by commercial interests of the companies owning the game being played, there is a conflict of interests that may negatively affect the health of both players and consumers of the sport (Chanda et al., 2021; Prakash et al., 2021).

11.3 Concluding Thoughts

Regardless of their relative effectiveness, performance enhancement is a part of competition and the question is what should be allowed (or not) in a competition, either due to ethical or health concerns. Regarding undesired and illicit performance enhancement procedures it will always be an arms race for regulators against potential users with regard to updating the policies, enforcement and the detection procedures. Furthermore, the perception of illicit enhancement (or lack thereof) is as important as the evidence for or against the usage (Friehs et al., 2024; Friehs et al., 2022a; Schubert et al., 2024). As long as esports fans, regulators and players perceive there to be problem, then there is a problem. Online discussions reveal that many community members not only talk about but also disclose personal use of enhancers, often justifying their use when they are considered safe, legal, or medically prescribed. A prevailing belief within the community is that professional esports players already make use of enhancers, reflecting broader mistrust of current drug-testing practices. The esports community differentiates between acceptable and unacceptable performance enhancers: pharmaceuticals, hard drugs, and brain stimulation are viewed as most concerning, whereas caffeine, food supplements, and other socially normalized enhancers are more tolerated. Perceptions of fairness are central to whether competitions and their outcomes are seen as legitimate, but the fragmented and sometimes untransparent regulatory landscape in esports threatens this perception.

References

Au, R. N. (2022). Neuro-Doping, tDCs and chess—are WADA's regulations under threat? *LSE Law Review, 8*(1), 52–119.

Bergmann, T. O., & Hartwigsen, G. (2020). Inferring causality from Noninvasive brain stimulation in cognitive neuroscience. *Journal of Cognitive Neuroscience*. https://doi.org/10.1162/jocn_a_01591

Blank, C., Kopp, M., Niedermeier, M., Schnitzer, M., & Schobersberger, W. (2016). Predictors of doping intentions, susceptibility, and behaviour of elite athletes: A meta-analytic review. *Springerplus, 5*(1), 1333. https://doi.org/10.1186/s40064-016-3000-0

Chanda, S., -, T., & Star, S. (2021). Contouring E-doping: A menace to sportsmanship in E-sports. *Turkish Online Journal of Qualitative Inquiry, 12*(8), Article 8.

De Hon, O., Kuipers, H., & Van Bottenburg, M. (2015). Prevalence of doping use in elite sports: A review of numbers and methods. *Sports Medicine, 45*(1), 57–69. https://doi.org/10.1007/s40279-014-0247-x

Dimeo, P. (2016). The myth of clean sport and its unintended consequences. *Performance Enhancement & Health, 4*(3–4), 103–110. https://doi.org/10.1016/j.peh.2016.04.001

Dimeo, P., & Taylor, J. (2013). Monitoring drug use in sport: The contrast between official statistics and other evidence. *Drugs: Education, Prevention and Policy, 20*(1), 40–47. https://doi.org/10.3109/09687637.2012.713412

Floel, A., & A., F. (2012). Non-invasive brain stimulation and language processing in the healthy brain. *Aphasiology, 26*(9), 1082–1102.

Franke, A. G., Gränsmark, P., Agricola, A., Schühle, K., Rommel, T., Sebastian, A., Balló, H. E., Gorbulev, S., Gerdes, C., Frank, B., Ruckes, C., Tüscher, O., & Lieb, K. (2017). Methylphenidate, modafinil, and caffeine for cognitive enhancement in chess: A double-blind, randomised controlled trial. *European Neuropsychopharmacology, 27*(3), 248–260. https://doi.org/10.1016/j.euroneuro.2017.01.006

Frias, F. J. L. (2022). The "big red bull" in the esports room: Anti-doping, esports, and energy drinks. *Performance Enhancement & Health, 10*(1), Article 100205.

Friehs, M. A., Dechant, M., Vedress, S., Frings, C., & Mandryk, R. L. (2020a). Shocking advantage! Improving digital game performance using non-invasive brain stimulation. *International Journal of Human—Computer Studies*, 102582. https://doi.org/10.1016/j.ijhcs.2020.102582

Friehs, M. A., Güldenpenning, I., Frings, C., & Weigelt, M. (2020b). Electrify your game! Anodal tDCS increases the resistance to head fakes in basketball. *Journal of Cognitive Enhancement, 4*(1), 62–70. https://doi.org/10.1007/s41465-019-00133-8

Friehs, M. A., Frings, C., & Hartwigsen, G. (2021). Effects of single-session transcranial direct current stimulation on reactive response inhibition. *Neuroscience & Biobehavioral Reviews, 128*, 749–765.

Friehs, M. A., Klarkowski, M., Frommel, J., Phillips, C., & Mandryk, R. L. (2022a). Enhanced esports: Community perspectives on performance enhancers in competitive gaming. In *Proceedings of the ACM on Human-Computer Interaction, 6*(CHI PLAY) (pp. 1–29).

Friehs, M. A., Whelan, E., Güldenpenning, I., Krause, D., & Weigelt, M. (2022b). Stimulating performance: A scoping review on transcranial electrical stimulation effects on olympic sports. *Psychology of Sport and Exercise, 59*, Article 102130. https://doi.org/10.1016/J.PSYCHSPORT.2021.102130

Friehs, M. A., Klarkowski, M., Frommel, J., Phillips, C., & Mandryk, R. L. (2024). Fighting fair: Community perspectives on the fairness of performance enhancement in esports. *Frontiers in Sports and Active Living, 6*, 1330755. https://doi.org/10.3389/fspor.2024.1330755

Grant, J. E., Redden, S. A., Lust, K., & Chamberlain, S. R. (2018). Nonmedical use of stimulants is associated with riskier sexual practices and other forms of impulsivity. *Journal of Addiction Medicine, 12*(6), 474.

Greenbaum, D. (2025). Unraveling Ethical Complexities: Transcranial Magnetic Stimulation (TMS) in Non-clinical Settings and the Dilemmas of Neuroenhancement. In V. Dubljević & J. R. Young (Eds.), *TMS and Neuroethics* (pp. 91–119). Springer Nature Switzerland. https://doi.org/10.1007/978-3-031-92401-9_6

Haccou, G. L., Nau, N., Johanson, C., Klooster, J. W. V., & Friehs, M. A. (2025). HD-tDCS in a gaming setting: Effects of polarity and timing in a visuospatial working-memory task. *Journal of Cognitive Enhancement*. https://doi.org/10.1007/s41465-025-00325-5

Hartwigsen, G. (2015). The neurophysiology of language: Insights from non-invasive brain stimulation in the healthy human brain. *Brain and Language*. https://doi.org/10.1016/j.bandl.2014.10.007

He, Q., Geißler, C. F., Ferrante, M., Hartwigsen, G., & Friehs, M. A. (2024). Effects of transcranial magnetic stimulation on reactive response inhibition. *Neuroscience & Biobehavioral Reviews, 157*, Article 105532. https://doi.org/10.1016/j.neubiorev.2023.105532

Henning, A. D., & Dimeo, P. (2015). Questions of fairness and anti-doping in US cycling: The contrasting experiences of professionals and amateurs. *Drugs: Education, Prevention and Policy, 22*(5), 400–409.

Holden, J. T., Kaburakis, A., & Wall Tweedie, J. (2019). Virtue (al) games—Real drugs. *Sport, Ethics and Philosophy, 13*(1), 19–32.

Johanson, C., Gutwin, C., Bowey, J. T., & Mandryk, R. L. (2019). Press pause when you play: Comparing spaced practice intervals for skill development in games. In *CHI PLAY 2019—Proceedings of the Annual Symposium on Computer-Human Interaction in Play*. https://doi.org/10.1145/3311350.3347195

Klaus, J., & Schutter, D. J. L. G. (2018). Non-invasive brain stimulation to investigate language production in healthy speakers: A meta-analysis. *Brain and Cognition, 123*, 10–22. https://doi.org/10.1016/j.bandc.2018.02.007

Kudlow, P. A., Treurnicht Naylor, K., Xie, B., & McIntyre, R. S. (2013). Cognitive enhancement in Canadian medical students. *Journal of Psychoactive Drugs, 45*(4), 360–365. https://doi.org/10.1080/02791072.2013.825033

Liang, C. S., Chou, P. H., Wang, S. C., Sack, A. T., & Su, K. P. (2023). Editorial: Non-invasive brain stimulation in psychiatric disorders: From bench to bedside. *Frontiers in Psychiatry, 13*, 1106558. https://doi.org/10.3389/fpsyt.2022.1106558

Machado, D. G. da S., Unal, G., Andrade, S. M., Moreira, A., Altimari, L. R., Brunoni, A. R., Perrey, S., Mauger, A. R., Bikson, M., & Okano, A. H. (2019). Effect of transcranial direct current stimulation on exercise performance: A systematic review and meta-analysis. *Brain Stimulation, 12*(3), 593-605. https://doi.org/10.1016/j.brs.2018.12.227

Machado, S., Sant'Ana, L. D. O., Travassos, B., & Monteiro, D. (2022). Anodal transcranial direct current stimulation reduces competitive anxiety and modulates heart rate variability in an eSports player. *Clinical Practice & Epidemiology in Mental Health, 18*(1), e174501792209270. https://doi.org/10.2174/17450179-v18-e2209270

McNulty, C., Jenny, S. E., Leis, O., Poulus, D., Sondergeld, P., & Nicholson, M. (2023). Physical exercise and performance in esports players: An initial systematic review. *Journal of Electronic Gaming and Esports, 1*(1), jege.2022–0014. https://doi.org/10.1123/jege.2022-0014

Momaya, A., Fawal, M., & Estes, R. (2015). Performance-Enhancing substances in sports: A review of the literature. *Sports Medicine, 45*(4), 517–531. https://doi.org/10.1007/s40279-015-0308-9

Ntoumanis, N., Ng, J. Y. Y., Barkoukis, V., & Backhouse, S. (2014). Personal and psychosocial predictors of doping use in physical activity settings: A meta-analysis. *Sports Medicine, 44*(11), 1603–1624. https://doi.org/10.1007/s40279-014-0240-4

Obeso, I., Oliviero, A., & Jahanshahi, M. (2016). Editorial: Non-invasive brain stimulation in neurology and psychiatry. *Frontiers in Neuroscience, 10*. https://doi.org/10.3389/fnins.2016.00574

Petersen, M. A., Nørgaard, L. S., & Traulsen, J. M. (2015). Going to the doctor with enhancement in mind–An ethnographic study of university students' use of prescription stimulants and their moral ambivalence. *Drugs: Education, Prevention and Policy, 22*(3), 201–207. https://doi.org/10.3109/09687637.2014.970517

Prakash, N., Modi, T., & Chanda, S. (2021). An analysis of board composition in national sport federations in the USA. *Journal of Sports Law, Policy and Governance, 2*(2), Article 2.

Roberts, C. A., Jones, A., Sumnall, H., Gage, S. H., & Montgomery, C. (2020). How effective are pharmaceuticals for cognitive enhancement in healthy adults? A series of meta-analyses of cognitive performance during acute administration of modafinil, methylphenidate and D-amphetamine. *European Neuropsychopharmacology, 38*, 40–62. https://doi.org/10.1016/j.euroneuro.2020.07.002

Schubert, M., Güre, A., & Haller, N. (2024). Performance-enhancement in esports—Players' perspectives on prevalence, legitimacy, governance and regulations. *Performance Enhancement & Health, 12*(3), Article 100290. https://doi.org/10.1016/j.peh.2024.100290

Sharpe, B. T., Sharpe, A., Poulus, D., Obine, E. A. C., King, R., Birch, P. D. J., & Gladwin, T. E. (2025). Enhancing pressurized esports performance: A pilot study on the combined effects of transcranial direct current stimulation and arousal reappraisal. *Anxiety, Stress, & Coping*, 1–17. https://doi.org/10.1080/10615806.2025.2502792

Toth, A. J., Ramsbottom, N., Constantin, C., Milliet, A., & Campbell, M. J. (2021). The effect of expertise, training and neurostimulation on sensory-motor skill in esports. *Computers in Human Behavior, 121*, Article 106782. https://doi.org/10.1016/j.chb.2021.106782

Wall Tweedie, J. (2022). Esports: There is a "red bull" in the room but it's a jungle out there. *Performance Enhancement & Health, 10*(1), Article 100215. https://doi.org/10.1016/j.peh.2021.100215

Warrier, A. A., Azua, E. N., Kasson, L. B., Allahabadi, S., Khan, Z. A., Mameri, E. S., Swindell, H. W., Tokish, J. M., & Chahla, J. (2024). Performance-Enhancing drugs in healthy athletes: An umbrella review of systematic reviews and meta-analyses. *Sports Health: A Multidisciplinary Approach, 16*(5), 695–705. https://doi.org/10.1177/19417381231197389

Yang, C. C., Mauer, L., Völlm, B., & Khalifa, N. (2020). The effects of non-invasive brain stimulation on impulsivity in people with mental disorders: A systematic review and explanatory meta-analysis. *Neuropsychology Review, 30*(4), 499–520. https://doi.org/10.1007/s11065-020-09456-2

Zhuang, W., Yin, K., Zi, Y., & Liu, Y. (2020). Non-invasive brain stimulation: Augmenting the training and performance potential in esports players. *Brain Sciences*. https://doi.org/10.3390/brainsci10070454

Chapter 12
The State of Esports Analytics: A Thematic Analysis of Tools, Challenges, and Emerging Directions

Laura Herrewijn and Sven Charleer

12.1 Introduction

Esports has matured into a global, professionalized industry where data have become an increasingly competitive advantage to teams (Rubleske et al., 2020; Werder, 2022). Dedicated analysts and coaches can help teams make proper use of this data for match preparation, post-match reviewing, and decision making on game and team strategy. However, despite this growing reliance on analytics, the tools available to esports teams remain fragmented, and in-house solutions often are not streamlined and aligned with day-to-day coaching practice. Metrics overlays, summaries, and post-match statistics are valuable, but these approaches rarely support current workflows and require teams to combine data from multiple sources and inconsistent formats, making them often useless under time pressure.

At the same time, data capture and sensing technologies have advanced thoroughly, especially in the development of psychophysiological methods that can capture people's objective bodily responses. Recent progress in multimodal sensing has made the simultaneous measurement of signals like electrodermal activity, heart rate (variability), and gaze behavior (i.e. eye tracking) more precise, portable, and computationally efficient (Ban et al., 2022; Sáez-García et al., 2024; Schmälzle & Grall, 2020). Innovations in biocompatible sensor materials and integrated data pipelines now make it possible to monitor player physiology in a continuous and non- or less-invasive way (Ban et al., 2022; Sáez-García et al., 2024; Schmälzle & Grall, 2020), allowing for more ecologically valid and context-aware measurement of player states.

L. Herrewijn (✉) · S. Charleer
Media, Design & IT, AP University of Applied Sciences and Arts, Antwerp, Belgium
e-mail: laura.herrewijn@ap.be

S. Charleer
e-mail: sven.charleer@ap.be

S. Bekir (ed.), *The Psychology of Esports*,
https://doi.org/10.1007/978-3-032-25090-2_12

However, although academic research has begun integrating such psychophysiological measures in esports studies in recent years (Berga et al., 2023; Leis & Lautenbach, 2020; Sadowska et al., 2023; Smerdov et al., 2021), their practical value in esports remains underexplored (Navarro-Lucena et al., 2025; Welsh et al., 2023) and without careful integration into existing workflows, such data risks of being perceived as curiosities and privacy threatening rather than actionable sources of insight (Seif El-Nasr & Kleinman, 2020).

To find better use of these data and improve its acceptance, this paper presents the findings from *BEAT* (Better Esports Analytics for Teams), an applied research project at AP University of Applied Sciences and Arts Antwerp focusing on how esports analytics tools are used in practice and where they fall short. Drawing on semi-structured interviews with analysts, coaches, players, and analytics providers from (semi-)professional esports teams and organizations, complemented by an analysis of commercial and community analytics platforms, the project identifies recurring challenges, needs, and expectations within the esports analytics ecosystem. This work offers a practice-oriented perspective on the current state of esports analytics and offers design implications for future analytics systems that move beyond current approaches and take into account teams' workflow to better support decision-making.

12.2 Background and Motivation

Current research on esports analytics focuses on gameplay modeling, visualization, sports science, and human–computer interaction and demonstrates the analytical potential of game metrics. While there is a strong focus on performance prediction and statistical pattern detection (Raetze et al., 2025; Rubleske et al., 2020), these approaches are often developed using public or non-professional datasets and offer limited insights into how analytical results are generated, interpreted, and applied within professional team contexts.

Dashboards and visual analytics systems can support sensemaking, reduce cognitive load, and foster trust when designed with users' goals and constraints in mind but when applied to esports, work has predominantly focused on spectator-facing tools, showing how real-time visualizations help audiences interpret fast-paced gameplay (Charleer et al., 2018a; Wang et al., 2025). Analysts, coaches, and players face similar challenges as their use case is embedded in time-critical decision-making contexts. Thus, dashboards could be leveraged similarly as a cognitive instrument for rapid interpretation, coordination, and tactical discussion under competitive pressure.

Because of the large diversity in esports games, esports teams' needs differ widely though (Białecki et al., 2024). On top of that, to support the development of dashboards and visualizations, we must first address the lack of standardized data formats and interoperable pipelines. Game data is typically exposed through proprietary APIs, replay files, or partial event streams that vary in granularity and stability, forcing analysts to rely on brittle workflows that frequently break with game updates (Charleer et al., 2018b). By contrast, standardization efforts in traditional sports and learning analytics have enabled richer tool ecosystems (Alonso-Fernández et al., 2022).

Furthermore, psychophysiological data can deepen our understanding of performance and stress in competitive esports: esports gameplay elicits interesting and measurable autonomic and endocrine responses, including increased heart rate, cortisol release, and altered heart rate variability, reflecting heightened arousal (Leis et al., 2024a; Leis & Lautenbach, 2020; Sadowska et al., 2023; Smerdov et al., 2021; Welsh et al., 2023). Additionally, recent research has begun to incorporate electrodermal activity as a complementary measure of autonomic arousal as well. For instance, Berga et al. (2023) showed that in-game events (e.g. kills, deaths, objective captures) can significantly modulate players' electrodermal and cardiac activity, with losing players showing stronger stress responses. While such studies show that there is a lot of potential for psychophysiological metrics to complement traditional performance analytics, they also reveal key challenges related to data interpretation, as arousal may signify both adaptive engagement and stress depending on both situational and individual factors. Finally, the methodological integration of psychophysiological data in esports research remains in an early stage as well. Standardized analytical frameworks that link psychophysiological signals to cognitive processes or in-game performance are still scarce, and more consistent approaches are needed to translate them into insights that are actually meaningful and actionable within esports contexts (Leis & Lautenbach, 2020; Welsh et al., 2023).

With this in mind, the *BEAT* research project (AP University of Applied Sciences and Arts Antwerp, 2023–2025) adopted a practice-oriented perspective on esports analytics. Rather than advancing new models or performance metrics, the project was guided by the question of how analytics systems can be designed to effectively support analysts, coaches, and players within the temporal, organizational, and competitive constraints of professional esports.

12.3 Practice-Grounded Research Approach

BEAT followed a design-based research approach (Reimann, 2011) with a user-centered, iterative design process to understand user needs, and explore possible solutions which are continually tested and approved by the target audience. This paper presents the results of the initial steps of this process: a qualitative, mixed-method approach grounded in professional practice to lay a foundation before moving onto design and implementation. Specifically, we conducted semi-structured interviews with analysts, coaches, players, and analytics providers currently or formerly affiliated with professional esports teams and organizations, including *100 Thieves*, *Team BDS*, *G2*, *Complexity*, *Heroic*, *Skybox Technologies*, and *GRID Esports*, focusing on day-to-day workflows, tooling choices, and perspectives on gameplay analytics and emerging psychophysiological data.

In parallel, we examined a range of commercial and community-created analytics platforms such as *GRID Esports*, *Skybox Edge*, *Augment*, *Blitz*, *Leetify*, *Leaguepedia*, *Ballchasing*, etcetera, to understand the current tooling landscape for esports games such as *League of Legends*, *Valorant*, *Counter-Strike 2*, and *Rocket League*. By analyzing current tools, we discovered recurring patterns, overlaps, and gaps across platforms, as well as emerging best practices. Both interview transcripts and platform analysis notes were evaluated using thematic analysis (Clarke & Braun, 2017) to identify shared challenges, expectations, and opportunities shaping esports analytics practice.

12.4 Insights from Professional Esports Analytics Practice

Prior work in esports research has investigated performance measurement frameworks and the conceptual space around what gets quantified, highlighting both the diversity of performance variables and limitations of conventional statistics in capturing complex competitive behaviors. For instance, Leis et al. (2024b) review performance indicators which illustrate the need for multidimensional measures that align with practitioner understandings of performance, but does not cover actual analytical practices used by teams. Therefore, our thematic analysis provides a new view of how the use of esports analytics specifically is practiced within professional teams. Rather than revealing a single dominant workflow, the findings highlight a fragmented ecosystem shaped by differences in game titles, competitive tiers, team resources, and individual expertise. Across interviews, analysts and coaches consistently described a tension between what is analytically possible and what is practically feasible within the constraints of time, tooling, and data availability. To unpack this tension, the findings are structured around three perspectives: the current state of esports analytics practice, the key challenges that constrain it, and the directions in which analysts and coaches expect the field to evolve.

12.4.1 Current State of Esports Analytics

We begin by outlining the current state of esports analytics practice, focusing on how in-game data is collected, processed, and used within professional teams.

Data Collection Tools and Platforms

Most teams rely on external platforms such as *GRID Esports* and *Ballchasing* to access in-game data, often supplemented by internally developed scripts or tools. These platforms form the backbone of many analytics workflows providing data across different games and genres, but add an extra layer of cost to the teams depending on the required scope and depth of the analytical tools.

Specialized tools like *Skybox Edge,* on the other hand, provide more advanced, game-specific functionality, particularly for *Counter-Strike*, such as 2D/3D replay analysis, automated match preparation, and voice communication details that are aligned with gameplay events. Analysts reported that such tools can reduce analysis time substantially ("*It can reduce what was ten hours work per match to three*"). However, these benefits are tightly coupled to specific titles and do not generalize across games or contexts.

Custom In-House Tools

Several analysts described building custom tools to compensate for not only the cost but also the limitations in commercial platforms ("*They give us data, but we need to process it. And I write my own app and the team uses it*"). These solutions ranged from lightweight scripts and spreadsheets to fully fledged web applications developed in-house to help them merge data from multiple sources ("*At the start you can use spreadsheets, but if you want to improve, you need to give the team more features*"). One analyst, for example, developed a *League of Legends* web tool combining data from *Leaguepedia* and *GRID Esports* to help the team with easier opponent scouting and pattern analysis.

This reliance on in-house tooling reflects both necessity for better solutions and team expertise with analysts frequently emphasizing that off-the-shelf tools rarely align with or suffice for their team's strategic focus and coaching style. As a result, customization becomes a core part of the analytics workflow rather than an exception.

Roles and Expertise

Across teams, responsibilities are typically distributed between analysts, assistant coaches, and head coaches although boundaries between roles are often vague. Analysts focus primarily on data collection, processing, and interpretation, while coaches will translate these insights into strategic decisions and feedback. In smaller teams, these roles often overlap and require individuals to balance technical analysis with tactical and communicative responsibilities ("*The separation between assistant coach and data analyst is not always strict. In some teams, especially with smaller budgets, those roles are combined into one person*").

This variety in division of labor strongly influences how analytics outputs should be designed, as expertise within the team, team size, and available resources define whether teams not only benefit from analytics but also have the means to process raw data and detailed statistics. In many cases, shrinking budgets put a further strain on this capacity ("*We used to have a small dev team, but now I'm the only analyst left. Most teams just don't have the budget for that anymore*"). As a result, teams are often better off with distilled, interpretable representations rather than complex or data-heavy outputs.

How Teams Use Data

According to our participants, data is primarily used for match preparation and post-match review. This includes playstyle analysis of the team and that of opposing teams as preparation for upcoming matches. Teams also attempt to identify recurring tactical patterns. In practice, this means that analysts will manually extract and analyze gameplay data and watch hours of videos to generate insights ("*I spend a lot of time watching early game VODs from opponents and trying to find punishable tendencies. A lot of that work is still manual*"). Those in turn must be translated into concise reports or presentations which coaches can leverage during player review sessions and team training ("*If you show players pure data, they won't understand it. You need to show it in a way they can actually use*").

Within these workflows, the interpretation of raw data plays an important role in tactical decision-making. Not only the validity of the conclusions, but also the process of turning data into actionable and comprehensible insights becomes a difficult and time-sensitive task. While it is important to understand what is measurable, a more important aspect of data analytics in esports comes down to what can be processed and which knowledge can be transferred, and how this can be effectively integrated into team discussions and the decision-making processes.

12.4.2 Challenges in Esports Analytics

In addition to providing insight into current analytics data gathering and knowledge transfer workflows, the interviews also surfaced a set of recurring challenges faced by analysts and coaches.

Manual Processing and Limited Automation

The continued reliance on manual data collection and processing provides a barrier for many teams. While automation is increasingly present (e.g. automated scouting reports, win-probability models, replay parsing), large parts of the analytical workflow remain time demanding, with many analysts often relying solely on large and brittle spreadsheets ("*Most of what I do is very manual. I download the CSV files, copy-paste everything into Excel, and then I start working from there. [...] It's basically just Excel sheets with a lot of formulas that I built myself*"). This is particularly true for teams without access to specialized or custom-built tools.

Participants mentioned that tasks such as extracting jungle paths, compiling opponent tendencies, or preparing review materials are demanding, time intensive tasks ("*A lot of the work I've done for coaches is just finding the moments for them: here are the timestamps, here's exactly what you want to watch*"). This time could be better used interpreting patterns, discussing implications with coaches, or exploring alternative strategies. As a result, participants are eager to see more of these tasks automated, which would result in better use of the limited time and resources teams struggle with.

Lack of Statistical Grounding and Standardization

From our interviews we learn that analysts often have limited formal training in statistics, leading to uncertainty about the validity and robustness of their analytical methods. Consequently, teams often rely on relatively simple approaches, such as descriptive statistics, correlations, and linear trends ("*Right now I'm using very simple models, like linear regression with basic statistics*"). While this makes translation of insights of the data to the team easier, the analysts also believe that advanced tools could provide deeper insights that could be beneficial to the success of the team.

At the same time, there is little to no standardization across teams and tools. Some organizations develop highly customized analytics pipelines, while others depend on basic metrics provided by third-party platforms. This uneven landscape creates a gap between teams' analytic capacity ("*Teams in the ERLs usually work with very standard things, while teams in the LEC or NA are automating a lot more*"). This certainly applies to smaller teams, where the lack of shared standards creates a high barrier to entry and reinforces inequalities in their analytical capability.

Fragmentation and Missing Data

Furthermore, access to gameplay data remains inconsistent and game dependent. While games such as *Counter-Strike* give the user detailed replay files containing every state change in the game, titles such as *League of Legends* provide limited ways to access the game data. Even when going through professional platforms such as *GRID Esports*, certain datapoints (e.g. creep movement) are not exposed, while being of major importance to proper analysis of *League of Legends* tactics. Analysts noted that publishers are often reluctant to release additional datasets due to technical, commercial, or infrastructural constraints ("*Riot doesn't share creep movement in their data. I asked them about it, and they said it's possible, but it's too much data to store, so they don't want to provide it*").

These gaps force analysts to rely on incomplete data, manual annotation during game time, or video-based analysis, each of which introduces noise and uncertainty, and are time consuming. Data scarcity is especially problematic when teams wish to scout for lower-tier or emerging talent ("*Once you get below tier one, it becomes really hard to find any information at all. A lot of the time the VODs are just gone*"). With low to non-existing tournament coverage and limited player data, only games with extensive data logging such as *Counter-Strike* can give insight into unknown players' skill and activities. Even then, scouring the web for these "demo" files and replays is a daunting task that not every team can afford to spend time on.

Privacy and Data Security

Concerns around privacy and data security were repeatedly emphasized, particularly in relation to scrim data ("*If you use an external company, scrim data can be leaked, and organizations are scared about that*"). Understandably, teams are highly protective of tactical information and expressed reluctance to upload sensitive data such as internal skirmishes and training data to external platforms due to the risk of leaks ("*A lot of teams are very paranoid about scrim data getting leaked, because it puts you at such a huge disadvantage*"). With the rise of the use of AI models training on available online data, risks are even higher as such models could learn tactics and get insights on their teams' playstyle.

These concerns directly impact the willingness to adopt new tools. Even if platforms offer clear benefits to the teams' analytical ability, these platforms may be avoided if teams cannot guarantee data isolation and confidentiality. For emerging data sources such as psychophysiological signals, these issues are further amplified. Transparency, security, and competitive trust are therefore of extreme importance when designing tools and platforms if we wish to see a broad adoption.

12.4.3 Expected Trends in Esports Analytics

Finally, we describe how analysts and coaches expect esports analytics to develop in the future.

Increased Automation and AI Integration

Analysts expect automation and AI-assisted analysis to play a growing role, particularly in handling repetitive and time-intensive tasks such as video analysis and strategic pattern recognition. Several interviewees already experiment with machine learning techniques to support win-probability estimation, opponent pattern detection, or early identification of strategic tendencies during matches ("*My goal is to create some AI or machine learning tools, for example to estimate win probabilities or to help with scouting players*"). However, due to their limited knowledge of AI and the severe time pressure and lack of resources, advancement in this domain remains limited ("*I would really like to work with someone who actually knows statistics or AI, because I feel like there's a lot more that could be done*").

Importantly, AI is not viewed as a replacement for analyst expertise. Instead, analysts emphasized its value as a filtering and prioritization mechanism. Instead of scanning through hours of videos, AI could highlight specific moments, patterns, or anomalies that warrant closer inspection ("*If something could automatically flag things that are unusual or worth looking at, that would save coaches a lot of time*"). This way, analysts can spend more time on the details, translating specific events in actionable items. As such, future AI integration is expected to favor interpretable, task-specific applications that complement existing workflows rather than fully automated decision-making systems.

Trust remains a central concern. Black box approaches, often the case as companies wish to keep their proprietary models private, cannot be trustworthy based on the track record of today's large data companies. Patches often change the game and its metadata, meaning the reliability of the tools will depend on how well every single game and its changes are followed up and implemented by such companies.

Advanced Visualizations and Player-Focused Insights

Data visualization approaches clearly help users understand and explore data but also assist in conveying messages and leveraging data to convince people of specific insights (Charleer et al., 2017; Claes & Vande Moere, 2015). A clear trend across interviews is the growing emphasis on visualization as the primary medium through which analytics insights are communicated. Participants noted that raw statistics are rarely effective when working with coaches and players, particularly under time pressure ("*A lot of what I do is just preparing things in a way that coaches can look at quickly, because they don't have time to go through everything themselves*"). Instead, visual abstractions such as heatmaps, pathing diagrams, and comparative timelines are essential for conveying tactical meaning quickly and convincingly ("*For things like jungle pathing or warding, I mostly use heat maps because it's easy to read for players*").

Therefore, existing platforms focus on reducing analysis time and offering customizable, role-specific reports. This shift reflects that esports teams require analytics systems that support communication and discussion. While data exploration is necessary for analysts, delivering and presenting the message to coaches and players is what eventually creates the needed impact in team behavior and play. Analysts hope future tools will offer greater flexibility in how insights are framed, enabling them to tailor visualizations to their specific needs.

Psychophysiological Data and Player Performance

Research interest in psychophysiological data (such as eye tracking, electrodermal activity and heart rate (variability)) is growing, particularly in relation to player focus/performance and stress (Berga et al., 2023; Leis & Lautenbach, 2020; Sadowska et al., 2023; Smerdov et al., 2021; Welsh et al., 2023). Most interviewees expressed clear interest in such measures as well. However, these initiatives had typically not progressed beyond early consideration ("*We talked about using trackers or smartwatches for stress or sleep, but right now it's kind of dead*") or small-scale experimentation ("*We actually got eye trackers at one point, but nothing really happened with it*").

Analysts expressed uncertainty about how to analyze and interpret psychophysiological signals as tools did not seem mature enough to use as is. They were also uncertain of their meaningfulness related to in-game events and performance data. As a result, psychophysiological data was described as promising but would require further research to understand its benefits.

Expansion to Lower Competitive Tiers and New Games

Finally, analysts anticipate a gradual expansion of analytics tooling toward lower competitive tiers and newer game titles. As current solutions are often tailored to elite teams with substantial resources, this leaves semi-professional and emerging teams underserved. Interviewees highlighted the need for affordable tools and standardization across games to lower the barriers to entry ("*It would be really helpful if there was something more organized for lower tiers, where data is actually stored and accessible*").

This includes simplified data ingestion and uniform data formats, and workflows and dashboards that can adapt to different games and tournament structures. With more esports teams across ranks receiving access to analytics, this will help mature the esports scene through sustainable talent development and more diverse competitive ecosystems.

12.5 Design Implications for Esports Analytics Systems

Building on the state-of-the-art and our findings from our thematic analysis, we put forward a set of design goals to help teams, esports data providers, and researchers design and create useful applications and systems that fit within and adhere to the complexity of teams' workflows.

12.5.1 Toward a Standardized Esports Data Exchange Format

Analysts spend a lot of effort to manually merge datasets originating from different sources. Video analysis needs to be logged, events can sometimes be extracted through demo files or APIs, resulting in multiple data formats that require consolidation and integration into e.g. spreadsheets or in-house tools. This fragmentation slows down analysis and constrains what analysts can feasibly explore within the limited time. While efforts are made to standardize data through providers such as *GRID Esports*, esports analytics remain largely siloed.

A standardized esports data format could address this structural bottleneck. Comparable to initiatives such as *Opta* in traditional sports (Liu et al., 2013) or xAPI in learning (Lim, 2018), such a format would enable analytics platforms, coaching tools, psychophysiological data systems and game-specific APIs to be developed and interoperate more seamlessly (Charleer et al., 2018b). Shared identifiers (e.g. players, matches), consistent metadata, and robust export mechanisms across game versions (i.e. patch acgnostic) could result in long term solutions instead of constant ad-hoc scripts and manual reconciliation. Importantly, standardization can create a platform for an ecosystem of more affordable and accessible tools which lower the barrier for smaller teams.

12.5.2 Integrating Psychophysiological Data as a First-Class Modality

Analysts expressed clear interest in psychophysiological data, yet the interviews revealed substantial uncertainty regarding its interpretation, practical value, and appropriate use in esports contexts. They described the possibilities of psychophysiological insights as promising, but also emphasized that their meaning depends on how well it can be connected to gameplay context; an observation that also mirrors ongoing methodological debates in esports research (Leis & Lautenbach, 2020; Welsh et al., 2023). Linking changes in psychophysiology (e.g. electrodermal activity, heart rate, eye gaze) to specific in-game events could make such data a lot more interpretable and relevant for performance analysis, which also echoes findings from Berga et al.'s

(2023) case study that showed how in-game events in *League of Legends* significantly modulate players' electrodermal and cardiac activity.

Building on this, the interviews also pointed to a gap between the capabilities of the technology and its analytical maturity. Although it is increasingly possible for esports teams to collect psychophysiological data in a non-invasive way (e.g. through eye trackers, smart watches), analysts felt that the current tools still lack the visualization and integration features that are needed to turn such data into actionable insights. What is still missing but direly needed are clear analytical frameworks and accessible interfaces. As a result, most teams of the interviewed analysts had not moved beyond early experimentation or internal discussions about using these technologies, even in cases where devices had already been purchased or briefly tested.

To make psychophysiological data truly useful, visual and analytical solutions are thus needed that situate psychophysiological signals within gameplay context. For example, mapping electrodermal activity (see Fig. 12.1) peaks to moments of heightened arousal during key competitive events (such as clutch situations, sudden team fights, critical decision points) could help analysts and coaches understand when players experience elevated stress or cognitive load and how these reactions affect team coordination and performance. To realize this potential, intuitive visualization and data integration tools are essential though. Data visualizations such as timeline overlays, annotated replays, or dashboards with aggregated summaries could help translate such complex psychophysiological data into interpretable patterns that can support reflection and post-match analysis. Finally, echoing broader ethical concerns about data-driven technologies in games (Seif El-Nasr & Kleinman, 2020), privacy-preserving design is essential: psychophysiological data are inherently sensitive and such information cannot leak to competitors.

12.5.3 Automating Repetitive Analysis Without Obscuring Insight

Manual processing remains a central part of everyday esports analytics work. Analysts described spending substantial time on repetitive tasks, usually in the form of video annotation or extracting data from files and APIs. With this data they can for example extract jungle paths (*League of Legends*), compile scouting summaries, generate heatmaps of player locations, and track other patterns, but often under significant time pressure. Reducing this manual workload therefore helps create space for more time to spend on deeper interpretation, strategic reasoning, and most importantly communication with coaches and players.

However, automation must be designed carefully. Black box models that produce outputs without transparent reasoning risk undermining analyst trust (Ribeiro et al., 2016), particularly in high-stakes competitive environments. First of all, automation should be robust across patches. If prediction models are for example trained on specific game versions, chances are that new game updates will break their logic

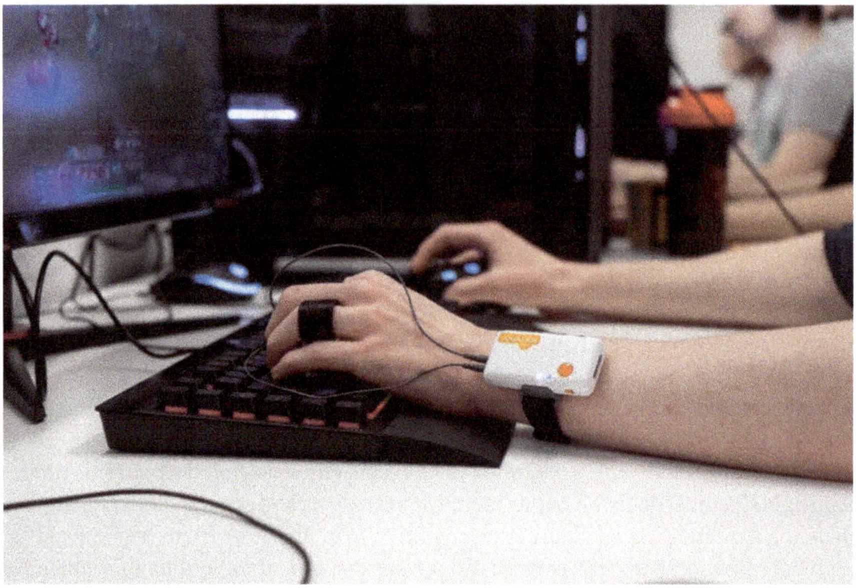

Fig. 12.1 Recording of electrodermal activity through the Shimmer3 GSR + sensing device (Shimmer Sensing), giving insight into stress and excitement in esports players while performing

and output. These platforms will have to be kept up-to-date simultaneously with the release schedule of game studios to expect any kind of acceptance by esports teams. Secondly, these tools will also require exposing intermediate steps providing analysts with insights of their inner working, not just to help understand the resulting data but also to build trust with its users (Gutiérrez et al., 2019).

12.5.4 Designing Visualizations for Action Under Time Pressure

While analysts may work with detailed statistics, coaches and players require comprehensible and effective analytical results as they often lack time and cannot afford to dig deep into the data. Review sessions are often short and decisions need to be made quickly. Interviewed analysts repeatedly emphasized that raw data is too complex and simple statistics are rarely sufficient in these contexts as they are often misaligned with the needs of the team.

As a result, effective esports analytics tools should require visual abstractions that highlight tactical meaning rather than raw metrics. For example, route diagrams, comparative timelines, heatmaps, and decision-flow visualizations allow recurring patterns to be identified at a glance (Glombik et al., 2025; Peché et al., 2025), reducing the need for statistical explanation. Importantly, these representations need to account for different roles within the team: analysts, coaches, and players engage with data at different levels of detail and for different purposes. Either role-specific tools or dashboard designs following an "overview first, details on demand" approach (Shneiderman, 2003) can ensure the data and reasoning are explorable and understandable by all parties.

12.5.5 Embedding Co-Design as an Ongoing Practice

One of the clearest patterns across interviews was that tools do not often meet the needs of the analysts and teams using them. Teams often fall back on building their own spreadsheets, scripts, and even dashboards to bridge the gap. This practice underscores a critical implication: co-design is important if tools wish to remain relevant over time.

Rather than involving users at a late stage, tool creation should follow an iterative approach where analysts, coaches, and players are involved from the start of design and through the entire development process. This participatory design approach also often results in higher acceptance rate (Hornbæk & Hertzum, 2017). Analysts should be involved in shaping the export tools, exploratory interactive visualizations, and explanatory dashboards, while the entire team should be involved in the design of privacy controls from the outset. Coaches and players must likewise be involved to ensure that insights are interpretable and relevant.

12.6 Conclusion

As esports continues to professionalize and data becomes central to competitive success, providing meaningful analytical support for teams becomes increasingly important. In this chapter we take a first step toward addressing this challenge by investigating how esports analytics is currently practiced and by identifying limitations in existing tooling and their uses. Findings suggest that although analysts and coaches rely heavily on data, current systems remain fragmented, manual, and are insufficiently aligned with everyday team workflows.

Our results show that there is clear interest in more advanced analytics, including automation, AI-supported pattern detection, and psychophysiological sensing. However, such innovations must be carefully integrated: automation should support rather than replace analyst expertise; psychophysiological data must be meaningfully connected to gameplay context; and visualizations must prioritize interpretability and trust. Otherwise, these tools risk increasing cognitive load, undermining decision-making, and ultimately failing to gain acceptance within the esports community. Based on these findings, we have outlined key design directions for esports analytics, including standardized and interoperable data formats, explanatory visualizations, transparent automation, integration of multimodal data, and the inclusion of teams in the design and development process. Our work highlights the opportunity for games research communities and analytics companies to contribute to the design and development of esports analytics by grounding technological innovation in real-world practice. By designing systems that acknowledge competitive constraints, esports teams' organizational realities, and the interpretive expertise of analysts and coaches, we hope to see an advancement in tools that support informed decision-making in professional esports. This chapter reports on the exploratory phase of a design-based research trajectory; subsequent prototyping and evaluation are needed to validate the design implications in practice. Nonetheless, the diversity of games, competitive tiers, and organizational contexts represented in our sample offers a grounded basis for the design implications we propose.

References

Alonso-Fernández, C., Calvo-Morata, A., Freire, M., Martínez-Ortiz, I., & Fernández-Manjón, B. (2022). Game learning analytics: Blending visual and data mining techniques to improve serious games and to better understand player learning. *Journal of Learning Analytics, 9*(3), 32–49. https://doi.org/10.18608/jla.2022.7633

Ban, S., Lee, Y. J., Kim, K. R., Kim, J.-H., & Yeo, W.-H. (2022). Advances in materials, sensors, and integrated systems for monitoring eye movements. *Biosensors, 12*(11), 1039. https://doi.org/10.3390/bios12111039

Berga, D., Pereda, A., Filippi, E. D., Nandi, A., Febrer, E., Reverte, M., & Russo, L. (2023). *Measuring arousal and stress physiology on esports, a league of legends case study* (arXiv: 2302.14269). arXiv. https://doi.org/10.48550/arXiv.2302.14269

Białecki, A., Michalak, B., & Gajewski, J. (2024). Esports training, periodization, and software—a scoping review. *Applied Sciences, 14*(22), 10354. https://doi.org/10.3390/app142210354

Charleer, S., Gerling, K., Gutiérrez, F., Cauwenbergh, H., Luycx, B., & Verbert, K. (2018a). Real-time dashboards to support esports spectating. *CHI PLAY 2018—Proceedings of the 2018 Annual Symposium on Computer-Human Interaction in Play*, 439–450. https://doi.org/10.1145/3242671.3242680/SUPPL_FILE/PLAY1028.MP4

Charleer, S., Gutiérrez, F., Gerling, K., & Verbert, K. (2018b). Towards an Open Standard for Gameplay Metrics. *Proceedings of the 2018 Annual Symposium on Computer-Human Interaction in Play Companion Extended Abstracts*, 399–406. https://doi.org/10.1145/3270316.3271529

Charleer, S., Vande Moere, A., Klerkx, J., Verbert, K., & De Laet, T. (2017). Learning analytics dashboards to support adviser-student dialogue. *IEEE Transactions on Learning Technologies*. https://doi.org/10.1109/TLT.2017.2720670

Claes, S., & Vande Moere, A. (2015). The role of tangible interaction in exploring information on public visualization displays. *Proceedings of the 4th International Symposium on Pervasive Displays, PerDis '15*, 201–207. https://doi.org/10.1145/2757710.2757733

Clarke, V., & Braun, V. (2017). Thematic analysis. *The Journal of Positive Psychology, 12*(3), 297–298. https://doi.org/10.1080/17439760.2016.1262613

Glombik, D., Beck, F., Agarwal, S., & Wallner, G. (2025). Visually exploring team communication and gameplay events in league of legends. *EuroVis Workshop on Visual Analytics (EuroVA) 2025*. https://doi.org/10.2312/EUROVA.20251103

Gutiérrez, F., Charleer, S., De Croon, R., Htun, N. N., Goetschalckx, G., & Verbert, K. (2019). Explaining and exploring job recommendations: A user-driven approach for interacting with knowledge-based job recommender systems. *Proceedings of the 13th ACM Conference on Recommender Systems, RecSys '19*, 60–68. https://doi.org/10.1145/3298689.3347001

Hornbæk, K., & Hertzum, M. (2017). Technology acceptance and user experience: A review of the experiential component in HCI. *ACM Transactions on Computer-Human Interaction, 24*(5), 33:1–33:30. https://doi.org/10.1145/3127358

Leis, O., & Lautenbach, F. (2020). Psychological and physiological stress in non-competitive and competitive esports settings: A systematic review. *Psychology of Sport and Exercise, 51*, Article 101738. https://doi.org/10.1016/j.psychsport.2020.101738

Leis, O., Praisan, G., Pedraza-Ramirez, I., Sharpe, B. T., Laborde, S., & Lautenbach, F. (2024a). Exploratory study of psychophysiological stress in esports: Training and competition in professional league of legends. *Journal of Electronic Gaming and Esports, 2*(1). https://doi.org/10.1123/jege.2024-0033

Leis, O., Sharpe, B. T., Pelikan, V., Fritsch, J., Nicholls, A. R., & Poulus, D. (2024). Stressors and coping strategies in esports: A systematic review. *International Review of Sport and Exercise Psychology, 0*(0), 1–31. https://doi.org/10.1080/1750984X.2024.2386528

Lim, K. C. (2018). Using the xAPI to track learning. In K. C. Li, K. S. Yuen & B. T. M. Wong (Eds.), *Innovations in open and flexible education* (pp. 233–242). Springer. https://doi.org/10.1007/978-981-10-7995-5_21

Liu, H., Hopkins, W., Gómez, A. M., & Molinuevo, S. J. (2013). Inter-operator reliability of live football match statistics from OPTA Sportsdata. *International Journal of Performance Analysis in Sport, 13*(3), 803–821. https://doi.org/10.1080/24748668.2013.11868690

Navarro-Lucena, F., Molinillo, S., Anaya-Sánchez, R., & Muñoz-Leiva, F. (2025). Levelling up esports research: Mapping the past, present, and future of a thriving digital arena. *Performance Enhancement & Health, 13*(4), Article 100354. https://doi.org/10.1016/j.peh.2025.100354

Peché, J., Tsishurou, A., Zap, A., & Wallner, G. (2025). Where are the frontlines? A visualization approach for map control in team-based games. *IEEE Conference on Games (CoG), 2025*, 1–4. https://doi.org/10.1109/CoG64752.2025.11114207

Raetze, S., Staedter, C., & Hüllmann, J. A. (2025). Taking aim at research on esports teams: A systematic literature review and cross-disciplinary future agenda. *Team Performance Management*. https://doi.org/10.1108/TPM-09-2024-0109/1256464/TAKING-AIM-AT-RESEARCH-ON-ESPORTS-TEAMS-A

Reimann, P. (2011). Design-Based research. In L. Markauskaite, P. Freebody & J. Irwin (Eds.), *Methodological choice and design: Scholarship, policy and practice in social and educational research* (pp. 37–50). Springer Netherlands. https://doi.org/10.1007/978-90-481-8933-5_3

Ribeiro, M. T., Singh, S., & Guestrin, C. (2016). "Why Should I Trust You?": Explaining the predictions of any classifier. *Proceedings of the 22nd ACM SIGKDD International Conference on Knowledge Discovery and Data Mining, KDD '16*, 1135–1144. https://doi.org/10.1145/2939672.2939778

Rubleske, J., Fletcher, T., & Westerfeld, B. (2020). E-Sports analytics: A primer and resource for student research projects and lesson plans. *Journal of Instructional Pedagogies, 23*. https://eric.ed.gov/?id=EJ1242004

Sadowska, D., Sacewicz, T., Rębiś, K., Kowalski, T., & Krzepota, J. (2023). Examining physiological changes during Counter-Strike: Global Offensive (CS:GO) performance in recreational male esports players. *Applied Sciences, 13*(20), 11526. https://doi.org/10.3390/app132011526

Sáez-García, J., Sáiz-Manzanares, M. C., & Marticorena-Sánchez, R. (2024). A proposed method of automating data processing for analysing data produced from eye tracking and galvanic skin response. *Computers, 13*(11), 289. https://doi.org/10.3390/computers13110289

Schmälzle, R., & Grall, C. (2020). Psychophysiological methods: Options, uses, and validity. In *The international encyclopedia of media psychology* (pp. 1–8). John Wiley & Sons, Ltd. https://doi.org/10.1002/9781119011071.iemp0013

Seif El-Nasr, M., & Kleinman, E. (2020). Data-Driven game development: Ethical considerations. *Proceedings of the 15th International Conference on the Foundations of Digital Games, FDG '20*, 1–10. https://doi.org/10.1145/3402942.3402964

Shneiderman, B. (2003). The eyes have it: A task by data type taxonomy for information visualizations. In *The craft of information visualization* (pp. 364–371). Morgan Kaufmann. https://doi.org/10.1016/B978-155860915-0/50046-9

Smerdov, A., Zhou, B., Lukowicz, P., & Somov, A. (2021). *Collection and validation of psychophysiological data from professional and amateur players: A multimodal eSports dataset* (arXiv: 2011.00958). arXiv. https://doi.org/10.48550/arXiv.2011.00958

Wang, L., Dormann, C., & Wallner, G. (2025). Player perception matters: Insights into the use of esports live companion tools. *Proceedings of the 20th International Conference on the Foundations of Digital Games, FDG 2025*. https://doi.org/10.1145/3723498.3723801/ASSET/5238DF24-1D21-4074-A6B3-C0DB3E3DACB3/ASSETS/IMAGES/LARGE/FDG25-49-FIG4.JPG

Welsh, M. R., Mosley, E., Laborde, S., Day, M. C., Sharpe, B. T., Burkill, R. A., & Birch, P. D. J. (2023). The use of heart rate variability in esports: A systematic review. *Psychology of Sport and Exercise, 69*, Article 102495. https://doi.org/10.1016/j.psychsport.2023.102495

Werder, K. (2022). Esport. *Business and Information Systems Engineering, 64*(3), 393–399. https://doi.org/10.1007/S12599-022-00748-W/TABLES/2

Index

S. Bekir (ed.), *The Psychology of Esports*, https://doi.org/10.1007/978-3-032-25090-2

www.ingramcontent.com/pod-product-compliance
Ingram Content Group UK Ltd.
Pitfield, Milton Keynes, MK11 3LW, UK
UKHW020934180926
475692UK00003B/36
9783032250896